DATE DUE

AP 14 '98			
AP 01 '99			
FE 14 '00			
FE 05 '00			
MR 21 '02			
MR 12 '02			
NO 21 '07			
OC 22 '08			
OC 09 '08			

#47-0108 Peel Off Pressure Sensitive

THE
ABORTION
PAPERS

THE ABORTION PAPERS

Inside the Abortion Mentality

Bernard N. Nathanson, M.D.

Frederick Fell Publishers, Inc./New York, New York

International Standard Book Number: 0-8119-0593-4
Library of Congress Catalog Card Number: 83-081126

For information address:
Frederick Fell Publishers, Inc.
386 Park Avenue South
New York, New York 10016

Published simultaneously in Canada by Fitzhenry & Whiteside, Limited, Toronto

Designed by Sheila Lynch

Manufactured in the United States of America

1 2 3 4 5 6 7 8 9 0

*For Sir William Liley, the first fetologist,
and for all our children, born and unborn,
to whom he dedicated his life.*

Contents

Prologue

It is four years since *Aborting America* was published. I had hoped that that book, an account of my odyssey through the byzantine world of abortion politics and the charnel houses of abortion technology, would have slowed the steam-roller a little. In company with the bright promise of the Reagan administration, that hope has died. The Abortion People, flushed with victories in Congress and in the federal courts, still rule the day. For those of us laboring in the pro-life cause, the prevailing state of mind might best be expressed in the lines of William Butler Yeats written in 1921:

> Turning and turning in the widening gyre
> The falcon cannot hear the falconer;
> Things fall apart; the center cannot hold;
> Mere anarchy is loosed upon the world,
> The blood-dimmed tide is loosed, and everywhere
> The ceremony of innocence is drowned;
> The best lack all conviction, while the worst
> Are full of passionate intensity.

This time I pick up my pen more in anger than in sorrow. *Aborting America* was a restrained and dispassionate treatment of a notoriously combustible subject. I took pains to avoid the conventional terms of the argument which have become part of the argument itself, such as "fetus" and "products of conception"; instead I used the term "alpha" to describe the person inside the womb. And the conclusion that abortion on demand is an unmitigated and unacceptable evil in a society nominally pledged to an over-riding respect for the value of life in any and all of its manifestations flowed inexorably from the

1

rigorously neutral, purely secular, predominately scientific arguments presented in that book. Significant advances in science and technology in the past four years, such as realtime ultrasound scanning, fetal medicine, intra-uterine surgery, and in vitro fertilization have all confirmed beyond a reasonable doubt that prenatality is just another passage in our lives — lives which commence with fertilization and end with death. Could any truth be more obvious, more self-evident? Yet infuriatingly, like the Bourbon kings, the Abortion People have learned nothing and have forgotten nothing. They cling to their flat earth credo, and would have the rest of us subscribe to it too.

Even following the publication of that book I continued to distance myself from the thick purple vein of emotion which pervades the abortion issue. I had great difficulty comprehending the impatience and often the rage with which pro-life advocates address the question. Then one day two years ago, following an address to a pro-life state convention, I queried a woman whom I respected for her otherwise calm and intellectual approach to complex questions as to why she became so heated and so intense on this particular issue. She looked at me almost uncomprehending for a moment, then replied: "Doctor, if you walked into a room in your hospital from which screams were emanating and found a woman beating her six-week old infant with a blunt instrument—blood everywhere and the infant grotesque and unrecognizable from the marks of the beating—and if you tried to stop it and were told that it was legal, good for the infant and even better for the mother, and if you came upon this scene daily for ten years and were powerless to put a stop to it, you'd get pretty heated up too." When articulated in these simple, visceral terms, the emotion generated by the issue became all too understandable. It was only then that I was able to commit my heart to the pro-life cause, and I passed from disinterested observation, through indignant protest, to angry resistance.

An incorrigible Joycean, I have chosen a title, *The Abortion Papers*, which applies equally to the three major sections of this book, but has a different meaning for each. After the Abortion People cashiered me from the highest councils of NARAL, I gathered up all my notes, internal memoranda, minutes of secret meetings, position papers, and policy documents and filed them under the heading "Abortion Papers." In the section which deals with the Catholic strategy a number of these papers are cited at considerable length in order to illuminate the dangerous alchemy whereby original humanitarian impulse was catalyzed by a poisonous bigotry to evolve into an effective, but ultimately corrupted, realpolitick. In *Aborting America* I had touched briefly upon the use of the "Catholic card"—the reader must forgive me a sense of dèja lu—but in this work I have dissected that strategy free of all the clever nuance and seductive ambiguity with which it was, and continues to be, so artfully employed by the Abortion People. Unmasked, that strategy stands revealed as shameful and deeply offensive to the high principles of the document which the Abortion People profess to respect so unshakably, the Constitution of the United States.

The lengthiest section of this book is devoted to an analysis of how the press and the electronic media have handled the issue. From the founding of NARAL and the launching of the abortion revolution, it was necessary to enlist the fourth estate in the cause in order to assure its success. Historical forces were working in NARAL's favor: the abortion revolution coincided neatly with the feminist tide overrunning the lower echelons of the media. Young women reporters, newly graduated from college and attractively radicalized in the campus tumults of the late 1960s, were assigned to cover the abortion issue, and we recruited them happily. That alliance between the Abortion People and the media was forged in 1969 and remains intact fifteen years later. The pro-life movement is armed with new scientific data and perceptions which demonstrate beyond question the humanity of the unborn child from the moment of conception. But if the pro-life movement is to have a fair share of the public attention, then the media, especially the national or mega-press, must be persuaded to renounce that alliance with the Abortion People and adhere to an impartial posture. If persuasion is ineffective then it may be necessary to resort to more drastic remedies, some of which are discussed herein.

Fetology is the study and science of the human unborn. It is perhaps the most exciting and dramatic specialty in the American medical community today. It is expanding at an astonishing rate and overlaps into areas of contemporary medicine such as cancer research, transplant surgery, laser therapy, immunochemistry, and fiberoptics. The number of textbooks and scientific articles dealing with fetology increases exponentially each year. I note with satisfaction that fetology has become such a comprehensive and well established medical specialty that it has even sprouted sub-specialties. In Great Britain Drs. A. J. Barson and J. A. Davis have co-authored a book entitled *Laboratory Investigation of Fetal Disease*, devoted solely to the recognition of diseases and disorders of the unborn in laboratory tests. In their preface the authors state the following:

> So numerous, diverse and sophisticated are the techniques for the monitoring of fetal disease that no single medical center can claim to be adept in all those that are in existence.

Imagine physicians sub-specializing in a medical field which did not even exist twenty years ago, and which only became recognized as a legitimate specialty ten years ago in 1973, the same year in which the United States Supreme Court decreed that the human being to whom this particular specialty was devoted did not exist.

I have spent my life in the practice of obstetrics and gynecology and have watched as the attention of the specialty has turned from a preoccupation with the maternal welfare to the welfare of the unborn child. It is a transcendent irony in the history of medicine that as increasing scientific attention and enormous resources were being assigned by the medical community to the protection and welfare of the unborn child, a new liberty was being quarried out of the United States Constitution which permitted and even encouraged the mass scale destruction of the child. This paradox becomes more insistent and more inexplicable daily. In the diabolic terms of Orwellian doublespeak the Abortion People would have us believe that destruction is preservation, that wrong is right, that human life is indefinable. And it is a crowning irony that 1984 is here, literally and figuratively.

The flowering of fetology as a major medical discipline is especially important to me personally. The data and perceptions arising from fetology formed the hinge of my thinking on the abortion issue. I have repeatedly denied that my pro-life position stems from religious convictions. It sprang from nothing but hard, reproducible, scientific facts and the application of the Golden Rule to those facts. But I must confess that I am a little less certain today that those scientific apercus upon which I relied to formulate my conclusions were merely the products of clever neurons clicking away in an existential disorder. And I find myself increasingly unwilling to believe that the ingeniously designed series of passages through which we progress from conception to death is only the work of random chance, of biological anarchy in a cruel universe.

No discussion of fetology and its relationship to the abortion issue would be complete without a tribute to Sir William Liley, to whose memory I have dedicated this book. He was the father of fetology. His brilliant and original research into the fundamentals of fetology are the underpinnings upon which the entire science rests. I recall a conversation with him in Auckland in February, 1981, in which he informed me that after his children had grown up and left his household, he and his wife had adopted a Down's syndrome child. He trained his bright, lively eyes on me, smiled that expansive smile which crinkled his face so attractively and said: "Do you know, we've had more enjoyment from that child than from any of our others?"

Before any of us, Sir William Liley recognized the irreconcilable antinomy between fetology and the abortion ethic:

> Our generation is the first ever to have a reasonably complete picture of the development of the human being from conception. In 1930 the liberation of a human egg from the ovary was observed. In 1944 through a microscope was seen the union of the human sperm and ovum. In the 1950s the events of the first six days of life were described, those critical first steps in a prodigious journey.
>
> For a generation which reputedly prefers scientific fact to barren philosophy, we might have thought that this new information would engender a new respect for the welfare and appreciation of the importance of intra-uterine life.
>
> Instead, around the world we find a systematic campaign clamoring for the destruction of the embryo and fetus as a cure-all for every social and personal problem. I, for one, find it a bitter irony that just when the embryo and fetus arrive on the medical scene there should be such sustained pressure to make him or her a social nonentity.

When I was leaving Auckland to board my plane back to the United States, he called to me almost plaintively as I started up the ramp: "Dr. Nathanson, when you return, ask them why they are killing our patients."

Why, indeed.

Part One

Abortion and the Media

THE PRINT MEDIA

Thursday, June 18, 1981, was a fine summer day in the District. In response to an invitation from Senator John East on behalf of his Sub-Committee on the Separation of Powers (Senate Judiciary Committee), I had taken the eight o'clock flight on New York Air to Washington's National Airport and taxied to the Everett M. Dirksen Senate Office Building to testify at the hearings on the Human Life Bill. The bill—an attempt by the pro-life movement and its legislative proponents to declare human life present from the moment of conception, thus making abortion a crime against the person—was in its second set of hearings, the first having taken place in April.

Those earlier hearings were covered by the *New York Times*, whose plenipotentiary, Bernard Weinraub, wrote the following:

> A Senate Subcommittee chairman who strongly opposes abortion bowed today to growing criticism that his hearings on an anti-abortion bill were 'stacked' in favor of the legislation and promised to extend the hearings to hear 'all points of view.'

In the article, illustrated with a photo of Leon Rosenberg, a geneticist who supports abortion on demand, Weinraub took considerable pains to list Rosenberg's academic credentials and achievements

(Chairman of the Department of Human Genetics at Yale University, and former President of the American Society of Human Genetics) but in listing those physicians who disagreed with Rosenberg— Dr. Jasper Williams and Dr. Alfred Bongiovanni—he did not adequately elaborate on their distinguished achievements, simply describing Bongiovanni as ". . . of the University of Pennsylvania Medical School" and Williams as ". . . a practising physician on Chicago's South Side." There was no mention here of Bongiovanni's not inconsiderable academic achievements or of the fact that Dr. Jasper Williams is black.

The description of Rosenberg's testimony occupied six paragraphs in the coverage; seven other scientists and medical men gave testimony on the pro-life cause. Unfairly, without giving a minimum of equal time for other views, these positions were ignored by the reporter. Further, Weinraub embellished Rosenberg's pro-abortion testimony with the following plaudit:

> In a statement that drew a prolonged round of applause from those who believe that a pregnant woman has the right to choose whether to terminate her pregnancy, Dr. Rosenberg said that there was not 'a single piece of scientific evidence' to determine when life begins.

Quite apart from the Lysenko-ish folly of the statement, the reportage of these events was at least as "stacked" as the hearings themselves. Responsible journalism has an obligation to present objective and unbiased reportage. In this case, this responsibility was cruelly offended.

The wire services fell into line, though perhaps a little less ardently than the *New York Times*. The *New York Daily News* (the largest general daily circulation in the United States) headlined "Life's Onset Is Religious Idea, Prof Tells Panel." The *New York Daily News* used the AP coverage which led off with four full paragraphs on Rosenberg's testimony, then gave three short paragraphs to Jasper Williams. The coverage however ended, dependably, with this statement: "Critics say such a law [the Human Life Statute] would make a woman who has an abortion subject to prosecution for murder." This statement was ignorant, irresponsible, and inflammatory.

Rosenberg's reductionism—let's not get into these heavy issues, it's just too complicated for us simple scientists let alone the soap opera and sitcom set—was a classic of its genre. It was a typical example of liberal casuistry on the subject of abortion: If one can avoid dealing with the definition of life then all those messy ancillary questions like abortion, in vitro fertilization, fetal research, and the like may just quietly go away. In addition it was a patronizing, condescending pat on the head from a distinguished geneticist arrayed in the unseemly lineaments of Uriah Heep, crooning mendacious reassurances to his adoring public.

Admittedly, there was something a little disappointing about the Human Life Statute. It was conceived in specious sin, designed primarily as a politically feasible end run around the pro-abortion opposition: If the anti-abortion camp could persuade Congress that life begins at conception then ipso facto abortion is unwarranted destruction of human life and as such impermissible. And unfortunately the anti-abortion forces allowed the circumstances in which the Human Life Statute was conceived, to become public (media) knowledge. For if they had been more subtle and more politically sophisticated they would have insisted that the public perception of the proposal was that of a necessary and compelling piece of legislation thus far lacking in our body of public law. For if there is no acceptable public definition of when life begins how indeed can we legislate logically in such knotty issues as in vitro fertilization? How can we decide on how much public support to give to premature infant centers concerning themselves with life support systems for smaller and smaller infants? How can we legislate on the countless issues of human genetic engineering, fetal research, the use of fetal organs for transplantation, intra-uterine surgery, and a host of other enormously challenging moral, ethical, and expensive issues. Some of these issues have not even been formulated yet because the technology is still uninvented.

Apply Rosenberg's reductionism in the matter of when life begins to its counterpart: When does life end (what is the definition of death)? The scene falls readily into focus: (The dialogue is taken verbatim from the Senate transcripts, but the word "death" is substituted for "life," and "ends" for "begins").

SENATOR EAST: What is the belief of the scientific community, Professor, regarding when life ends?

ROSENBERG: The great majority of scientists believe that it is impossible to determine when life ends, Senator.

SENATOR EAST: Do we have no evidence or information on that question, Professor?

ROSENBERG: There is not a single piece of scientific evidence to determine when life ends, Senator. Some people argue that life ends at death, but others say that life ends when brain function ceases, or when the heart stops beating, or when a person can survive without a life support system, or when natural death occurs.

SENATOR EAST: I really don't understand, Professor—but do go on.

ROSENBERG: Thank you, Senator. There is no single simple answer. If I am correct in asserting that the question of when actual life ends is not a scientific matter, then—you may ask—why have so many scientists come here to say that it is?

SENATOR EAST: Yes, Professor. Why indeed?

ROSENBERG: My answer is that scientists, like all other people, have religious feelings to which they are entitled. I believe they have failed to distinguish between their personal biases and their professional scientific judgments.

Now follows a second scene, entirely the creation of the author but singularly fitting.

SENATOR EAST: But Professor, we really have got to know when life ends. After all, how are we going to know when to pronounce someone dead? We may prematurely bury someone who isn't even dead if we can't come to some reasonable agreement on this question.

ROSENBERG: Senator, I believe that the notion embodied in the phrase "actual human death" is not a scientific one but rather a religious, metaphysical one.

SENATOR EAST: But Professor, do we have to wait for putrefaction to occur—as they did in the eighteenth century—before we can pronounce someone dead? The French surgeon Louis once wrote: "The opinion that the signs of death are uncertain is too injurious to Medicine to be true. One cannot doubt that the art exists. The faults that are committed in practising it prove this. But if the limits of this art were such that it would be impossible to know if a human were dead or alive, what idea would one then have of the rules of science?" Now that was written in 1752, Dr. Rosenberg, but it seems to my admittedly ingenuous mind that that declaration applies equally well here.

ROSENBERG: Well, Senator, it's really a question of freedom of choice. Each person—each doctor, each surviving relative, each undertaker, demographer, insurance company, spouse, court, and judge—should be able to exercise a freedom of choice in this matter. The right of freedom of choice is guaranteed in our Constitution—or at least I think it is . . . and if it isn't it should be.

SENATOR EAST: But if there are no rules, no guidelines at all on the question, won't we have utter chaos Professor? Let me give you an example to clarify: I can envision someone who needs a kidney transplant finding out that his doctor has another seriously ill patient in the hospital with the same tissue type. Then by bribing or persuading the doctor to declare his patient dead, he can get the kidney. Don't we have to have laws regulating this sort of surgical chicanery?

ROSENBERG: Senator, I believe that everyone should have control of their own body. It's a matter of privacy too; after all death is a private matter and government has no right to intrude upon it. And besides, I don't like you imposing your religious beliefs on me.

Admittedly I have taken a bit of dramatic license here and there, but the point is, I believe, inescapably made. Though the definition of the end of life (physicians with their no-nonsense clinical training cling to the simple stripped-down term "death") may well be a philosophical, religious, or metaphysical concept, it is and must be *primarily* a medico-legal one. Decisions must be made by physicians within a coherent legal framework regarding the onset and the moment of death. Within my own clinical experience I recall one case in which the moment of decision was solely mine. A woman in her ninth month of pregnancy had suffered a massive cerebro-vascular hemmorrhage, a stroke, and was deeply comatose in a hospital bed. The brain damage was of such an extent that she was expected to die momentarily and her husband had indicated to me that all reasonable measures should be taken to preserve the life of the baby (the fetal heart, and presumably the fetal health, were still good). This episode occurred in the mid-1950s, and we had no criteria for the establishment of brain death, nor did we then have any of the sophisticated technology we now have with which to evaluate the fetal health. I recall hovering over this woman's bed, watching and listening to the machine-like rattling of the agonal respirations which precede death, and planning the post-mortem Caesarean section (you may well ask why we didn't do the Caesarean section while she was still alive in order to rescue the baby. The answer to that question is that the procedure itself would certainly have hastened her death, and the prevailing medical ethic—*Primum Non Nocere*, or *first, do no harm*—forbade us to hasten her death, even in the interests of the fetus).

The rattling finally subsided, and my stethoscope on her chest indicated no further heart action. I seized the scalpel; my hands had broken a cold sweat. I was struggling in a metaphysical black hole with one life rushing toward death and another bubbling brightly upward. Trembling, I drove the scalpel the length of the lower torso from umbilicus to the pubic bone. I then peered at her face. It was the first time I had ever operated on anyone without any anesthesia at all and it was a scene out of a medieval medical text, an atavistic nightmare. With one more slash (not a twitch of the corpse—my confidence renewed) I plunged the knife through the remaining layers of muscle and fascia straight on through the thick meat of the uterine wall to the amniotic sac. Ouspensky taught that there are seven layers of consciousness, and in the first five we are only partially awake or conscious. It is in that sixth layer, seldom achieved by most of us, that we have access to a consciousness so dazzling that whatever we are doing is impressed forever on the mind as an unrelieved and vivid memory: an epiphany. The absence of bleeding and the lack of any reaction whatever was such an epiphany to me; surgeons are so accustomed to the cruel depredations of the scalpel evoking a scarlet weeping of the tissues that the absence of bleeding is an alarm bell which cannot be turned off even though one knows—or definitely thinks—that the patient is dead. Of course we have all dissected cadavers and performed autopsies in medical school, but there the medico-legal reality of death has been defined by others more experienced at it. Here I was operating on this poor woman without an anesthetic in what amounted to an aggressive criminal assault (axe murderers do comparable work; in the ordinary Caesarean section the skin, various layers of the abdominal wall, and the uterus itself are entered slowly, deliberately with meticulous attention to bleeding vessels and the preservation of tissue integrity), with no regard for the traditional surgical niceties. The alarm bell would not be turned off, and it kept me continually aware of the enormity of the act. Even the setting was wrong: Surgery is done in operating rooms, not in beds on maternity wards. Richard Seltzer, the Laureate of the Scalpel, in writing about surgery speaks reverently about the stillness of the bodily recesses in which the surgeon plies his art, calling it an ". . . awful quiet of ruin, of rainbows, full of expectation and Holy Dread." He compares surgery to a Mass served with body and blood and this Mass was here being served in a strange and inappropriate place with the surgeon's ancient enemy, Death, in vile dominion.

The knife, now racing more urgently through the final frail layer of the amnion, sliced into the sac and an ominous green pea-soup fluid oozed out. I had lost. The surgeon defines his art, at least in part, as a contest between himself and Death. The green slime was meconium, the content of the fetal intestine passed from the fetal anus into the amniotic sac in the extremity of that tiny life, and its presence in the amniotic fluid freezes the blood of the doctor. The fetus was ripped from what was its mortal chamber, flipped upside down (the umbilical cord was pitifully thin, its blood vessels collapsed and without a pulse) and the green slime also oozed from the nostrils and the mouth. No heart-beat, no respiration. Apgar score zero-zero. Too late.

The sight of a lifeless newborn lying livid and broken in the resuscitation crib in a delivery room—all the gleaming tangled life-support machinery laid aside and impotent—is a heartbreaking one in ordinary circumstances. But where the mother is already dead—even though the death was anticipated—it is an inexpressibly poignant scene, and the oppressive silence of that room defined my own visceral understanding of death. Had I acted too late? Had I been intimidated by death, unwilling to draw my sword at the instant of the challenge? I knew that only half of all infants born by post-mortem Caesarean section survive (we have no satisfactory explanation for this) but the pervasive doubt remained: I had missed the moment. Death had not only intimidated me but it had deceived me and had claimed another life as well. There had been one moment, one crossing-over, and I had failed to apprehend it.

We must have a practical and universally acceptable definition of death. This need has been recognized increasingly in the past dozen years or so, and we now have a report by the President's Commission for the Study of Ethical Problems in Medicine, Biomedical and

Behavioral Research in which concrete criteria are set forth for a uniform definition of death. Indeed, the necessity to define death clearly and in *purely* biological terms (no philosophical musings or metaphysical acrobatics) has not only resulted in general agreement that the definition may encompass both the ancient heart-lung function as a standard and/or the newer brain death as another standard. It also has generated a new conflict which in itself is a testimony to society's desire to define death in as precise biological terms as possible: whether brain death means only death of the higher cerebral centers (consciousness) or whether it means whole-brain death. No matter—the significant feature of this disagreement is the intensity of the effort to define death in the most refined biological terms.

To return to the esteemed Professor Rosenberg and his cheering claque in the pro-abortion forces, we have this curious, inexplicable diffidence about defining the other extremity of life: the beginning. Don't the same perplexing questions present themselves at this extremity of life as at the other? Who is this "person" referred to repeatedly in Section 1. Article XIV of the Constitution? At what point did this "person" come into being and ascend to his rights? We have as compelling a desire and need to know the answer as we do to know when that person ceases to be, that is, when those rights are withdrawn.

Now comes forth George Ryan, M.D. of Memphis, Tennessee, president of the American College of Obstetrics and Gynecology (he assumed this post in 1981). This is, of course, an elective post, not one gained through the fruits of scientific endeavor or medical expertise. The college, founded in 1951, is a national organization with a membership of approximately 18,000 obstetricians and gynecologists, and the membership comprises the great majority of physicians practising that specialty in the United States. (In rural areas there are still to be found general practitioners delivering babies, and there are increasing numbers of midwives plying the trade but the enormous numbers of certified young specialists being churned out of the residency machine in the past dozen years dwarfs the latter.) I have been a Fellow of the college since 1957, and within my memory the college has historically been virgin-timid in expressing views on controversial matters or political questions. But in 1981, the college, without bothering itself with such democratic frivolity as a consultation with or a polling of the membership, shed its virginal timidity and roared forth like Mona Stangley, the proprietress of the best little whorehouse in Texas. The Executive Board of the college, speaking through the estimable Dr. Ryan, released an official statement of policy during its annual beer-bust in Las Vegas in which it roundly condemned the hearing on the Human Life Bill and opposed the proposed legislation.

Now, there are several unprecedented features to this aggressively political excursion by the college. To begin with, a careful reading of the current by-laws of the organization reveals that the executive board is rather explicitly restricted in its powers and duties (Article XII, Section 2) to the conventional dithering and harmless corporate gabbling which mark such massive professional congresses. Nowhere in the section which defines the powers and duties of the executive board is there any mention concerning the expression of policy statements on such controversial political matters as abortion; even in the all-purpose omnibus clause designed to cover exigencies not set forth in the rest of the section: "Transact all business not otherwise provided for that may pertain to the College," there is no provision for such flagrant propagandizing. Nor does Article XI, Section 5, which defines the duties of the president, charge that officer with the responsibility to embroil himself or the college in such difficult issues.

Beyond such quasi-legal considerations (I shall refrain from commenting further on imperial behavior of the Executive Board and/or Ryan himself in writing and releasing the statement without attempting to elicit some expression of opinion from the ordinary membership) there is the issue of the American College of Obstetrics and Gynecology arrogating to itself some special wisdom in the public matter of abortion. As if the Institute of Electrical and Electronics Engineers were to hold itself out as expert in the question of capital punishment merely because an electric chair is utilized as the instrument of destruction. I am perfectly willing to concede that obstetricians and gynecologists are in general the personnel who wield the instruments in the process of abortion and undeniably have the technical expertise to comment upon the uses of the machinery. But in the complex arena of public policy (in this case the legal and ethical acceptability of permissive abortion) they possess no special insights. To the contrary, a statement of policy on the question of abortion from an organization whose membership has an immense financial investment in the maintenance of the status quo (abortion is a half a billion dollar a year industry) is at least strongly indicative of some substantial conflict of interest.

But what of the policy statement itself? In part, it states the following:

> In taking this definitive stand [opposing the Human Life Bill] the College is affirming its belief that the issue of when life begins which is the purported basis for this legislation is a broader concern than any of the recent testimony on biological or cellular development would indicate. It is not a question that can be answered strictly scientifically.

This from an organization—*my* organization—which concerns itself solely with the origins, the earliest stirrings of life and the protection and advancement of that life. It is as if neurologists, cringing abjectly, refused to define brain death because they lacked the necessary technology to ascertain the precise micro-second at which the last neuron expires. Even Dr. Alan Guttmacher, the longtime respected president of the Planned Parenthood Federation and avowed proponent of permissive abortion, stated in his book, *Pregnancy and Birth: a Book for Expectant Parents*, the following on this sample issue, which seems to have passed Dr. Ryan's understanding:

> The essential step in the initiation of a new life is fertilization, the penetration of the ovum by a spermatozoon and the fusion of the two cells into a single cell.

Or this, from a brochure published by the Planned Parenthood World Population circa 1965:

> An abortion kills the life of a baby after it has begun. It is dangerous to your life and health. It may make you sterile so that when you want a child you cannot have it.

Admittedly, these statements were made and published in the comparatively peaceful days of the mid 1960s. And I myself have changed *my* own mind on the question of permissive abortion. But what persuaded me to change my mind, and what should have strengthened those precepts and beliefs of the Planned Parenthood organization and Dr. Guttmacher in particular, was the development of the marvelous new technology which has served to define beyond reasonable challenge the nature of intrauterine life, the unarguably and specifically human quality of that life. Where is the scientific evidence, where are the new developments which would serve to convince an obstetrician to the contrary view, that what is in the uterus from the beginning of pregnancy is less human today than that which we perceived in 1965? We had no real time ultrasound in those years, no fetal heart monitoring, no fetoscopy, no in vitro fertilization. Science marches inexorably toward a deeper understanding of the uniquely human qualities of the fetus, and George Ryan and the American College of Obstetrics and Gynecology are floundering in the netherworld of revisionist biology. Cowed by the media, oppressed and intimidated by the increasing numbers of militant feminists in the new membership rolls of the American College of Obstetrics and Gynecology and its affiliate organizations (the Junior Fellow Division of the American College of Obstetrics and Gynecology and the Nurses Association of the American College of Obstetrics and Gynecology) Ryan and the executive board have capitulated to internal and external political pressures and have joined the ranks of the soft revolutions of feminism and abortion. Orwell once remarked that to understand a revolution one must first join it, but in joining it one then inevitably becomes a propagandist for it.

More to be censured than pitied, the policy statement—listing dangerously to and fro like a foundering life raft—goes on with this curious caveat:

> There is no question that there is biologic life in the first cell. But when that developing fetus actually becomes human, when it should have civil rights is certainly another question.

Here is Ryan the metaphysician, the eminent legal scholar holding forth in his best pro-abortion form; no wonder the Sub-Committee on the Separation of Powers responsible for the hearings insisted that Ryan confine his testimony to strict definitions on the commencement of life, and that he speak only as an individual and not for the American College of Obstetrics and Gynecology. Ryan and the American College of Obstetrics and Gynecology sulked under these reasonable restraints and at first refused to testify. Eventually we were treated to the privilege of hearing an explanation of this politically inspired twaddle, this caving in to doctrinal cant.

On July 9, 1981, the bill was approved by Senator East's Sub-Committee on the Separation of Powers of the Senate Judiciary Committee, 3–2. East, Orrin Hatch of Utah, and Jeremiah Denton of

Alabama voted for the bill while Baucus of Montana and Heflin of Alabama opposed it. In its final form the bill states the following: "The Congress finds that the life of each human being begins at conception." In itself this is a truism to which no one with the most rudimentary knowledge of high school biology could take serious exception, but the simple, majestic power of the statement had been so diluted and squandered by the perversely political direction of the debate from which the statement had emerged that it was now ineffective.

The anti-abortion forces had unwittingly stumbled on a brilliant tactic: To force Congress and the nation to a comprehensive apolitical consensus on the definition of the beginning of life. Had they confined the hearings to this one pure issue, and had they insisted on keeping the testimony to that issue only, then even though the pro-abortionists would undoubtedly turn the debate into political channels (the central theme of permissive abortion), the hearings could have proceeded in the purity of a bio-medical and bio-ethical quest. Thus, the too-obvious effort of the pro-abortionists to turn the proceedings into a political circus would have netted substantial capital for the pro-lifers. Instead, the pro-life forces erroneously defined the issue in the expected political terms from the very beginning and therefore blew what had been a glorious opportunity for a legal and public relations breakthrough; the pro-abortionists gleefully picked up the cudgels. It was as if Charles Darwin, having concluded his work with barnacles in 1844 and realizing that species are not immutable, had decided to utilize his discovery in a petty vendetta against the teachings of the Church of England instead of allowing it to stand as a monumental milestone in the synthesis of *Origin of the Species*.

Or picture, if you will, the hearings before the President's Commission on Death seized by the euthanasia lobby, insisting that there is no absolute or definable moment of death—that death is a continuum —and therefore that mercy killing is really not killing at all but merely an exogenously applied easement to what is essentially a continuing biologic transition state; that the comatose or quadriplegic or cancer-riddled relative is dead anyway, but since death is not a definable phenomenon, a bolus of 400 cc of air into the vein is nothing but a signature, even a post-script. The hearings would then have been turned into an unparalleled political adventure for the euthanasia forces and the original laudable purpose of the hearings would have been grossly perverted. Worse, if the hearings had been announced by the commission as a tactic to blunt the efforts of the forces of euthanasia then the resulting partisan squabble would have effectively nullified the impact of any substantial scientific testimony adduced in the proceedings.

The mega-press coverage of the sub-committee was predictably partisan and irresponsible. The *New York Times*, again represented by Mr. Weinraub, gave it a four column coverage but led off the piece with the by-now typically deceitful line pushed by Planned Parenthood:

SENATE UNIT VOTES BAN ON ABORTIONS
Declares 3–2 That Life Begins at Conception
Bill Would Allow Murder Charges

The lead paragraph continued:

> A senate subcommittee today approved legislation that could allow the state to prosecute abortion as murder, a first Congressional step toward overturning the 1973 Supreme Court decision that a woman has the right to terminate her pregnancy.

The article went on to quote Senator Baucus extensively. He was one of the two who voted against the bill. In particular, this article quoted his view that this bill if passed ". . . would have the practical effect of barring such contraceptive measures as the intra-uterine device which is believed to act after conception." This is not only the standard party line of the Planned Parenthood virtually verbatim; it is also deliberately deceptive. In fact the scientific community simply does not yet understand exactly how the intra-uterine device works. There are any number of theories at present ranging from the theory that the device in some way acts to interfere with capacitation of the sperm, to the observation that the device promotes a chronic inflammation in the endometrial lining of the uterus thus rendering it inhospitable to the fertilized ovum. No responsible scientist working in the field today suggests that the device has any direct lytic action on the fertilized egg which would destroy it. Senator Heflin of Alabama was also quoted to the effect that he felt the bill was ". . . an exercise in futility" since the United States Supreme Court would in any case refuse to overrule the 1973 Roe v. Wade decision. Senator

Hatch who voted for the bill was quoted only with respect to his reservations regarding the bill (. . . obvious unhappiness with the bill and his prediction that the abortion issue would probably not reach the Senate floor until next year). Senator Denton who also supported the bill was evidently considered not sufficiently distinguished. He wasn't quoted at all, nor were any other anti-abortion sources. You may be sure however that those dedicated leaders of the pro-abortion cause— Suellen Lowery, legislative director of the National Abortion Rights Action League and Fay Wattleton, president of the Planned Parenthood Federation of America were extensively quoted. Even the gun control issue was dragged kicking and screaming into the coverage, presumably to certify the liberal credentials of the coverage.

But the most flagrantly offensive feature of the coverage to those who would demand at least an even-handed reporting of such a concededly inflammatory issue was the use of the word "murder" in the reportage. In the remote past this word was the heavy artillery of the early stereotypical anti-abortion nuts parading thin-lipped and snarling outside abortion clinics and Planned Parenthood enclaves. They would hurl the word at those entering and leaving these establishments and the pro-abortionists, quite correctly, labelled these people as emotional and hysterical. Now, the anti-abortion forces have evolved into a quietly reasonable and politically sophisticated group with a deeply committed but judicious leadership intent upon lowering the volume of noise and increasing the level of understanding in this volatile and complex issue. Cleverly the pro-abortion forces have commandeered the word which anti-abortionists now shun, and are insisting on continuing to identify the latter with that now repugnant term. (When the word "murder" enters into the abortion issue it is reflexively identified with the anti-abortion extreme right and evokes that repulsive stereotype in the mind of the reader.) There was no mention of the word "murder" in the actual bill. Murder is a legal term, the subject of a prodigious literature on its meaning and interpretation; in fact the Helms-Hyde Human Life Bill S 158 is utterly devoid of any clauses or sections describing sanctions or punitive measures. The currently proposed Hatch-Eagleton amendment is a model of clarity and simplicity, and avoids use of words such as "murder," and omits all reference to legal sanctions. "Abortion" is a word which connotes only the destruction of a human being without reference to intent or punishment, and has none of the gaudy Hollywood-inspired prurience of the term "murder." I submit that the writer of the piece knew exactly what he was doing when he invoked that term.

But that nagging question will not—for all the tasteless propagandizing of the pro-abortion left and the lunatic violence of the anti-abortion extreme right—go away: What is the fetus? And what is the act of destruction of the fetus? "Abortion" after all is only the act of giving premature birth, i.e., the expulsion of the human fetus prematurely. And "fetus" is defined by *Webster's Second International* (as lovely and apolitical a treatise as to be found in the galaxy) as: "The young or embryo of an animal in the womb or in the egg." A fine, neutral definition which might be equally applied to the developing snail-darter as to the human.

An article tucked away in the *New York Daily News* on December 19, 1981, poses the question in its most compelling legal terms:

> A New Jersey Appeals Court ruled yesterday that killing a fetus cannot be considered a homicide. The court ruled in a case stemming from a June 1980 auto accident in which a young man's car struck a pregnant woman's car. The woman miscarried and the man was charged with causing the death of the fetus . . .

The lower court had thrown out the charge on the grounds that the fetus was not a human being, at least not within the meaning of the criminal homicide law. Presumably it is not a human being because we refuse to define exactly when the life of a human being begins. If, for example, a President's Commission were convened to work out such a definition (exactly as has been done with the equally difficult though admittedly less combustible issue of death) and the commission could bring to the public a comprehensive, apolitical, and ultimately reliable definition (not subject to the caprices of the next scientific paper to appear in the *American Journal of Obstetrics and Gynecology* or even the *New England Journal of Medicine*), we would finally bring a moral peace to what Paul Ramsay has termed the "Edges of Life." The central problem now is that the pro-euthanasia forces are not nearly as powerful or as well funded as the pro-abortion forces, and, most important, they do not have the neat theoretical link with a political movement as powerful as the feminist revolution. But if the elderly should organize themselves in the near future (their numbers are growing in proportion to the rest of the population, and their political power proportionately—witness the strategic retreat of the Reagan administration on the question of reductions in social security benefits) and formulate a sweeping manifesto on the question of newly perceived rights and ancient abuses, then look out: The definition of death, the matter of euthanasia, the perplexing problems of organ transplant, and the whole unresolved issue of allocation of limited medical resources in a finite, closed economy will be re-opened in a blast.

One of the major striking points which now torments legal scholars, philosophers, and physicians is the tacit interment of the old dividing line, birth. Only in the reaches of the statutory law does that dividing line which distinguishes life from non-life persist (What is non-life? Is the fetus a non-human life, or a human non-life?). The statutory law clings to what scientists and, increasingly, ethicists now perceive to be an ephemeral and unreliable definition of when life begins (birth) only because it has nothing else to lean on. Regardless of what absurdities and inconsistencies the law is led into by adherence to this now-defunct border, it will continue to rely on birth as the definition of life until the bio-ethical community delivers something else— something workable, reliable, and generally acceptable. Scientists unencumbered by the shopworn baggage of political dogma understand that life begins when life begins.

Room 6226 in the Dirksen Senate Office Building is a large hearing room but it was packed to overflowing, largely with youngish women. Senator John East (Republican, North Carolina and Chairman of the Judiciary Committee's Sub-Committee on Separation of Powers), a burly, balding man confined to a wheelchair since the age of twenty-four with advanced spinal cord damage as a result of extensive poliomyelitis, presided at the center of an immense semi-circular elevated rostrum. He was not only presiding, he was the only senator present. However, from time to time Senator Max Baucus, a thin leathery man with a sardonic grin and a pronounced pro-abortion bias, would straggle in and lounge indolently in one of the numerous empty seats at the rostrum, a careful two or three places from East, a pro-life advocate. A cadre of aides, secretaries, messengers, and other assorted hangers-on were ranged in stern straight-back chairs behind the senators. Three television cameras stared from the right wall at the speakers table directly in front of the senatorial aerie.

Congressman Henry Hyde was the first witness and commenced his testimony at ten o'clock. He was composed, and presented the pro-life view with his usual skill. Hyde is a genial gentleman, a spell-binder, a nineteenth century Fourth of July orator, an honorable and passionately committed man who believes deeply in his cause.

Hyde had been accorded the distinction of commanding the speaker's table alone. The next speakers, a rank of appellants of both views, were seated at the long tables facing the senatorial rostrum, four abreast. In the first file was Judy Collins, a singer of some renown; Sarah Weddington, a plump, cherubic blonde attorney who had argued the Roe v. Wade case in the United States Supreme Court thereby achieving a certain celebrity status in the feminist ranks, (she had more recently served in the Carter administration as an advisor on Women's Affairs); a quiet person named Mary Meehan who described herself as a pro-life feminist; and Dr. Caroline Gerster, an Arizona physician, formerly the president of the National Right to Life Committee, and a dedicated, bright, and enormously effective spokeswoman for the pro-life cause. The tenor of their respective statements was predictable save for that of Judy Collins who had never before, to my knowledge, been publicly identified with the abortion conflict. In her prepared statement which was chanted in a sepulchral rise-and-fall she modestly designated herself to be the *soi-disant* advocate for all women everywhere. She proceeded to read an interminable series of meticulously recorded case histories of women who had had abortions for the usual reasons (unplanned pregnancies, limited economic circumstances, and so forth); her closing number was a disappointingly pedestrian plea for more and cheaper abortions, done with the subtle hint of a sob in the voice. Science and/or logic it was not, but it was good show biz.

That file having retired, the next—mine—advanced into place at the table. I sat in the middle with Dr. John Willke, currently the president of the National Right to Life Committee on my extreme left. To his right was a Dr. Naomo Goldstein, a psychiatrist who was representing the American Psychiatric Association—no surprise there. To my right was a Dr. Joseph Boyle, president of the Board of Trustees of the American Medical Association. Seated immediately to Boyle's right, so closely that it appeared they were conjoined twins, was an oatmeal-faced somber man who was identified by Boyle as an attorney for the A.M.A. Boyle was obviously laboring under great duress; his face pulsed with a flush and his hands trembled visibly. Why he had brought an attorney with him was not immediately clear. The attorney, for his part, kept his lips glued to Boyle's right ear in a manner reminiscent of the Roy Cohn-Joe McCarthy tango in other circuses of senatorial seasons.

Again, the content of the prepared statements which each of us read to Senator East regarding S 158, the Human Life Bill, was predictable. Willke and I made our strongly pro-life remarks: Goldstein dithered on about social conditions and unwanted pregnancies as if the continued legal existence of contraception were at issue (the Planned Parenthood full-page advertisements would have us believe that is the case, but serious thinkers on the issue know this line of argument is pure cant) and Boyle, in a rather uncertain voice declared that life does not begin at conception. He came out four-square in favor of the existing abortion ethic. The present position of the A.M.A. as stated by Boyle is at odds with the historical stance of that organization; as recently as June 1973, five months after the Roe v. Wade decision, the A.M.A. refused to commit itself to either side of the abortion controversy and instead issued a statement affirming the "traditionally favorable attitude of the medical profession toward pregnancy and motherhood." What significant medical advances have emerged that would nullify that position in the past eight years had escaped my notice. Senator East questioned Boyle rather closely on his statement and shook him with several rather caustic rebuttals to his answers. East appeared especially nettled by Boyle's timidity on the issue of amniocentesis and late abortion for defective fetuses. Boyle for his part shrank from jousting with the lawmaker in the wheelchair.

The last witness for the morning was John Ashcroft, Attorney-General for Missouri. I was under a considerable time limitation and had to leave before he testified.

The *New York Times* covered this set of hearings in characteristic style. The piece, written by Bernard Weinraub, appeared on page A 16 of the Friday, June 19, edition and was illustrated with a soulful photo of Ms. Weddington. The heading of the piece was "Senate Hearings on Abortion Close on Emotional Note," a sardonic reference to Dr. Gerster recounting her miscarriage and her examination of the wasted fetus.

Hyde's testimony was accorded three paragraphs in the lead of the piece. Weddington also got three paragraphs. Gerster got two paragraphs. Boyle, Goldstein, and Collins received a paragraph each. Meehan, Willke, and Ashcroft were simply listed as having appeared.

My name did not appear in the coverage. And again, my name did not appear in the *Washington Post* coverage of the hearings, whereas all other participants were listed. The *National Catholic Register*, also covering these hearings, managed to list *all* the participants—even me. Why did the *New York Times* fail to list me as participant? Possibly an oversight. Let's examine the record further: At the invitation of Senator Orrin Hatch (Rep. Utah), I journeyed once again to the Dirksen Senate Office Building on Wednesday, October 14, to testify regarding the proposed Hatch Amendment. Dr. Carl Tyler, who preferred to identify himself for the press as the ". . . Assistant Science Director for the Center for Disease Control in Atlanta" and with modesty avoided his more accurate designation as the then Head of the Abortion Surveillance Branch of the Center for Disease Control, was the first witness before Hatch's Senate Labor and Human Resource Committee. He droned out the body count: 1.6 million abortions in 1978, the last year for which there were complete statistics, a 7% increase over 1977. He commented that the typical woman who has an abortion is young, white, and unmarried. He neglected to state of course that there are more abortions per capita among blacks than whites, but perhaps Tyler with the crafty political wisdom that bureaucrats cultivate knew enough to circle warily around *that* hot potato. Departing only once from his fabled prudence, he did concede that there are thirty to thirty-five million abortions performed world wide every year, and this has resulted in abortion being the most frequently used form of *birth control*. Pro-abortion politicians must have twitched visibly when *that* particular cat bolted out of that particular bag!

Dr. Irving Cushner, a well-respected gynecologist from the UCLA Medical Center, followed with a peroration on abortion, love, and interpersonal communication that would have done the Reverend Jim Jones credit. Listen to this rather recondite link between abortion and human communication:

> That is the simple truth. There is a need for abortion . . . so long as we humans continue to occasionally communicate affection and love through sexual intercourse.

I followed Cushner to the witness table. Hatch was rather more difficult to read with respect to his attitude than Senator East. East had been skeptical, even a little belligerent, with the pro-abortion witnesses before his committee, but Hatch was carefully neutral, according each witness an equal measure of respect and even deference.

Hatch had seized what he probably conceived to be the cooler middle ground in this incendiary issue, to wit:

> Section 1. The right to abortion is not secured by this Constitution. The Congress and the several states shall have the concurrent power to restrict and prohibit abortions: Provided, that a law of a state more restrictive than a law of Congress shall govern. . . .

This proposed amendment was a brilliant example of Realpolitik, a masterly compromise in this seemingly insoluble conflict. Even ardent abortioneers would concede that the so called right to abortion resides in the perception by recent courts of a right to privacy in the Constitution, and the nexus between an alleged right to privacy and a claimed right to abortion is as shaky as a skid row derelict doing a microsurgical anastomosis. So the choice of the word "secured" in that first sentence was an exquisite subtlety; the unwary would assume that the word indicates that the right to abortion is not to be *found* in the Constitution, but in its correct usage the word means "to guard or make safe." What a precious ambiguity we have here: The right to abortion may after all reside in the Constitution for all we know but it is not beyond uprooting by this amendment. In short, a little something for everybody.

By entrusting the regulation of abortional practices to both Congress and the individual states ("several states" is an antique term, redolent of colonial Philadelphia: elegant gentlemen with aquiline profiles wigged and floured to a fault, plucking delicately at lace handkerchiefs in the cuffs of their splendid satin morning coats— reassuringly quaint), Hatch reached for the mantle of the "Great Pacificator," Henry Clay. To have suggested that only the states could regulate abortion practices would have conjured up in the press and the media a reactionary image, an antebellum mentality; to have left it to Congress alone would have alienated the right and virtually assured a bitter struggle in Congress every two years. What he proposed in fact was that the South, the Southwest, and the Midwest could be entrusted to formulate restrictive laws while the naughty bi-coastal areas would have to be propped up by Congress. Further, the passage of such an amendment would be lubricated by giving each of the major consenting parties to the amendment a role in the application of the amendment to abortion practices. Hatch-Eagleton carefully avoids this treacherous issue entirely.

Well and good. What does the phrase "concurrent power" mean? Or, as we used to ask when we were kids entering a haunted house, who goes first? Does Congress, possibly every two years, formulate a "model law," and the states conform to the Federal example? Or do the states pass their own laws—a more likely probability since they do not function in the national eye, and the political machinery in state legislatures is at once more efficient and more organized—and Congress trails badly behind in a welter of filibusters, power-brokering, horse-trading, and governmental paralysis, as the abortion law is tied to the national budget or to the defense budget or to the social programs budget? What such an amendment augured—no, guaranteed—is a round dozen or two of explosive, venomous fights in Congress and the legislatures of the more volatile states in the realm on the abortion issue every two years. Meanwhile, other equally important or more important affairs of state remain in enforced limbo.

Contrary to what the National Right to Life Committee argued, this amendment virtually guaranteed the germination and creative migratory shuttling of abortion sanctuaries in the nation, especially in the bi-coastal areas. It is reasonable to assume, for example, that states like New York and California (at this writing two of the eight states still supplying government subsidy to abortion in the form of medicaid payments) would provide statutes which are elastic and compliant, on the order of the Old American Law Institute Model allowing for abortion where there is incest, rape, fetal deformity, and/or serious threat to the maternal health. Anything is possible under such a law. While Congress is wrangling on abortion with each new House of Representatives and infusion of new Senators every two years, these sanctuaries would be in and out of business like street peddlers hawking "genuine" Swiss watches for four dollars each.

Now I am no constitutional scholar, but even someone as unschooled in the law as I am can foresee innumerable problems and litigation of the issue of what the phrase "more restrictive" means. Does it mean that if a state passes a law which bans all abortions after

twelve weeks but allows abortions up to twelve weeks for no reason—
that is, permissive abortion in the first trimester—that this law is
more restrictive than a federal statute which allows abortion in any
stage of the pregnancy for rape, incest, and the rest? Or if a state
passes a law which permits abortion up to the sixteenth week for fetal
deformity while Congress has mandated that abortions can be performed up to the twelfth week for rape, incest, or the health of the
mother, then which law prevails? The fine Elysian fields for abortion
litigation which this provides for Roy Lucas and Frank Sussman,
attorneys who have specialized in abortion law litigation and are
enormously effective at it, fairly beggar description.

In medical malpractice ligitation, the desideratum for the plaintiff's
lawyer is the situation in which the defendants—frequently the
hospital and the physician—are finally manipulated into wrangling
with each other as to who bears the major portion of the liability
for the damages alleged to have been suffered at their hands by
the client. Once the defending parties are set at each other's throats
it is Fat City for the plaintiff. With the Hatch Amendment, I
could easily envision the federal government and the state legislatures devoting a disproportionate and utterly unacceptable amount
of time bi-annually to the challenge of formulating laws which
attempt to supercede or in some other way outdistance each other.
Whole political careers would be made and broken on this issue,
and the courts would be brought to a standstill with the prodigious volume of litigation generated by such an ambiguous amendment. Meanwhile the descendants of C*R*A*S*H*, the third
generation of abortion clinics, would continue to function in what
would amount to a legal limbo, opening here and closing there in
response to the last and latest nuance in the last and latest interpretation of the law and the conflict between the federal government and
the individual states. A three-card monte game with millions of tiny
lives at stake.

But give Senator Hatch this: his timing was impeccable. While the
media were gagging over Senator East's Human Life Bill—potentially
the more workable legislation in its clarity and logic, but politicized
to the point of uselessness—Hatch arrived like the cavalry with an
amendment clearly distinguishable as anti-abortion, but pragmatic
and soft enough to seem moderate and statesmanlike. Here was an

umbrella wide enough to allow the National Right to Life, the National Conference of Catholic Bishops, the fundamentalists, and the Mormon Church to huddle under it uneasily. Indeed, even the *New York Times* delivered a compliment to him in its best left-handed tradition, calling him the "Point Man For The Right." In addition to his abortion pacificating, he has also sponsored a bill against forced busing, restraining federal judges from ordering busing to promote integration in schools. He has in the fire an amendment to outlaw affirmative action in hiring and education; he also reportedly has plans to hold hearings on the Federal Voting Rights Act to dilute its force with an amendment that would require the proof of intent of discrimination in the application of the act.

But the Hatch anti-abortion amendment was fundamentally unworkable—too broad, too tempting to legal gymnasts and sharp-shooters, and most important, virtually insuring turbulent and unceasing legislative conflict to say nothing of a thirty-year judicial war in the abortion arena. Give the Great Pacificator credit for trying to keep his coalition intact with a sop for everyone—that coalition is so volatile it makes the Entente Cordiale look like a couple of the guys down at the local watering-hole for a friendly beer—but it simply wouldn't wash.

In comparison to the Helms Amendment supported by Nellie Gray and her March for Life, the Hatch Amendment was a model of sweet reasonableness. In the Helms version, abortion was to be outlawed completely with no provision even for those admittedly rare cases in which the mother's life is at stake as a result of the continuation of the pregnancy. When Gray approached me with her proposal for support several years ago I told her quite candidly that I could not, as a physician, accept such an uncompromising solution to the problem. Nor for that matter would the American public, since it invoked an image of the anti-abortion movement as a bloodless monolith drained utterly of the humanitarian values which it professes to represent in its battle against the engineers of fetal destruction. Gray replied that in practice such an amendment would bend a little, allowing abortion in the most extreme life-threatening circumstances. If that is so, then the amendment is not what it seems and is thus an exercise in cynicism on the order of the old restrictive laws of pre-Roe v. Wade. This law we perverted to our pro-abortion uses in

1968 and 1969, using the old suicide-and-psychiatry caper in those dear dead days. Otherwise, Gray was indulging herself in the politics of cajolery with me.

At least the proposed National Right to Life Human Life Amendment engaged the central issue fearlessly and with sharp focus. It reads as follows:

> *Section 1.* The right to life is the paramount and most fundamental right of a person.
> *Section 2.* With respect to the right to life guaranteed to persons by the fifth and fourteenth articles of the Constitution, the word 'person' applies to all human beings irrespective of age, health, function or condition of dependency including their unborn offspring at every stage of their biological development including fertilization.
> *Section 3.* No unborn person shall be deprived of life by any person: Provided, however, that nothing in this article shall prohibit a law allowing justification to be shown for only those medical procedures required to prevent the death of either the pregnant woman or her unborn offspring as long as such law requires every reasonable effort be made to preserve the life of each.
> *Section 4.* Congress and the several states shall have power to enforce this article by appropriate legislation.

This proposed amendment is a model of logic and an exemplar of clarity in its first two sections in that it sets forth in the first section the pre-eminent right inherent in the United States Constitution, the right to one's continued existence: "the right to life . . . of a person." The second section thereupon defines the word "person" as it occurs in this amendment and in other apposite portions of the Constitution —that is the Fifth and Fourteenth Amendments. The definition is at once precise enough to include the unborn at all stages of maturation including fertilization itself and sweeping enough to embrace the many permutations and combinations of life which may soon spring from the burgeoning science of experimental embryogenesis (in vitro fertilization, for example) and genetic engineering. The pro-abortionist might obfuscate a bit by reading Section One of the Fourteenth Amendment substituting the definition of person proposed by the amendment, in this manner: "All unborn persons born or naturalized in the United States and subject to the jurisdiction thereof. . . ." To be charitable, there is a trace of ambiguity here, not to say outright nonsense, but I assume that the framers of the proposed amendment would insist that the definition of "person" as it applies in the proposed amendment and to the Fourteenth Amendment is to be limited only to that portion of Section One which concerns the following (and only this): ". . . nor shall any state deprive any person of life, liberty or property without due process of law."

Regrettably Section Three of the proposed amendment is burdened with an infelicity of phrasing which renders it all but impenetrable except to those who intuit the intent of the section. I presume that this section reserves to the physician the option of recommending—and if commissioned to do so by the pregnant woman, carrying out—a termination of pregnancy where the object of the procedure is to prevent the death of the pregnant woman. The phrasing

> . . . Provided however that nothing in this article shall prohibit a law allowing justification to be shown for only those medical procedures required to prevent the death of either the pregnant woman or her unborn offspring. . . .

is clumsy and opaque. If the intent was to set out the one set of circumstances in which abortion can be countenanced under his article, why not say it, viz:

> The individual state legislatures will be acting within the intent of this article if they devise laws allowing abortion to prevent the death of the pregnant woman.

How to devise a law allowing for an abortional procedure to prevent the death of the unborn offspring in the state of our present technology—every first trimester abortion involves the death of the fetus—is a legal mystification which eludes my untutored mind completely. If a pregnancy is terminated after the twentieth week—say, in the twenty-fourth or the twenty-fifth week—for a fetal indication, it is *not* an abortion but rather an induction of labor and a premature delivery, provided of course that the induction of labor is carried out with an agent compatible with fetal life such as pitocin and not with a lethal agent like hypertonic saline. But the notion that a true abortion—that is, a termination of pregnancy before the twentieth week—can be carried out to save the life of the child is simply rubbish, and this provision needs re-statement and/or clarification.

The final phrase in Section Three of the proposed amendment, "as long as such law requires every reasonable effort be made to preserve the life of each," is a judicious and eminently practicable cautionary. Conscientious obstetricians have always practiced in this manner, attempting always to preserve life where we find it. There is nothing in this section which binds the obstetrician to favor the fetal life over the maternal life despite the irresponsible shotgun casuistry of Dr. George Ryan who, in a return match with the United States Senate in October, 1981, declared that the establishment of legal personhood for the fetus would precipitate an intolerable conflict of health interests between the fetus and the mother, causing unsolvable problems for the pregnant woman and her physician. Perhaps what Ryan meant was that his assumption of any other posture but shameless grovelling before the liberal-intellectuals of the pro-abortion movement would pose an unsolvable problem between feminists and the male obstetrical community. In an age in which sound becomes image, light is tamed to penetrate the most secret recesses of the human body, and the lethal excrement of the nuclear beast is converted into the most marvellous diagnostic machinery, how a physician charged with the vigil for two lives can pervert this priestly charge into a politically convenient dissemblance is exceedingly difficult to comprehend. Well, as Saul Bellow said: "A great deal of intelligence can be invested in ignorance when the need for illusion is deep."

Neither amendment was perfect; not the all-purpose Hatch job nor the paunchy National Right to Life creation. And they were perhaps the two best of the breed. The flaw in the ointment may well have been that the subject—abortion itself—is unfit for constitutional amendment. The Thirteenth Amendment prohibiting slavery is a model of clarity and brevity: slavery may not exist in the United States. Why not then an equally clear, equally uncompromising constitutional declaration about abortion? (Hatch/Eagleton strives for this standard of excellence, but may be entirely too terse, too non-specific.) For one thing, abortion is not an unmitigated evil; there are certain admittedly rare circumstances in which abortion is justifiable. These instances would have to be set forth, not in any detail (it is not necessary to state in such an amendment that a fulminating malignant hypertension or end-stage renal disease is an appropriate indication for abortion) but at least as an operative principle. Slavery on the other hand is an unmitigated and unrelenting evil and under no conceivable circumstances can it be countenanced. Furthermore, slavery was a moral, economic, legal, and ultimately national political issue which was properly within the public domain at all times, so much so that it finally evolved into a dreaded and tragic public disagreement—civil war. But abortion, while similarly a moral, economic, legal, and moral issue and also quite properly within the public domain, has been tacitly ceded to two forces: to organized medicine in the mistaken belief that abortion is primarily a medical issue, and to the forces of radical feminism in an unforgivable genuflection by opinion-making liberal intellectuals to affirmative action on behalf of oppressed womanhood.

I have long doubted that an issue as complex and as multi-faceted as abortion will yield itself to crystallization within a restraining constitutional amendment. Perhaps we should bring another series of tests before the United States Supreme Court, but not on the timid periphery of whether there should be Federal funding of permissive abortion or whether there should be parental notification before abortion of a minor. No, the next series should be right on the money. Here, Ladies and Gentlemen, look at this television tape and deny that that responsive, thumb-sucking, ear-scratching breathing little fellow (ultrasound is now refined enough to determine sexual apparatus as well) in there is a human being. Watch him sleep, see him waken with a start, jump at the sound of a noise, cock his ear at soothing music. Draw close as we insert the fetoscope into the uterus and minutely inspect his features, count his fingers, draw blood from his umbilical vein, inject him with thyroid extract for his underactive thyroid, transfuse him with blood for his anemia, and even operate on him for his obstructed bladder and his malfunctioning kidneys. And that's only today's technology! Tomorrow's will be more convincing, more demanding. Discard the Blackmun Gilgamesh of Roe v. Wade and open the Sixteenth Edition of William's *Obstetrics*; Robert Goodlin's *Care of the Fetus* (1980); Longo and Reneau's *Fetal and Newborn Cardiovascular Physiology* (1978); Quilligan and Kretchmer's *Fetal and Maternal Medicine* (1980). The latter is a 680 page textbook put together by Dr. E. J. Quilligan, Professor of Obstetrics and Gynecology and Associate Vice President of Health Affairs at the University of Southern California School of Medicine, and Dr. Norman Kretchmer, the Director of the National Institute of Child Health and Human Development in Bethesda, Maryland. Approximately two-thirds of *Fetal and Maternal Medicine* deals with the function and disorders of the fetus and one-third with the newborn infant. I will volunteer my time to tutor Mr. Blackmun and his recalcitrant cronies on that Olympian bench in the elements of the New Science of Fetology which has flowered entirely since the Roe v. Wade decision.

It is certainly not unprecedented for the United States Supreme Court to overrule and reverse itself in the passage of time: In the last one hundred years it has reversed itself on major issues in over one hundred cases. For example, in 1942 in Betts v. Brady, the Court had held that the due process clause of the Fourteenth Amendment did not require a guarantee of counsel for indigents in state criminal trials. However, twenty-one years later in Gideon v. Wainwright (Gideon v. Cochran), the Court reversed itself and declared its original error, insisting that in 1963 the right of counsel to any and all accused in state criminal trials was guaranteed by the United States Constitution. Even more significant here is the observation that nothing significant or relevant to the issue had transpired in the intervening twenty-one years to elicit new facts, offer new insights, or in any way alter the substance of the arguments. Indeed, Justice Hugo Black who had participated in the deliberations and decision of Betts v. Brady is reported to have stated after the Gideon decision was announced: "When Betts v. Brady was decided I never thought I'd live to see it over-ruled."

Now, in the deplorable matter of Roe v. Wade we have the emergence of a New Science since the decision, a science which concerns itself solely with the substance of the argument; we have, in addition, a less suggestible national mood with the 1960-ish bellowing of rights muted to a civilized level of discourse. The bitterly divisive Vietnam War is behind us; the strident sandwich board Malthusiasts have been shown to be apocalyptic apes, with the birth of the green revolution and the aging of the population; the fundamentalist groups have developed a political voice; there is an increasingly conservative cast to the political complexion of the country; and even a few of the heavy hitters in the situationist team of ethicists are beginning to make revisionist noises. When Daniel Callahan of the Hastings Center publishes a rueful piece in the Report of the Center on "Minimalist Ethics," a piece in which he examines a little more critically the withering state of our ethical system in the past twenty years and finds it seriously ill, it may be time for a judicial reconsideration of the matter. This time the pro-life forces must take the offensive and

continue to press forward with all the careful preparation of a Mont-
gomery at El Alamein.

* * * *

The national referendum is a mode of political expression which
has never been utilized in this country. Referenda have been submitted to the electorates of many individual states on a variety of
issues ranging from the legalization of casino gambling to abortion
itself (in Michigan and North Dakota where the anti-abortion forces
prevailed and in the state of Washington where the pro-abortionists
won). One might offer that the bi-annual congressional elections
serve as referenda for the American electorate in that the candidates
have identifiable views on the subjects and topics in the national
spotlight. However the clarity of the process is to some extent blurred
for the voters by the personality attributes and liabilities of the
candidates, some waffling in imprecision on the plurality of issues for
which each candidate stands. For instance, a candidate may take a
strong pro-abortion stance but may also pump *for* busing or gun
control or some other posture putatively incompatible in the conventional political spectrum with anti-abortion posture. Here the pro-life
voter is torn between conflicting loyalties, and this failure to delineate
the issues sharply enough for the average voter has led in part to the
flowering of "single-issue" candidates and parties. The voter who pulls
the lever for the single-issue candidate is the purest political animal
imaginable: The candidate is the issue and vice versa. Still it is a little
ludicrous to envision the candidate of the National Rifle Association,
once elected to Congress, having to grapple with the rather more complex problem of the international control of nuclear weapons (he
would probably be in favor of it provided they weren't in the form of
conventional firearms). A successful democracy requires a breadth of
vision in its leaders which the single issue candidate cannot supply.

But the elected representative must be in touch not only with the
attitudes and wishes of his constituency, his over-riding obligation, he
also has a higher duty—the health of the nation. To that end the
congressman or the senator legislates for *all* the people, not just for
his own constituents. And to that end the colossal polling industry
has taken root and flourished. But a poll is not a referendum any
more than an anthology is an organic novel. Furthermore, the American public itself has grown sufficiently sophisticated to understand
the flaws inherent in polling: the selection of the sample, the size of the

sample, the wording of the question, the attitude of the questioner, the season of the year, even the barometric pressure of the day. More to the point, the respondent to a poll has no time to formulate the answers; he or she is usually confronted by a questioner who demands an immediate answer to the question. With a widely-advertised referendum question to be conducted at some time in the future, there is an opportunity for the voter to seek out advice, research the factual base of the question, crystallize attitudes, and then register the answer in the secrecy and isolation of the voting booth. Ergo, a national referendum is a more reliable and more accurate expression of opinion on a public issue than is an infinity of polls.

The national referendum had been used to advantage in Western Europe on a variety of public issues. In May, 1981, in Italy the abortion issue was put to referendum with a set of three clearly phrased questions to the voters. Should the abortion laws remain as they are (free abortion up to twelve weeks for any woman over eighteen)? Should the laws be expanded to allow abortion at any stage of the pregnancy? Should the laws be abolished and abortion once again totally outlawed? The electorate opted for retention of the present laws, and having spoken put the quietus on the issue, at least for the present. Admittedly the results of the referendum did not automatically force the pro-life forces in Italy into immediate liquidation, but these results served notice that until a new or more forceful collection of arguments is adduced, the issue will be placed on the back burner and the current laws will prevail. A tacit moratorium was established, and the warring parties withdrew to the old drawing board.

In contrast, in the United States with no provision or precedent for a national referendum and with no national single issue candidate to stand, we have no clear expression of the national opinion. Instead we have nasty little skirmishes on the local and state levels which never seem to end; we have marches, demonstrations, sit-ins, fire-bombings, unrelenting barrages of poll results, rallies, and parades. We have a national referendum of nine people perched in a judicial cloudland determining the national will, a plebescite so fragile and so pitifully inadequate that, far from setting the issue to rest for a time, it merely stirs up more furor by the nature of the result and the frailty of the process. No, if ideas and arguments are the currency of change, then the referendum as expression of national will may be the quoin of the realm.

Some will argue that the process by which an amendment to the Constitution is adopted is an ultimate plebescite, requiring approval by two-thirds of both House and Senate and three-quarters of the states. But here we have a different mode of expression, an electoral-college phenomenon in which thirty-eight states may approve but the majority of the electorate may not. Furthermore, the process of ratification may take a considerable length of time. In the matter of Articles XI through XXVI, the average interval between passage by Congress and final ratification by the states was 1.5 years, not including the time necessary to conduct the various hearings in the Congress prior to passage. The Equal Rights Amendment slogged along for seven lean years, and in that time voter sentiment may change to the extent that a state which ratified the proposal three or four years before now wishes to change its vote. In addition, this procedure keeps the issue before the public far too long and does not allow for a lengthy period of quiet following defeat by referendum in which the opposition may withdraw, reorganize its presentation, and come before the electorate with new ideas. One may well hold that the very length of time necessary to adopt an amendment virtually guarantees that the adoption is not a frivolous expression of the national will but a slow-maturing, deliberate determination. Still, the Eighteenth Amendment was ratified in January, 1919, and a scant fourteen years later it was repealed.

The national referendum is a useful and reasonable mode of political expression, perhaps clearer and more precise than anything we have employed until now. While I do not advocate that laws should be formulated by this means alone, the referendum would certainly be an unambiguous and reliable guide both to those who would legislate in the true democratic tradition (in an Aristotelian equilibrium between the duty to one's conscience and the assertion of the popular will) and to those in the judicial ionospheres who would make law in the guise of interpreting law. Bored as we may be with the maxims of Mr. Dooley, it's still inescapable that ". . . the Supreme Court follows the election results."

* * * *

Hatch was clearly in his element. He had now emerged as a redoubtable conservative statesman, and he lounged easily behind the rostrum like an iguana on a hot rock. I read my prepared statement, and he seemed to be paying attention, except for when some flunky would whisper into his ear or he would turn and summon another aide to carry memoranda for him. Hatch proceeded to ask me questions, the same ones he had asked Cushner and Tyler before me and would ask Thomas Hilgers after me. The questions were pedestrian, largely concerned with the deleterious effects of second-trimester abortions, but one of the questions was provocative and interesting.

Q. What suggestions would you have as to how this sub-committee can best contribute to an intelligent or rational debate in the Senate? Some think that our debates in the Senate and House have been somewhat irrational. I guess it depends on which side you are on and who is winning at the time. How could we have the most rational intelligent debate on this subject?

A. As you know, Mr. Chairman, this is an extraordinarily incendiary issue.

Q. It sure is.

A. Everybody has an expert opinion in it. I suppose that the first thing one has to do is examine very carefully those statements which pass for argument but in fact are nothing but slogan and shibboleth. Examine them very critically, because most of them are hollow. I have pointed out some of them in my little statement to you: that a woman's right to control her own body is a deceitful slogan. I say this because of the recent advances in the area of immunology [which has demonstrated repeatedly and conclusively that the white blood cells of the immune system have the unique ability to distinguish between "self" and "non-self," and as a consequence refrain from attacking and destroying one's *own* organs such as the heart and kidneys; but these same white blood cells surge to the site of implantation of the conceptus in the uterus at the ninth day, recognize it as an alien, a "non-self" (half of its chromosomes are derived from the father) and mount a concerted attack to destroy it and cast it out of the maternal body. Over the eons the fetus has of course evolved a sophisticated and effective defense to this attack, and in ninety per cent of cases a stalemate results. The attack wanes as the fetal defenses repel it, and the fetus continues to grow and develop in its immune sanctuary. This is a classical example of the biological facts belieing the political fiction.]

The whole argument has proceeded past all those 1960-ish rallying cries (I was the author of a great many of these, in conjunction with Friedan and Lader) that we used. I have attempted in my book (*Aborting America*) to examine those passwords and slogans very carefully.

The state of the art today is so different from what it was in 1967 and 1968 when I and a few others sold permissive abortion to the American public that one must concentrate only on the exponential advances in fetology and perinatology as of today—1983. It is time-wasting and unprofitable to dredge up those ancient myths and slogans of the 1960s. We are long since past that, and I do not think we should allow ourselves to be stuck in that mire anymore.

Hatch wanted to move the senatorial storm over abortion off dead center. He perceived one side noisily asserting feminist doctrine with endless keening over the impending loss of "abortion rights" (conceived in ignorance and dedicated to the proposition that everything created may equally be destroyed). He envisioned the anti-abortion opposition yielding no ground whatever. The serene middle ground that he had seized might be only four microns wide and as dangerous as a sally into no-man's land at Verdun in 1916, but he had evidently consulted my maps, cased the terrain, and decided that it might be just the ground from which to launch himself into the presidential firmament.

During my testimony, there had been some angry stirrings from time to time from the assemblage behind me. Pro-abortion forces outnumbered the pro-life contingent in that hearing room by a considerable margin if one were to judge by the volume of mutinous muttering accompanying my witness. At one point there was an outbreak of hissing and a few catcalls when I firmly denied that the re-criminalization of abortion would lead to carnage among women seeking illegal abortions. I took some considerable pains to describe the extremely efficient abortifacient drug prostaglandin and predicted that women would purchase prostaglandin suppositories on the black market if abortion were proscribed. They would then have their abortion swiftly, safely, and privately in their own bathrooms without recourse to the archetypal drunken defrocked doctor, scheming midwife, or filthy crone practicing kitchen-table gynecology. It continues to be an incongruity to me that feminists will insist upon their putative right to a hazardous surgical procedure for interruption of pregnancy when for the first time in recorded history science has finally developed a simple, safe, efficient, and low-cost abortifacient drug such as prostaglandin. This obstinate and muddle-headed fidelity to the surgical procedure with its attendant risks and its relatively astronomical costs is quite inexplicable. With typical revolutionary myopia they are proceeding on the dubious basis that if it was good enough for our mothers, now that the doctor doesn't have to peer over his shoulder at the door any longer, it's good enough for the sisters. I am of course not advocating abortion by prostaglandins as a procedure any more ethically acceptable than abortion by suction; I am merely predicting what would happen if abortion *were* proscribed in the United States.

Hatch hushed the mutiny with a stern injunction that he would tolerate no partisan support or vocal demonstration from the audience. My testimony then concluded, and I retired to my seat at the press table. The room was so crowded that it was the only seat available.

Dr. Thomas Hilgers, Associate Professor of Obstetrics and Gynecology at the Creighton University School of Medicine in Omaha and Director of the Creighton University Natural Family Planning and Educational Research Center, sat himself at the speaker's table at Hatch's invitation. Hilgers is a distinguished physician with impressive academic credentials in the field of obstetrics and gynecology and has made some interesting demographic studies on abortion particularly with respect to abortion statistics prior to 1973. With some rather arresting statistical studies carried out over the past several years, he and his colleagues have shown that contrary to what we in the National Association for the Repeal of Abortion Laws (NARAL) were feeding to the public and the media in the late 1960s, that there were at least a million or so illegal abortions a year in the United States. In fact, there was an average of 98,000 abortions per year for the years 1940–1967. Compare that figure to the 1.5 million abortions performed annually on a legal basis at present, and it is inescapable that 1.4 million of those women would probably have opted to have their children in a less permissive era, and 1.4 million children would have been spared. Thus it would seem that the dominant factor in the decision for abortion is *not* maternal health, *not* economic circumstance, *not* psychological and emotional distress. The dominant factor is the legality or illegality of the operation. Hilgers' statistics seem to confirm that when women conceive, a great number of them are of several minds regarding the fate of the pregnancy, and if the political, moral, and legal climate is such that irresponsibility and permissiveness is the order of the day, then they will choose abortion. However, if abortion is illegal and disapproved of by the pregnant woman's peers and by the general public, then she will probably resolve to carry the child to term.

In the vast majority of cases, women elect abortion not out of physical, emotional, or financial considerations, but primarily from the consideration of whether it's easily and legally available. The pro-abortionists are fond of declaring that one cannot regulate morality and invoke in their behalf the abysmal Prohibition experiment in the United States. The Volstead Act criminalized the drinking of alcohol but human nature could not be changed, the argument goes, so people simply drank underground, in the speak-easies. But during Prohibition there were no profound issues at stake, no questions or doubts regarding human life and its destruction. In the abortion dilemma women become pregnant through a natural process (drinking alcohol is *not* a natural process), and carrying the pregnancy to term is a natural process. Abortion is a factitious and violent disruption of that natural process, and in other less permissive times society has generally rejected it in all but a comparatively few cases—according to Hilgers, ninety-five per cent of the time. Now in these affluent times with ubiquitous governmental support programs and subsidized medical care, that same ninety-five per cent are choosing abortion because it is convenient, legal, and evidently no longer disapproved of. I say "evidently" because there seems to be a persistent public uneasiness with abortion despite what the Roe-Doe Court said. Look at the results of the *Life* magazine poll: a majority of respondents confessed to their interviewer that they still regard abortion as immoral, but in response to another question posed, they asserted that it should be kept legal.

Hilgers pressed forward. With his remorseless figures he pointed out that far from the 5,000 to 10,000 deaths from illegal abortion annually which we in NARAL had fastened upon in our political campaign as a nice, round, shocking figure, the actual number in the twenty-five year period prior to Roe-Doe averaged 250 and the

highest figure for any one year was 388 in 1948. With the enormous
advances in antibiotic research and development, anesthesia techniques, and diagnostic modalities since 1948, it is no surgical ex-
travagance to assert that today at least seventy-five to eighty per cent
of those women would have been saved. So that the projected toll of
deaths from illegal abortion, even assuming women returned to the
back alley, would now probably be seventy-five or so a year.

Hilgers paused. There was no dramatic hush, no sharp intakes of
breath in the wake of his revelations. Hatch was a little glazed, but
imperturbable. No fellow committee members had shown up for this
portion of the hearings. The audience was sullen; brows were bee-
tling, and a collective snarl bloomed on the upturned faces. All
oblivious to the lowering air of the packed chamber, Hilgers strode
over to a television screen at the right lateral extremity of the rostrum
and announced that he was going to show a ten minute tape of a realtime ultrasound picture of a sixteen week old fetus in utero. The
crowd began to boil. The feminists, the pro-abortionists, and the
liberal press had seen this material before, and they sensed correctly
that it was dynamite. It was the aseptic, cooled-down, rigorously
non-partisan 1981 scientific counterpart of these old four-color flam-
ing placards depicting the fetal auto-da-fe brandished by another
steamier generation of pro-life workers. It was the Abortion War
brought into the living room.

Hilgers' tape of the real-time ultrasound on the sixteen week old
fetus was, predictably, compelling. The child could be seen shifting its
position, sticking its thumb into its mouth, and breathing. Some of
the feminist cadres stared fixedly at the floor but other less disciplined ones concentrated on that screen with rapt attention. After
all, for a generation born and brought up to regard the electronic
media as baby sitter, mealtime companion, and evening jester, that
screen represents immediacy. The printed word is a longish trip to the
memory banks. It may still be the staple of formal education, but the
masses are learning from the small screen, and the anchorman-host-
moderator is the professor. The young shock troops of the pro-
abortion camp were being pelted with electronic pamphlets, and a
few wavered. In that packed room the day belonged to Hilgers and
his close encounter with the unborn.

What was the press coverage of this proceeding? The *New York*

Times, the so-called "newspaper of record," did not cover the proceeding. Not a word. Whether the *New York Times* was signalling that the failure to cover was, in effect, an Olympian dismissal of the whole grubby disagreement which in any case had been decided for all time by the Roe-Wade decisions of 1973, was not determinable from the journalistic silence. It is simply inconceivable that the *New York Times* was unaware of the hearings. No, I believe that someone on an editorial level had decided that the abortion argument was distillable into the political kickapoo of Women's Rights and Freedom of Choice, and that there was nothing new under the sun. The failure to cover was surely not attributable to my presence at those hearings; there were many other witnesses, some pro-abortion, and certainly their testimony was of interest.

Contrast if you will the patrician disregard which the New York press lavished upon these Hatch hearings with the slavish adoration it showered upon the Equal Rights Amendment. When the cooling corpse of the E.R.A. gave off a posthumous twitch (on December 1, 1981, a handful of desperate feminists encamped in Times Square to act as a "message brigade" to persuade New Yorkers to write to and work in states which have failed to ratify the amendment) the New York press made sure that there was full coverage of this homerically insignificant event.

But examine if you will the coverage provided by the *Washington Post*. On the following day, October 15, the *Post* printed an eight paragraph, thirty-four line piece in the second section of its Thursday edition. The piece was not by-lined by one of its own reporters but was a story from the wire of the United Press International. There was a reporter from the *Washington Post* at that hearing. Nor do I doubt that that reporter turned in copy on those hearings to the *Post*: What happened to the copy? Was it too non-partisan and unsuitable for printing in that bastion of democratic social liberalism?

The UPI piece which did appear in the *Post* mentioned Tyler and summarized his testimony in some detail. Cushner was covered in two paragraphs. Neither Hilgers nor I were mentioned.

There are two separate but related aspects of this journalistic malpractice upon which I shall comment. The first is the question of whether a specific event, be it accident, fire, conference, funeral, or election should or should not be covered by the press; the second is the quality of the coverage. These two questions of course subsume at least a significant portion of the function of an ethical press in a free society.

In regard to the first, the free press is constantly called upon to exercise choice in the selection of events to be covered and words to be printed. As an example, the *New York Times* receives 2.5 million words daily in its editorial offices and can print only 185,000. Decisions must be made daily and often hourly regarding assigning reporters to specific places for coverage of specific events. These decisions are made by human beings, not by machines; as the unjustly persecuted protagonist put it rather sardonically to the crusading reporter in the film "Absence of Malice": "Who puts out the paper—nobody?" *Someone* up there decided that the senatorial hearings on the Hatch amendment were simply not news-worthy and more important were not fit ("All the news that's fit to print") for consumption by the decision-making electorate. This judgement was made—clearly mistakenly—in light of what was emerging as a politically feasible and workable compromise between the more militant and the more pragmatic forces on the anti-abortion front. The Hatch amendment was endorsed, albeit reluctantly, by the National Conference of Bishops, and in proposing to return law-making power on the abortion issue to the sovereign states and to Congress, Hatch had geometrically increased the chances of passing an anti-abortion amendment during the Reagan suzerainty. But someone up there abused his fiduciary duties to the electorate and decreed that there would be no coverage. Whether the decision was made from the doctrinal posture of the newspaper; whether it was made from a purely personal consideration on the part of an editor stemming from personal bias or political frenzy; or whether it was a combination of the two is not determinable. The issue of whether this question should be determinable, and if so, how, will be discussed presently.

For the press *does* have a definable fiduciary duty to the electorate, and no amount of First Amendment belligerency or Fourteenth Amendment razzle-dazzle can refute this relationship contention. The electorate is willy-nilly forced into a trust relationship with the working press upon which it depends entirely for the information it needs in the public—and even private—area of decision-making. The relationship, however, is an unequal one, resembling the relationship between a doctor and a patient. In the latter case, the doctor has a superior knowledge of medicine and the patient has a medical need, most often urgent, without the ability to bargain for it. In the case of the press and the public, the former has superior knowledge of events and the massive resources to disseminate this knowledge while the latter needs this knowledge and is also in no position to bargain for it. After all, can you afford to go to Washington yourself and listen in on all the congressional hearings, conferences, debates, votes, and cloak-room scuttlebutt on every public issue which may substantially affect your life and your well-being? Can you as a responsible and conscientious citizen foreswear the news and make your decisions in a vacuum?

Over the centuries the law has taken note of the question of unequal relationships, whether in contracts, in guardians and incompetents, in trustees and dependents, or in executors and heirs. It has formulated a considerable body of law regarding these basically unequal relationships between fiduciaries and beneficiaries. In addition, the law has provided appropriate punishment for those who abuse the relationship. If I, a gynecologic surgeon, fail to explain to my patient the risks, consequences, benefits, and "complications" of a proposed surgical procedure, the law regards this as an abuse of the fiduciary relationship between me and the patient (called lack of informed consent: The patient could not make an informed decision regarding the proposed surgery without this information, and in the law no one can make a decision regarding your body except you). I, the physician, may be severely punished.

But the fiduciary relationship between the press and the electorate is the only such relationship in which there are no legal safeguards to regulate it. The libel laws are totally ineffective here since they do not cut to the heart of the issue: what to tell the electorate and what not to tell it. In addition, the libel laws prevail only in acts of commission. For instance, in general one may sue the press for libel only when the press has made a false and injurious statement with malice. The silence of the press cannot be interpreted as libelous, but it is nonetheless as injurious to the electorate and as firm an abuse of its fiduciary obligation to the public as a deliberate misstatement.

But even more serious than the breach of good faith on the part of the press here, beyond the abuse of the fiduciary relationship, is the seemingly purposeful suppression of the news. The *New York Times* has been quite openly committed to the permissive abortion ethic in its editorial columns. However, when someone up there in the decision-making stratosphere of the paper decrees that senatorial hearings should not be covered because they might be the source of new and startling revelations in the abortion arena that are inimical to the stated editorial policy of the publication, we have now crossed into the Orwellian world of suppression of the news, or *internal censorship*. Was it that the testimony of Hilgers and Nathanson was not fit to print? Or was it that a reporter listening to my statement and the answers to Senator Hatch's questions, listening to Hilgers and watching that bombshell of a tape on the television, might be unexpectedly swayed to write a fair, reasoned, and informative piece for the public indicating that the 1969 passwords can no longer suffice for pro-abortion arguments in 1981?

Now it would be disingenuous indeed for me to pretend that partisan suppression of the news—internal censorship—has not been practiced from time immemorial by the press. But in the coverage of an issue of the immediacy of the Abortion Wars in which twelve million or so lives have been lost thus far, it is a particularly offensive and reprehensible act. To suggest to the press that full and frank disclosures of all aspects of congressional debate on, say, capital punishment, in which the innocent lives of perhaps ten people a year may be taken, should be modified or selectively suppressed to fit editorial policy would likely provoke a collective seizure or worse. And yet in the abortion issue the practice continues unabated.

The abuse of the fiduciary relationship and the internal censorship of news hostile to editorial policy is especially dangerous when practiced by the mega-press: the all-powerful eastern liberal newspapers such as the *New York Times* and the *Washington Post*, the three television networks, the wire services of the Associated Press and the United Press International, and the news magazines such as *Time* and *Newsweek*. Not only are these the eminently visible opinion-makers of our society, but they are colossal multinationals infiltrating and colonizing the information industry of the western world.

To cite an example: In New York City, the *New York Times* circulates to 900,000 readers daily, with an edition printed in Chicago flown to most of the major cities in the West, Southwest, Northeast, and South. It has a Sunday circulation of 1.4 million copies. It owns and operates eighteen other daily and weekly newspapers throughout the United States. It owns and operates five major magazines including *Family Circle*, the largest-selling woman's magazine in the country, and two magazines in Australia. It owns and operates three television stations in the South and one major radio station in New York City. It owns and operates its own news service which is the leading supplemental news wire service in the country and distributes material from the *New York Times* to over 500 dependent publications around the world. It owns two publishing companies, an information bank, a micro-film company, two companies which manufacture audio-visual materials for educational purposes, four huge paper mills, and a substantial interest in the *International Herald Tribune*. In its Annual Report 1980, the *New York Times* harumphs a little, puffs contentedly on its cigar while knitting its brows thoughtfully, and discloses with irreproachable modesty that the operating profit for the newspaper itself was ". . . the highest ever for the newspaper—31.4 million dollars, a fifteen per cent increase over 1979." And the revenue for the New York Times corporation in 1980 was $733,237,000, somewhat higher than the total take for the entire abortion industry in the United States in the same year. This is not exactly your average Mom 'n Pop country weekly that James Stewart takes over when he resigns in a sanctimonious huff from the corrupt *Big City Daily* and turns the weekly into the rural equivalent of the *Manchester Guardian* after three weeks of Herculean effort and the devoted and adoring efforts of June Allyson. Not to put too fine a point on it, but don't you think the *New York Times'* behavior is a mite hypocritical in accepting all that full-page, four-color advertising by the cigarette companies, while on its editorial pages it's fulminating mightily over the public hazards and costs of smoking and calling for instant revocation of federal subsidies to the tobacco farmers?

It would be pointless—perhaps even tasteless if you happen to be a liberal and have your gag reflex easily activated by what the *New York Times* delights in calling "windfall" or "obscene" profits—to list the holdings, annual revenues, and net profits of its cronies in the mega-press. Let it suffice to say that they are on the self-same mega-scale as those of the *New York Times* save for the *New England Journal of Medicine* which practices a Jesuitical restraint, plucking a dainty handkerchief from its sleeve, and holding it ever so disdainfully to its elegant Back Bay nose at the merest hint of a profit motive. The *Journal*, however, qualifies itself for that august company by its transcendent medical statesmanship and its editorial love-feast with the liberal establishment.

In the late 1960s, the *New England Journal of Medicine* began its romance with the mega-press. The *Journal* radiated an unmistakable aura of Harvard respectability but trailed a seductive spoor of girlish daring that roused the mega-press to a fevered pitch. The *New England Journal of Medicine* began to publish all manner of arcana ranging from unbearably arch little pieces such as a clinical description of the Chinese Restaurant Syndrome to my own editorial article "Deeper into Abortion" in which I raised some perplexing questions concerning the permissive abortion ethic but, probably to the *Journal*'s ineffable relief, still came down foursquare on the side of legal abortion. I had of course calculated that, in submitting my piece to the *New England Journal of Medicine*, it would get the widest possible circulation in the mega-press as the romance was by that time out of the closet; in that judgement I was not disappointed. I was deluged with correspondence, interviewed to a fare-thee-well, and courted shyly by the pro-life movement.

The *New England Journal of Medicine* has continued to act like a moon-struck middle-aged gamine in a sweaty love-affair with the liberal Lothario. Following the conviction of Dr. Kenneth C. Edelin for manslaughter, the *New England Journal of Medicine* published an editorial in its March 27, 1975, issue in which it termed the trial itself a "fiasco" (in truth the only fiasco was poor Dr. Edelin's horrifying misconception of what an abortion is); appealed to cheap racist sentiment in carefully pointing out that the pregnant woman involved was black; blurred the issues in determining the fetus at "twenty to twenty-eight weeks old" (we can pinpoint the fetal age more accurately than that; it was in fact twenty-five to twenty-six weeks old); martyred Edelin by terming him a ". . . sacrificial victim of the continuing bitter strife between pro-abortion and anti-abortion forces" when, to put it plainly, he was a victim of his own infelicitous lack of judgement; suggested that the whole Edelin matter was set into motion by the pro-life forces ("Hence it is reprehensible that a movement in pursuing what it perceives as a high ethical goal resorts to guerilla tactics to undermine the 1973 Supreme Court decision. . . ."); trundled in my article, "Deeper into Abortion," in a clumsy lunge at even-handedness; and finally, hurling caution to the winds, passed the hat around in behalf of the Kenneth Edelin Defense Fund.

Nor does it feel itself constrained to confine itself to comment only on medical matters. With a fine Churchillian sweep it will not hesitate to pronounce on affirmative action, nuclear politics, or Federal budgetary matters. In the October 8, 1981, issue the *New England Journal of Medicine* published a piece by Faith T. Fitzgerald, M.D., Associate Dean for Students and Curricular Affairs at the University of California at Davis, entitled "Three Years After Bakke: A Reaffirmation." It is a ringing social manifesto deploring the reputed racist standards for admission to medical school of past generations (keeping to just this side of a nakedly reverse-racist appeal, for example: "minority students may evidence more commitment and more perseverance than the average white student in professional school. . . ."); proposing an entirely new and avowedly politico-racial set of standards ("Because of the unending demands of medicine we want to recruit people who have the ability to endure and overcome opposition. . . ."): implying that intelligence, scholarship, and ability have little or nothing to do with the mastery of the medical arts ("minority students who have had academic difficulty with the preclinical curriculum may do very well in the clinical years when subjective judgements of personal relationships with patients are a substantial factor in the assessment of student performance. . . .") and a coda on the impending reductions in federal funding and scholarships for "disadvantaged and poor applicants to medical schools" (are all the "disadvantaged" poor? or visa versa?).

Now I have no serious quarrel with the *New England Journal of Medicine* allotting its editorial space to a plainly political pamphlet like this one, and I am not disconsolate that Fitzgerald seems unaware that medical student loans have the lowest rate of repayment (by the currently affluent recipient-graduates practicing high-cost, high-tech medicine in the opulent suburbs of a hundred cities in this nation) of any federal loan program extant. Thirty-three per cent of the 167,000 recipients who benefited from the Federal Health Professionals Student Loan Progam are delinquent at this writing. It has depleted the resources of the program by twenty-three million dollars. Seventy per cent of the delinquents had perfect credit rating in their *own* commerce, so it is just "ripping off Uncle." If we compare *this* program, say, to the National Direct Student Loan Program, the latter has a default rate of only thirteen per cent. Ergo, the three-fold increase in delinquency in the medical borrower's group probably represents, at least in part, a response by blacks and other "disadvantaged" to white middle-class breast-beating and general mortification of flesh.

I am not moved to protest when Fitzgerald invokes that old chestnut "medical schools may soon be open only to rich kids," though Trotsky did it with more éclat; it is, after all, only political pamphleteering and any old chestnut goes into *that* fire. I am not even especially disturbed that Fitzgerald seems ignorant of the fact that at her own medical school there has been a sharp decline in black enrollment since the 1978 Bakke decision, so sharp that the college has had to hire a consultant and has obtained a Federal grant to help attract students from the minority groups. At first glance that might seem cause for rejoicing for those conservative forces which view affirmative action as unjust and unconstitutional. I view it as an affirmation that black students want no social charity from the white power structure, want no paternalistic condescension from the likes of Faith Fitzgerald, and hold to a higher standard of dignity, self-worth, and self-respect than even the United States Supreme Court in its whiggish waffling gave them credit for.

No. I am deeply offended by the *Journal*'s failure to maintain balance. I am affronted by the inexcusable suppression of heterodox opinion in the pages of this issue of the *Journal*. Had the editorial staff contented itself to publish purely scientific papers ("Defective EBV-Specific Suppressor T-Cell Function in Rheumatoid Arthritis") or irascible medical correspondence ("Upshaw-Schulman Syndrome and Fibronectin") there would be no justifiable grievance. But when the *New England Journal of Medicine* moves to transcend the modest limits of any respectable professional publication and strikes instead for pundit status right up there with Walter Lippman and "Foreign Affairs," in effect burrowing in as the runt of the mega-press, it incurs a decent obligation to showcase dissenting opinion. Even its beloved big brother, the *New York Times*, once printed an anti-abortion piece on its Op-Ed page, although in all fairness one must point out that the author of the piece, Dr. Walker Percy, is a physician, an internationally renowned novelist, and possible Nobel Prize winner in literature. The Op-Ed page could hardly turn *him* down as a right-wing nut writing irascible anti-abortion tracts (all in all, though, it *was* a pretty testy piece, especially impatient with the pro-abortion doublespeak).

During my militantly pro-abortion days, the keys to the city were pressed upon me by the *Journal*: in 1972 it published as a "Special Article" my paper on "Ambulatory Abortion: Experience with 26,000 Cases" which was a reprise of the history and mechanics of C*R*A*S*H, and in addition established for the first time the feasibility and safety of mass-scale ambulatory abortion. In November, 1974, it published as an editorial piece the "Deeper into Abortion" essay. In February, 1975, it presented a collection of critical letters on "Deeper," and allowed me to issue a rebuttal letter. With what now seems pitiable naivete I believed that the *New England Journal of Medicine* would continue its hospitality toward my changing views on abortion. I had maintained for many years that medical journals serve as marketplaces for ideas and that these bazaars are necessary for those researchers and clinical investigators who would traffic in novel hypotheses and innovative ideas in medicine. I was more experienced in the field of abortion (the political, surgical, and ethical arenas) than perhaps any other physician in the United States. True, I had written what could be interpreted—at least by the more febrile pro-abortion legions—as an anti-abortion treatise (*Aborting America*), though I maintain that it is a scrubbed and neutral treatment of a profoundly perplexing question (so neutral that I took pains to depersonify the fetus in my book, calling it "alpha" throughout). And there is no denying that I had addressed a great number of pro-life gatherings in the two years since the publication of that book, although I had clung to what I believed to be an ethically sound, non-doctrinaire posture on the issue. I had refused to join formally with any pro-life organization, emphasizing my considerable differences with the organizational dogma. I support more funding for contraceptive research, better and safer contraception, exception for the mother's life in proposed abortion law, and refusal to condemn the intrauterine device and the oral contraceptive "pill" as abortifacient agents. For these reasons I held fast to a belief that a seemingly apolitical medical publication like the *New England Journal of Medicine* would not shrink from exposing its not inconsiderable audience to a carefully worked out and astringently apolitical dissent. *Aborting America* had been refused for review by the *New York Times* on at least five separate submissions, while Lader's book, *Abortion II: Making The Revolution*, and a skimpy little paperback by Arlene Carmen and the Reverend Howard Moody, *Abortion Counselling and Social Change,* had been most favorably reviewed by Jane Brody in the *New York Times* in company with—what else?—*Abortion: A Woman's Guide* by the Planned Parenthood of New York City. No, the adamant impenetrability of the *New York Times* was all but expected. I was a little miffed at the *Journal* for not having at least taken notice of the publication of *Aborting America* (a harbinger?) in its Book Review section, but put this down to oversight. The title was by no stretch of the imagination a medical one, and it could therefore have easily escaped the notice of those entrusted with monitoring the medical and paramedical press for the *Journal*. Even so, the editors do take note of a wide range of books in that Book Review section of the *Journal*. For example, *Budgeting Fundamentals for Nonfinancial Executives*, by Allen Sweeny and John N. Wisner, Jr., and *The Joy of Running*, by Thaddeus Kostrubala, M.D., are not exactly pure science. Slighted, even feeling a little rebuffed, I still believed in the quintessential fairness of the *New England Journal of Medicine*.

I was wrong. Egregiously, infuriatingly wrong. "Morbus Abortiensis and the Quaquaversal Ethic" taught me *that*.

The human brain and spinal cord float freely in a bath of straw-colored fluid called the cerebro-spinal fluid. Your brain consists of two hollow chambers—the lateral ventricles, one on each side—which are surrounded by brain substance, or "white matter." It is in each of these chambers that a little cluster of blood vessels called the choroid plexus secretes this fluid, and the fluid then travels, like a lake emptying down into a falls, through a narrow passageway in the back of the brain, the aqueduct of Sylvius, into a smaller lake, the fourth ventricle, which surrounds the hind brain, the medulla. From there the fluid circulates around the spinal cord and is finally picked up by little veins around the spinal cord to be returned to the general circulation. The fluid serves a number of vital functions. It acts as a shock absorber for the brain and cord; it supplies nutrients to the brain and cord; and it even helps maintain a constant temperature around these structures. There are about two ounces of this fluid in the average adult human; in the fetus and newborn, there is only about a teaspoonful.

Even the ancient Egyptians knew about the cerebro-spinal fluid. They were a clever lot and did an impressive amount of probing of the brain, particularly in people who had sustained injuries of the head. In 3000 B.C. they wrote down their findings on papyri called the Edwin Smith Papyri, named after the explorer who discovered these writings. Hippocrates, the oath-giver, also recognized the unique characteristics of this fluid and described it quite well. But it was not until comparatively recently, in 1842, that the actual circulation of the fluid from the front end of the brain to the bottom of the spinal cord was understood and described by a Frenchman named François Magendie, who was rewarded by having the outflow passageway for the fluid named after him—foramen of Magendie. Small cheese indeed—he died penniless.

Very well. The fluid circulates around the brain and spinal cord from front to back, up and down. What happens if the circulation is interrupted and there is an obstruction to the orderly circulation of the fluid? Simple. If the obstruction, or the dam, is at the narrowest portion of this river, or the aqueduct of Sylvius, then the fluid will back up in the big hollow chambers on each side of the brain. After a while the accumulating fluid, with no means of exit, will balloon out the hollow chambers; as a result, the brain substance around the chambers will be compressed into a thin shell. This is a condition known as hydrocephalus which is Greek for "water-brain." Normally the brain substance around the water-filled hollow chambers or lateral ventricles is perhaps an inch thick, but in advanced degrees of hydrocephalus it may be reduced to only one-twentieth of an inch. The obstruction or dam may be the result of an infection in the brain, or in the unborn it may be the result of a faulty formation of the system of passageways for the fluid.

In hydrocephalus, the fluid continues to form and back up, and the developing brain becomes more and more compressed by the fluid inside it. At term the fetal head can measure ten or more inches across —an adult head measures about six inches across—and it simply cannot proceed down the birth canal for ordinary delivery. In the pre-World War II era when Caesarean section was considered a hazardous operation, it was customary to allow the woman bearing a hydrocephalic baby to go into labor and, when the cervix was dilated enough, the obstetrician would poke a huge needle into the head and drain off all the fluid. The skull was perforated with a long, thick, spear-point instrument known as a basiotribe and then crushed after all the fluid had run out with another instrument known as the cranioclast—even the names are chilling. The skull and brain would then collapse; the baby would die almost immediately as a result of this procedure; but the Caesarean section would have been avoided. In the interests of the mother the unborn would have been sacrificed. In those dark and tragic days in the history of obstetrics, the Roman Catholic obstetrician was confronted with one of his most wrenching dilemmas: to save the mother by performing this destructive operation on the unborn, or to reject the destruction of the unborn and watch both mother and infant die as a result of a labor which was impossible to terminate in the normal way. The mother would simply continue to labor until her uterus finally ruptured, the unborn was cast out into her abdominal cavity to die, and she herself would die from internal hemorrhage. Hence the cruel—though in some cases deserved— cautionary which circulated among the female population in the early years of the twentieth century: Don't go to a Catholic obstetrician, he'll watch you die before he'll kill the baby.

With the brilliant advances in surgical technique and blood re-placement technology and with the advent of the specialty of anes-thesiology, Caesarean section became a relatively safe procedure after World War II, and that excruciating dilemma, at least for the Catholic obstetrician, became a thing of the past. Curiously, one still hears that canard now and again, though it has been remodelled and applied to the abortion question. One of Planned Parenthood's favored pieces of agitprop, exemplified in a series of full-page ad-vertisements in the *Sunday New York Times* between June and October of 1981 and costing upwards of 25,000 dollars a throw, was the sly appeal to that viciously anti-Catholic fiction that the attempt to re-impose abortion restraints was the work of a dark Papist conspiracy which would preserve fetal life at the expense of the maternal existence: "radical right wing political and religious forces . . . want to impose their beliefs on you." I leave it to the reader to imagine what the *New York Times's* advertising department would say in response to a petition by a pro-Arab group here in America to place a series of full-page advertisements in the newspaper accusing American Zionists of constituting a "radical right wing political and religious force wanting to impose their pro-Israel beliefs on the American electorate."

"Grand rounds" in obstetrics and gynecology are today neither grand, nor are they rounds. In the first half of this century, medical education depended to a great extent on bedside teaching. In my years in medical school at McGill in Montreal, grand rounds were conducted by the Professor, an articulate, erudite gentleman as much at ease discussing the monads of Liebnitz as he was in discoursing on the etiology of Toxemia. He was accompanied by his retinue of young attending physicians, residents, interns, and finally us lowly medical students trailing in his wake.

These were the old open wards of twenty or so beds, and the only privacy one could find there was within the precincts of a heavy canvas screen suspended from a trilateral overhead track which, when drawn, would shield the patient from her neighbors. The caravan would stop at each bed on the ward and the case would be "presented" to the professor by the chief resident as he referred to the hospital chart on a clip-board hanging at the foot of the bed. Following the presentation, the patient would be observed, questioned and, if necessary, examined; then selected members of the retinue would be sharply questioned by the professor. The caravan would move on, and the process would be repeated until each patient had been visited. The entire group would then go to a conference room off the ward, and the professor would lead the general discussion. The ineradicable lessons of these rounds have remained with me throughout my professional life.

Today, grand rounds is a euphemism for "staff conference," the desultory weekly gathering of attending physicians and residents to discuss various "cases of interest." The "time-wasting practice" of observing and examining patients, living human beings, has been eliminated, and instead we deal only with the hospital chart, that paper incarnation of the patient. The attendance at these meetings is generally poor, the quality of presentation even poorer (the resident or medical student who narrates the case is frequently unfamiliar with the case and often inaccurate in his narrative), and the discussion which follows is perfunctory and pathetic. In all, this is as anemic and as dull a teaching method as one will find in a day's hard march from the Orthodox cheder of Ottowa circa 1901.

On a Monday in October, 1979, the grand rounds concerned itself with a case of a woman bearing what had been diagnosed by ultrasound as a hydrocephalic fetus. The degree of hydrocephalus of the infant appeared to be moderately severe, as well as one could determine from the ultrasound images. But these of course are computer-generated shadows and not actual photographs. Instead of revolving around the challenge of how to deliver this infant to afford it the best chance possible at future corrective surgery for the blockage of the cerebro-spinal fluid in the nervous system, the discussion was confined to how best to thrust a large-bore needle through the abdominal wall of the mother into the child's skull in order to collapse the skull and destroy the infant. This fetus was at thirty-six weeks gestation, and I was astounded at the passive receptivity of the audience of residents and medical students to what was clearly a gratuitous and colossally unethical act of ultimate violence. I reacted savagely, holding forth for some considerable length of time on the wanton destruction of a human being merely because it *seemed* imperfect, on the safety of Caesarean section for delivery of such an infant (indeed, the act of blindly thrusting such a large needle into and through the abdominal wall in the uterus might well be as risky, or even riskier, as carrying out a section); and on the failure of such a cruel judgement to take into account the enormous advances in neurosurgery which now allow us doctors, as useful citizens, to salvage such affected babies. I even quoted the latest work of Dr. John Lorber, a neurologist in Sheffield, England, who has been until recently in the forefront of those who would deny any medical or surgical treatment to infants and children seriously afflicted with disabling neurological defects such as hydrocephalus, spina bifida, and meningocele. Lorber *now* recants his former pronouncements, citing the instance of an extremely bright student at his university who had an I.Q. of 126 and had won first-class honors in mathematics despite having been afflicted since birth with hydrocephalus of such an advanced degree that the massive accumulation of fluid in his skull had virtually obliterated any brain tissue present. The pressure of the accumulating fluid within his brain had so compressed the surrounding brain substance that finally, with special measuring techniques such as the ultrasound apparatus, no brain tissue could be made out at all. Picture, if you will, inserting a balloon into the middle of the forebrain (the cerebral hemispheres with which we think, see, and move) and inflating that balloon continuously until the surrounding shell of brain is so thin and so stretched that it cannot even be seen any longer as an identifiable structure. That was this young man's situation. Musing on this profoundly disturbing—to him, anyway—phenomenon, Lorber only half-jokingly concluded that maybe the brain isn't necessary at all for intelligence.

I was joined in my rather vocal resistance by a resident physician who, like me, was opposed to abortion and personally offended by the complaisance of the staff members in this affair. We met after the grand rounds were over and resolved to register our indignation formally and publically. That infant was, in fact, soon thereafter destroyed and the mother delivered of a dead baby by vaginal delivery. Together we wrote a paper entitled "Morbus Abortiensis and the Quaquaversal Ethic" in which we deplored the decline of ethical standards in the obstetrical discipline in the United States, examined the permissive abortion ethic in its relationship to obstetrical practice, and cited the management of the hydrocephalic fetus as another repellent instance of selective harvesting more appropriate to a winery than to an obstetrical service. The article (Appendix A) concluded with the following coda:

> The destruction of a living being—embryo, defective fetus, neonate —is an act of irretrievable finality. One life is not fungible with another, and the value of each human life transcends ordinary measuration. To justify the destruction of a life by invoking the puny reach of our current scientific knowledge—as the quaquaversal ethic would have us do—is to traverse a quicksand on ballet slippers. Physicians should declare a moratorium on the destruction of life until we have explored unceasingly every feasible alternative, and until we more fully comprehend the inexpressible divinity of existence.

We finished researching the article in January, 1980, and the writing in May. I felt it was a fair and even-handed presentation of the decline of ethical standards in my own field of expertise, and the resident and I agreed that the most suitable outlet for the piece was the *New England Journal of Medicine*. It was read internationally, it was scanned by the media, and it had had the courage to print my "Deeper into Abortion" piece seven years earlier, a piece which articulated serious doubts about the permissive abortion ethic in the United States. We sent the piece on to the *New England Journal of Medicine* with a letter which stated, in part:

> We also recognize that the senior author has assumed a public stance against permissive abortion. Nonetheless we disclaim any partisan

interest in the matter within the corpus of this piece. Further, the issues raised herein are—to the best of our recollection—new and original, and demand the attention of the medical community. Finally, we concede that this is quite possibly the most eristic, incendiary public controversy of our time, about which there is more chiliastic fustian written and thundered than any other. Still, we believe that reasonable voices should have their forum.

The piece languished with the *New England Journal of Medicine* for over three months. In the middle of August I received a letter from Dr. Arnold Relman, the editor of the *New England Journal of Medicine* since 1977, which stated in part that the editors had "considered your thoughtful piece carefully but decided that they simply could not give it a high enough priority to warrant publication in the *Journal*."

What did the term "high enough priority" mean? The editors did not seem to be telling us that the article was poorly written. It had been read by a professional journalist prior to submitting it to the *New England Journal of Medicine*, and he pronounced it eminently suitable for publication on the merits of the writing. They did not declare that the research evidenced in the piece was inaccurate or incomplete. Like the *New York Times*, what the editors implied was that the *New England Journal of Medicine* considered the abortion issue to have been interred with the 1973 Roe v. Wade decision. Fini, ausgespielt. One could almost forgive this disdainful attitude in an organ as resolutely single-minded as the *New York Times*. However, in a publication which pretended to a grand hospitality to all responsible medical and ethical points of view and presumably was up-to-date with scientific advances in fields such as fetology, it was a poor show indeed.

The *New England Journal of Medicine* has been carrying on a cozy little relationship with the other brothers in the mega-press sodality. As an example, in the December 31, 1981, edition of the *New York Times*, an article from the *New England Journal of Medicine* dealing with a heart pump designed to assist a failing heart was abstracted on page A-8 ("Failing Hearts Saved by Small Pump"). In the same edition of the *New York Times* on page A-14, a cute little letter in the correspondence section of the *New England Journal of Medicine* was picked up by the *New York Times* and abstracted ("A Bitter Medicine Cures The Hiccups"). The letter, written by a bartender and a physician, proposed that a lemon wedge saturated with Angostura bitters is an effective treatment for the hiccups. But the article solemnly cautions the reader not to eat the rind. This is, of course, the sort of giddy frippery one would expect to find in the Living or Home section of the *New York Times* but hardly in a scientific publication of international repute. Almost swooning with delight, the *New York Times* then goes on, in that same edition, to quote the *New England Journal of Medicine* regarding an article that the *Journal* had published on the use of progesterone, a female hormone, to reduce the risk of cancer in women taking estrogens for the relief of menopausal symptoms ("Cancer Risk Cut By Hormone") on page B-4.

Not to be outdone, the *New York Daily News*, which has been vacillating between its longtime conservative blue collar constituency and the pressure of an increasingly liberal metropolitan marketplace for the past dozen years, threw in its lot with the *New England Journal of Medicine.* Page 14 of the *New York Daily News* headlined: "Heart Pump Hailed For Saving Five Lives" and went on to declare that the report on a new mechanical heart pump had been developed at the Pennsylvania State Medical School. The report on the research was published in the *New England Journal of Medicine.*

Now this is not to denigrate the *New England Journal of Medicine.* It is concededly a carefully produced scientific publication which maintains a reasonably high standard for material printed within its covers. But also consider that in the same week that the mega-press was adoringly abstracting the above material from the *New England Journal of Medicine,* the *American Journal of Obstetrics and Gynecology* had published an article on the prenatal detection of cystic fibrosis, an article of potentially far greater importance in the field of pediatrics and public health; and *Obstetrics and Gynecology*, the official organ of the American College of Obstetrics and Gynecology, had published one article on a critical analysis of Cesarean sections and another on the use of out-of-hospital birth centers. And in another issue in December, the *American Journal of Obstetrics and Gynecology* ran an article entitled: "Induced Abortion: A Risk Factor for Placenta Previa" in which researchers at the Vanderbilt University Medical Center had concluded the following from a careful study of their patient population: "Induced first trimester abortion is seen as a significant risk factor predisposing to placenta previa." Placenta previa is a fearsome condition in which the placenta implants itself in the lower portion of the uterus in front of the infant and frequently results in massive hemorrhage which may be lethal to mother and baby.

Now these articles, which are of considerable importance to the public at large, were to be found in only two of the more than 400 reputable medical journals published monthly in the United States. How much else of significance was missed is difficult to say. While the decision of which sources should be culled for news is admittedly not a simple one, nevertheless the continued disproportionately heavy reliance of the mega-press on only *one* journal among 400 is more than coincidence and less than responsible and unprejudiced journalism. How to account for the seemingly irresistible effect of the *New England Journal of Medicine* on the mega-press?

Not to be outdone, the other brethren in the sodality press their suit. On the CBS Six O'clock News, the *New England Journal of Medicine* was mentioned twice in the course of an hour in connection with medical stories. One concerned the possible relationship between toxic shock and the diaphragm. The other dealt with the development of a drug to control precocious puberty. Now one can concede that the toxic shock story has always been good for media mileage with the radical feminists carping over their menstrual misfortune and droning on about how the male-dominated drug industry has devised lethal tampons to continue the international subjugation of defenseless womanhood. But precocious puberty? What sort of choice is that for a story on the evening news? It is such a rare phenomenon that in my twenty-five years of gynecological practise I have never seen it, and I am aware that when a case of this rarity turns up on the teaching service of a hospital it is always presented to the staff as a most unusual matter. One can only conclude that the networks are also hopelessly enamored with the *New England Journal of Medicine*, and if the *Journal* should publish an article next month on the transmutation of lead into gold using only bio-feedback techniques, we'll see it on the evening news just before sports and right after the weather. Why, with over 400 reputable medical journals published monthly, the media cling embarrassingly to the *New England Journal of Medicine* is difficult to fathom until one examines more closely the editorial policy and political cast of the *Journal*.

Well, the attraction of, let us say, the *New York Times* is not entirely one-sided. The *New England Journal of Medicine* apes the *Times* by adhering to a white glossy cover with an ascetic logo set in an austere typeface reminiscent of the *Times'* old English logo. It has a correspondence section which might very well be cloned from the Op-Ed page of the *Times*; it ranges far and wide in the sweep of the material it accepts for publication (articles on medical education in China are mixed with surveys on the prevalence of hysterectomies in Saskatchewan), and invites best-selling authors like Norman Cousins to contribute a "special article." It concerns itself unremittingly with matters pertaining to medical ethics, unfailingly adhering to the liberal dogma, and even makes the occasional foray into the historical aspects of medicine. In short, an amusing hybrid of *Foreign Affairs, People* magazine and *Nature*.

The *New England Journal of Medicine* has had for many years a column entitled "Law-Medicine Notes" in which it commented editorially on medico-legal issues. Until 1969 it was written by one Neil Chayet, then assistant professor of legal medicine at the Law-Medicine Institute of Boston University. Chayet is a frequent contributor to CBS Radio for which he does periodic broadcasts entitled "Looking at the Law." In 1969 William J. Curran, armed with a veritable alphabet after his name—J.D., LlM., S.M. Hyg., took over the column and has been its proprietor since. Curran has the customary impeccable northeast liberal credentials, having been educated variously at Harvard's Schools of Law and Public Health as well as at the Boston University law school. He has been active in the American Public Health Association (recall please that this organization was one of our earliest allies in the late 1960s and early 1970s when I and my cohorts at NARAL were fighting to repeal all abortion laws) and even served a term as chairman of its Health Administration Section. Indeed Curran, working the other side of the street, wrote and continues to write a medico-legal column for the *American Journal of Public Health*, the organ of the American Public Health Association. In August, 1969, Curran weighed in with a column in the *Public Health Journal* in which, discussing "Illegal Therapeutic Abortions: The Modern Dilemma," he delivered himself of this rather thinly-veiled sentiment: "This type of law [law of New York State restraining abortion] has been regarded by a large portion of our pluralistic society for many years as too restrictive."

Curran delivered himself of an article in July, 1971, in the *New England Journal of Medicine* entitled "Abortion Law in the Supreme court" in which he commented on the decision of a Federal District Court judge, one Gerhard Gesell. This decision declared the district abortion law unconstitutional on the grounds of "vagueness." Curran complained that the real issue in the matter—the question of right of privacy in the abortion arena—had not been dealt with by the Court. Furthermore, he argued that the decision, favorable to the pro-abortion groups, was not broad enough as it pertained only to the district. He followed up in 1973 with two articles dealing in general with the Roe-Doe decisions, and in spite of the homeric stateliness of the pieces there is no doubt that in Curran's opinion justice had been done and all was right with his world.

It is probably superfluous to cite the editorials on the Edelin case at this point having commented on them earlier, but in March, 1975, the *New England Journal of Medicine* labelled the Edelin trial a "fiasco." The dictionary defines "fiasco" as a crash, a complete or ridiculous failure, especially of a dramatic performance. The true failure here was on the part of Edelin to understand the core issue involved, that is, what is an abortion. An abortion is the separation of fetus from mother; the term does *not* connote willful destruction of either parties. Curiously the same editorial goes on to confess that the Massachusetts Medical Society—the *New England Journal of Medicine* is the official organ of the Massachusetts Medical Society— refused to take any stand on the Edelin matter and even refused to endorse a plea for financial support for his defense. Lest the reader experience an incontrollable urge to take the Massachusetts Medical Society to his or her bosom, recall please that that esteemed organization wrote laudatory letters of recommendation for a physician-member (affiliated with the Harvard Medical School) convicted of raping a nurse. This singular act of ethical myopia—some might even call it plain old-fashioned lying—came to the attention of the press. Even the *New York Daily News*, editorially holding its nose, commented: "Never let it be said that the Massachusetts Medical Society and the Harvard Medical School aren't ready to deal with lapses in ethics—provided the slips are thrown in their faces." The

News closed with this cautionary: "But just in case, anyone asking Harvard for a rundown on a doctor might be well advised to add a little post-script: Please include rap sheet, if any."

The *New England Journal of Medicine* doggedly pressed on in condemning the conviction of Edelin for manslaughter. It levelled an appeal to all individual readers who felt that the trial was a monstrous injustice, and that—in the delicious words of the editor, Dr. Franz J. Ingelfinger—" it abrogated Dr. Edelin's right to a normal life." The editorial tactfully refrained from commenting on Edelin's pre-emptive role in abrogating that infant's right to a normal life.

One final note: Curran weighed in with an editorial piece in the *New England Journal of Medicine* in February, 1975, on the subject of fetal research. He was pouting that the Supreme Court did not seem to be "aware of the importance of the fetus, alive and dead, to scientific study and experimentation." In particular, he seems to have registered dismay over the laws prohibiting research on the live human fetus in the Commonwealth of Massachusetts. He goes through a good deal of agonized hand-wringing over how to distinguish between a live fetus and a dead fetus, something a third-year medical student could lend him a helping hand on; moans a little over the stringency of the laws; and complains that making fetal research on the live fetus a felony is excessive. He asks: "Would not a non-criminal penalty have accomplished the objectives of the law. I must say I come away from laws of this type with a very uneasy feeling." Perhaps the act of experimenting on the live fetus—or on any other defenseless, mute, living human being without advocacy—should be on a par with, say, a traffic violation or breaking a window in a school. After all, what's a little biological vandalism between friends?

There is no need to labor the point any farther. The *New England Journal of Medicine* is the *New York Times* of medical publications: powerful, trendy, wealthy, imperial (it goes to 130 countries), and irremediably liberal in the most perjorative sense of that word. For those who may argue that this assault on the *New England Journal of Medicine* is an ill-tempered, small-minded act of revenge, I can only reply that the rejection of the paper which the resident and I wrote only served to draw attention to the recent phenomenal ascent of this publication to a well-deserved niche in the ranks of the mega-press.

One final irony: In March, 1978, the Massachusetts Supreme Judicial

Court, acting in the Saikewicz matter, declared that all decisions on the discontinuation of life-support systems or administration of life-extending ministrations for the dying in the case of legal incompetents or minors must be adjudicated by the Probate Court in the Commonwealth. Saikewicz was a sixty-seven year old, profoundly retarded man terminally ill with leukemia, and the question arose as to whether to administer chemotherapy in an effort to prolong his life. In so ruling, the court arrogated to itself those wrenching decisions which formerly had been the preserve of the physicians in conjunction with hospital ethics committees and of families of the dying. Arnold Relman, the current editor of the *New England Journal of Medicine*, roundly condemned the incursion of the judiciary into what he perceived as the exclusive domain of attending physicians and responsible family. Now Dr. Relman, like Curran, is another accredited member of the northeast liberal establishment in good standing, having been educated at Columbia University's College of Physicians and Surgeons and having had his postgraduate training in the Yale and Harvard medical communities. He has made no secret of his approval of judicial activism in the matter of permissive abortion and in the matter of barring family from any substantive role in consent for abortion for minors. Well, Dr. Relman; what the Court giveth the Court taketh away.

But the *New England Journal of Medicine* is now more to be censured than pitied. Uncritically it published two articles on cardiac research from a Dr. John R. Darsee of the Harvard Medical School and Emory University. The findings in the articles were admittedly fabricated by Darsee, and the *New England Journal of Medicine*, blushing deeply, has printed retractions of the articles.

The medical press remains adamantly committed to the Abortion People. In August, 1982, Dr. Aubrey Milunsky, writing with an attorney named Leonard Glantz, published an editorial article in the *Journal of the American Medical Association* (JAMA) entitled "Abortion Legislation: Implications For Medicine" (Appendix D). Milunsky is a pediatrician long active and prolific in the area of amniocentesis for discovery of fetal defect. He has published an enormous body of work on the subject and could fairly be characterized as one of the principle architects of the heinous search-and-destroy mission in modern obstetrics. He is ardent on the subject of abortion, particularly late abortion. The editorial article is so brazenly pro-abortion that it reads like the standard handout of the Planned Parenthood mill. He and Glantz inveigh against the proposed amendments to the Constitution limiting abortion; they protest the withdrawal of the requirement for federal funding for abortion; they ridicule the Hatch Amendment and the Human Life Bill; they flatly deny that human life begins at conception; and they erect that tired old straw man, equating abortion with murder if the Human Life Bill were passed and pontificating with great solemnity that abortion will be a capital crime if any of these legal curbs are enacted. They whimper that the passage of any remedial legislation on abortion would have a "negative effect" on fetal investigation, an Orwellian euphemism with frightening implications—what more terrifying direction could this man's so-called research take? The windup of this exemplary, balanced, and neutral article was a rousing exhortation for the Abortion People:

> At the very least we believe that people should retain the freedom of reproductive autonomy and in particular the rights to save the life and secure the health of the mother rather than the fetus [that familiar anti-Catholic line so successful in other campaigns], to enable victims of incest or rape to abort a pregnancy, and to allow parents the option of aborting a pregnancy when the fetus is seriously defective or deformed. We believe that physicians and patients must not allow the life and health of the mother to become subordinate to her fertilized ovum.

The reference to the unborn child as nothing but a "fertilized ovum" not only reflects a vicious air of contempt for pregnant women and their babies, but is gratuitously mean-spirited since Milunsky deals exclusively with the unborn after the sixteenth week, a date perilously close to the line of viability set in 1982. In all the years I have subscribed to the JAMA I cannot recall having read such a tasteless, stridently anti-pregnancy article. I was moved to write a strong reply in which I pointed out the numerous inaccuracies, false premises, overt politicking, and misleading histrionics which pervade the article and are the hallmark of pro-abortion pamphleteering. In the cover letter which accompanied my reply I conceded that although:

> ". . . official policy of the American Medical Association (of which I have been a member for many years) endorses abortion on demand, I am also aware that a substantial portion of the membership disagrees

with that posture. Therefore I believe that in the interests of balance and fairness the dissident view . . . should have equal access to these pages and to the readership.

Original articles to the JAMA are generally submitted to a putatively impartial reviewer on the editorial board for evaluation and recommendation. I am reasonably certain that this article was never submitted to the editorial board. After an indecently short interval it was returned to me accompanied by an impatient note signed by Harriet S. Mayer, a senior editor of the journal. The tone of the note can be appreciated from this excerpt:

> We think that it [the article] overlaps substantially with material recently published in response to the Milunsky commentary . . . and opinions frequently aired in the general news media. Thus we cannot accord it a high enough priority for publication at this time.

The short interval between the mailing and rejection of the article would reasonably preclude its submission to an independent reviewer for evaluation. The rejection of this pro-life rebuttal to the Milunsky manifesto seems to have been a pure knee-jerk liberal response from the medical press. Equally arresting was Mayer's implication that media coverage of the abortion issue has been predominantly pro-life. Has she been on Mars these past ten years? And the material to which she referred as having been published in response to Milunsky consisted of two short, respectfully restrained letters of protest answering several of the arguments made by Milunsky but falling short of countering the pro-abortion political dogma which marked his article. Milunsky required a full-scale refutation, nothing less. The JAMA then proceeded to rub a little saline into the wound by running a reply from Milunsky to these two relatively inoffensive letters which occupied as much editorial space as the letters themselves and stood by itself as yet another pro-abortion fulmination.

Incensed, I resubmitted the article to the JAMA accompanied by a lengthy letter to the editor, Dr. George Lundberg, (Appendix D), in which I requested reconsideration. This time the article languished with the editorial board for three months before it was returned accompanied by the comments of an obviously nettled anonymous reviewer who rejected the article in these rather classic pro-abortion terms:

The author has decided that the issue of abortion is purely a social problem and comfortably ignores the obvious that it is an extremely personal matter as well as obviously directly in the medical arena. He also seems to ignore the different indications for abortion such as genetic disease, psychological problems or psychiatric impairment . . . This is a disappointingly strident commentary, lacking a sense of objectivity. . . .

Is it any wonder that this monumentally insensitive ingenue would take pains to preserve his or her anonymity? I confess to the vagrant thought that Milunsky had been the reviewer and had written the comments himself.

The major newsmagazines, *Time* and *Newsweek*, are members in good standing in the opinion-making mega-press. They of course do not report the news any more than chefs produce food. They buy the news (from their own reporters, from the wire services, networks, major newspapers, professional publications, and a host of other informational agribusinesses and truck-farms), process it, arrange it in a palatable and tasteful presentation, and then distribute it. They read history at the shortest possible focal distance. In Darwinian terms they have found a comfortable niche somewhere between the clatter of the machinery of information-gathering and the tranquillity of the working historian. They are quite simply an indispensable anodyne to this society provoked by the morning newspaper and belted by the evening network news. (What does it all mean? *Timeweek* will put it together.)

The *Time* magazine chronicle, its founding by the redoubtable Henry Luce, and its remarkable adolescence and comfortable middle age, are too familiar to readers for me to describe here. Assuredly others have done it at much greater length and with far more expertise than I. It is necessary, however, to establish beyond serious question the truly impressive dimensions of these mammoths in order to understand just what muscular opinion-makers they are.

Time Incorporated—the company, not just the newsmagazine —is a publicly owned corporation with annual sales of just over 2.5 billion dollars. It employs 25,000 people. The corporation owns and operates seven magazines including *Life, Fortune, Money, People, Sports Illustrated,* and *Discover,* but *Time* magazine is the flagship publication. It owns the Book-of-the-Month Club, the Quality Paperback Book Club, the Little, Brown & Co. in Boston,

The New York Graphics Society, The St. Paul Pioneer Press, and until very recently the ill-fated *Washington Star*. It also owns and operates the American Television and Communications Corporation which in turn has forty-one cable television companies under its aegis. It also owns and operates the Home Box Office Co. and the Manhattan Cable Television company. It owns the Inland Container Corporation which is a giant in itself, controlling ten other sizable companies including one real estate company. It owns the Angelina Free Press and the massive Lumberman's Investment Corporation which in turn controls eight other businesses including several mortgage companies, an insurance company, and a hotel corporation. It owns libraries, oil companies, steel companies, music publishing companies, and, for all we know, the state of Oklahoma. It owns eleven foreign companies from Australia and New Zealand to Tokyo and Korea, to Mexico and Canada, and then across to the Netherlands. In short, it is one heavy hitter.

The *Washington Post-Newsweek* company, on the other hand, is a privately held corporation with 50.1% of its stock in the hands of Katherine Graham. This company is no lightweight, enjoying annual sales of almost six hundred million dollars and employing 5,200 people. It owns three newspapers including the *International Herald Tribune*; television stations in Hartford, Detroit, and Miami; its own paper company; and a newsprint manufacturing company. What legitimizes the credentials of this corporation for admission to the ranks of the mega-press is the smoothly synergistic play between the *Washington Post*—one of the two most influential newspapers in the United States—and the newsmagazine *Newsweek*. Like owning your own munitions factory and your own army too.

Let's examine how the newsmagazine segment of the mega-press handled the abortion issue over the years in which it emerged, in the words of *Time* magazine in 1972, "the most volatile issue in American politics." The newsmagazines function at the interface of journalism and history and are potent opinion makers for the thoughtful college-educated segment of the electorate who pretend to a fine contempt for television. This segment declares a preference for the educational public access channels, admits to infrequent viewing of sporting events and films, and confesses, if pressed, to occasional secret indulgence in pure junk such as sitcoms and entertainment "specials," it also professes a dissatisfaction with the daily newspaper (too superficial, not analytical enough). This segment of the electorate—

business and professional people, community leaders, and politicians —is opinion-making in itself. The information it absorbs—from a respected source such as the newsmagazines—is often disgorged virtually unprocessed and undigested, as advice and revelation. Periodic surveys by the newsmagazines themselves, as well as by other marketing firms and sociological machinery, confirm the above.

Time magazine first awakened to the abortion issue in 1965 when, in a September issue in the Medicine section, it commented on the formation of the Association for the Study of Abortion (A.S.A.), a creation of Dr. Robert Hall. Hall was an obstetrician and gynecologist connected with the Presbyterian Hospital and the Columbia College of Physicians and Surgeons—a man of impeccable reputation. He found himself in the mid-1960s chafing under the restrictions of the old anti-abortion statute in New York State which allowed abortion only when the maternal life was in danger. He organized the A.S.A. along with others such as Dr. Alan Guttmacher. Styling itself as an educational enterprise devoted to an almost monastic pursuit of research and data on the subject of abortion, it denied any hint of political involvement in the issue. Occasionally it would dare to offer approval of the American Law Institute model law which allowed for abortion for reasons of maternal health, rape, incest, and/or fetal abnormality, but mostly it fussed with its pince-nez, thoughtfully stroked its beard, and looked exceedingly wise. *Time* noted its emergence with a faint air of satisfaction, and three months later *Newsweek* in its Medicine section also remarked upon its appearance but with somewhat less sangfroid than *Time*. *Newsweek's* carefully neutral tone was marred only by a quote from a psychiatrist on the subject of abortion to the effect that "a woman is worse off after her abortion because of her remorse than if she goes ahead and has the baby." (*That* psychiatrist has probably repented his words in some professional gulag by now.)

From 1965 on, the coverage of the issue begins to heat up, along with the gathering turbulence on a great many other political issues in the United States including the birth of NARAL the first group devoted to political action in abortion reform. In examining the tone and content of the coverage it is useful—necessary, in fact—to take careful note of the heading of each article, the photography accompanying the article, and the last paragraph of the article—the "wind-up." From these one can divine the tone of the article.

While *Time* dozed in 1966, *Newsweek* took note of the prosecution

of two obstetricians in California for performing abortions on women
who had had Rubella (German measles) during the pregnancy. Four
months later in October, they covered the American Public Health
Association convention in San Francisco at which Hall delivered
himself of an impassioned oration against the current abortion laws.
Both articles were faintly approving, and both were carried in the
Medicine section of the magazine. The article was accompanied by a
photograph of Hall in his white coat lounging negligently against a
gynecologic examining table complete with stirrups, and the caption
read "Hall, the woman is the victim."

Time roused itself in 1967 to comment—again, in the Medicine
section—on the passage of a liberal American Law Institute (A.L.I.)-
type law in the state of Colorado. The tone of the piece was approving, and, as if to shore up its spindly-legged confidence in the
issue, quoted a poll carried out by the magazine Modern Medicine
which found that out of 40,000 physicians, eighty-seven per cent
responded in favor of liberalizing the abortion laws. The results of
this poll were the purest type of infantile wish-fantasy, somewhat on
the order of the fabricated pap we delighted in feeding the press from
our NARAL dream factory and may help explain why Modern
Medicine is no longer whinnying with us.

In October, 1967, in an unsigned essay, Time magazine burst out of
the closet and declared itself unequivocally in favor of the repeal of
restrictive abortion laws. Henry Luce had died in that year, and
Hedley Donovan had taken command of the enterprise. The Vietnam
anti-war movement was geysering out of the radical underground and
erupting into the streets, and authority was being challenged everywhere. "Why not?" was the slogan of the day.

From that point on, Time remained resolutely in the pro-abortion
vanguard of the mega-press, shoulder to shoulder with the New York
Times and the Washington Post. In covering abortion over the next
several years, it kept the issue in the comparatively obscure ghetto of
the Medicine section as if the only substantive questions were those of
a scientific nature. The science of fetology had not yet emerged; it
probably dates its emergence from 1972, with the development of a
new generation of ultrasound equipment and the gradual introduction of electronic fetal heart monitoring into the clinical practice of
obstetrics. Science thus knew conveniently little about the unborn.
Until around 1972, we could confidently award primacy to the ma-

ternal interest and only secondarily take note of the fetal presence. But with the emergence of fetology as a full-fledged discipline, the scientific data suddenly became quite unpalatable to the pro-abortion forces and a potent weapon for the anti-abortion side. With the unborn then looming larger and larger as a person to be reckoned with, the whole issue had to be moved out of the Medicine, Law, and Religion sections of the magazine and onto the National stage. For the first time, in December, 1972, *Time* grudgingly cedes a place in its section "The Nation" to the abortion question in its coverage of what it called "The Bitter Abortion Battle" in the Pennsylvania legislature over a proposed anti-abortion bill. In addition, 1972 was an election year, and the abortion issue, for the first time in American politics, had become a factor of no little consequence. Senator McGovern had made clear his own pro-abortion stance (remember the rallying cry of the Nixon forces in that fateful year in referring to the McGovern campaign platform: Amnesty, Acid, and Abortion), and Ellen McCormick had run for President balanced precariously on a platform with a single plank—anti-abortionism.

The Roe-Doe Decision of January, 1973, evidently signalled to the mega-press that the abortion battle had been decided and that only small housekeeping details were necessary thereafter. The issue was once again relegated to the journalistic boondocks. *Time* covered it in the fluffy little boutique section it devised called "The Sexes" as well as in Medicine and Religion. It languished in these sections until July, 1977, when it again burst onto the national stage with the United States Supreme Court decision declaring that the individual states were not obligated to fund non-therapeutic abortions. *Time* reported this story in the front section "Issues," headlining it with "The Supreme Court Ignites a Fiery Abortion Debate." A month later, hurling denunciations with indignation, a signed *Time* essay deploring the decision ("discriminates against the poor; not only unfair but absurd") appeared. It was signed by a senior writer, Lance Morrow. At least as far as *Time* is concerned, the issue has remained in the national arena since 1977. Of fourteen articles on the subject from 1977 on, only twice has it appeared in the Medicine section and once in the Religion section.

One other item of interest: As one analyzes the coverage of the issue in *Time* from 1969 on, almost without fail there are four stories each year, usually spaced one for each season. In 1969 there were stories in March and September and two in November; in 1970 there were stories in February, March, April, and September; in 1971 in March, May, September, and November; and in 1972 in March, May, September, and December. There were only two in 1973 during January and February. But in 1974 the pattern resumed with deadly regularity, with stories appearing in February, May, September, and December issues and in February, March, April, and December issues of 1975. That pattern has continued virtually unchanged up to the present. It is difficult to believe that significant stories on the issue crop up exactly four times a year—and interestingly September seems to yield a bumper crop. Rather, it would seem that an editorial judgement had been made somewhere down the line that abortion stories were to be rationed out on a quarterly basis, and perhaps if there were no story one would be created from some old material lying around. This is an odd way to keep the electorate informed on an issue which this magazine itself had termed one of the most volatile issues in American politics.

Newsweek, too, kept the abortion issue caged in the Medicine section, with an occasional foray into the Religion section. In a long article in the Medicine section in July, 1967, entitled "Easing Abortion Rules," the writer took note of the change in the policy of the American Medical Association toward a more permissive stance, endorsing the model A.L.I. law. The abortion issue remained for the most part consigned to the Medicine section until October, 1972, just about the date on which *Time* declared it a national issue, when a strongly pro-abortion piece entitled "The Politics of Abortion" with the by-line of Shana Alexander in National Affairs. Since that time the issue has remained almost exclusively in the National Affairs section, and from time to time the magazine has published other signed opinion pieces from exponents of both the pro- and anti-abortion camps: George F. Will, John D. Rockefeller, III, Nick Timmesch. The pattern of coverage in *Newsweek* has been more distributive, ranging from two pieces (1968) to none (1979) to six (1967). In general, as one surveys the *Newsweek* coverage, one finds it more responsive to the breaking of newsworthy events in the issue, with less of the rigid, duty-bound regularity of the *Time* coverage.

As the science of fetology developed and our society's increasing perception of the unborn as a person strengthened the resolve of the anti-abortion groups, the issue could no longer be contained within the medicine or science ghettoes of these magazines. The boundaries of the debate could no longer be limited to citing maternal mortality statistics for illegal abortions and dismissing the unborn as an insignificant lump of meat. Now the editors of the newsmagazines moved the issue into the larger arena but qualified their acceptance of it as a bona fide issue by wreathing it in conflict and controversy. The desideratum for every story evidently was "balance." Each side of the issue was presented by the most strident, most zealous advocates (I include myself circa 1970 here): Bill Baird on the pro-abortion side and the fire-bombers of the abortion clinics on the other side. The coverage for the most part remained superficial, emotional, and quite discernibly pro-abortion.

This continued in *Time* until 1978. In an article which appeared in the Nation section in April, 1978, entitled "Stacy's Day at the Abortion Clinic" in which the reporter follows a young girl named Stacy through her transit in an abortion clinic, a snide, ironic note creeps into the coverage for the first time. Note the conclusion of the article: "But now that it [the abortion] is over, she and her mother are off to Alexander's . . . for a shopping spree." The same tone of weary irony prevails throughout much of the coverage thereafter. In the coverage of the Waddill trial in California, the article concludes: "The day after the mistrial was declared, Kathy Davis [a twenty-one year old secretary on the jury] got married with four of the other jurors in attendance." Dr. Waddill had aborted the fetus of a woman who was somewhere between twenty-two and thirty-one weeks pregnant, and he was accused of having strangled the infant when it was delivered alive. In another article in November, 1978, dealing with flagrant abuses at Chicago abortion clinics, the piece concludes: "In 1973 the Supreme Court legalized abortion. As it turns out, what they legalized . . . is the highly profitable and very dangerous back-room abortion." *Time's* coverage has remained doggedly pro-abortion but with a numbed, slightly ironic counterpoint to it.

Thereafter, in story after story in *Time*, one detects the increasing weariness, the omnipresent cynicism about the issue. In an article in July, 1979, headed "The Fanatical Abortion Fight," *Time* conceded that the momentum had swung to the anti-abortion groups. It discussed the role of the pro-abortion clergy in the struggle and concluded: "The aroused [pro-abortion] ministers quickly discovered that the politics of abortion is a bruising business." Again, in a story on the McRae vs. Califano case over Medicaid funding of abortion, *Time* pondered the Dooling ruling (the Hyde Amendment, in the opinion of Federal District Judge Dooling was unconstitutional) but wearily conceded in the last paragraph of the piece: "Even if the Supreme Court does agree with him, the abortion battle was far from over." Even the Medicine section which had been a party-line perfect ideologue on the issue for all these years began to waver. In reporting the debacle at Mount Sinai hospital in New York in 1981 in which one fetus was killed ostensibly to save another (the Orwellian circumlocution dragged up to support this indefensible leaching baffles the brain) *Time* headed the piece: "Saving One, Dooming Another." Quite apart from the present concession by the magazine that one fetus counted enough to be described as "doomed," the photo accompanying the article was one of Dr. Kerenyi, the architect of the procedure, lounging negligently back in his chair, the picture of Hollywood directorial insouciance as he flicks a cigarette and arrogantly lectures the press. Not your ideal illustration of the medical savior. Even the quote in the concluding paragraph was, to be charitable, ambiguous: "The mother looked forward to the birth as a delightful event, and the other aspect didn't bother her," Kerenyi said. Subtly disapproving, with a fine veneer of Swiftian irony.

Newsweek caved in rather more suddenly. It too had adhered to the pro-abortion line since discovering the issue, although some signed columns had expressed a disciplined opposition to that posture. Then in January, 1982, neatly timed to coincide with the ninth anniversary of the Roe-Doe decision, *Newsweek* experienced its epiphany and trumpeted it all over its cover. The science of fetology, now ten years old, was finally granted recognition in the mega-press. *Newsweek* called it: "How Life Begins: Biology's New Frontier" and headlines the piece itself: "How Human Life Begins." Mind you, not *when* does it begin—the concession was finally made that life begins at the beginning—but *how*. There was a disclaimer to the main piece entitled "But Is It A Person," but even here *Newsweek* seemed to have lost its heart for the struggle. After vascillating about when legal protection should begin for the intrauterine occupant, it finally concluded with this confession: "Even many doctors who believe that abortions are justified will concede that life begins at fertilization, and that the fetus becomes human at any point the anti-abortion groups care to specify; the problem is not determining when actual human life begins, but when the value of that life begins to outweigh other considerations such as the health or even the happiness of the mother."

Exactly. Now it's only a matter of Time.

Like a vivacious young debutante pausing long enough in her giddy social whirl to deliver herself of a serious thought—perhaps something like a breathless five minute exegesis on the relationship between Wittgenstein and the hermeneutic elements in the latest Bugs Bunny cartoons—*Time*'s younger sister *Life* ran a straight-faced editorial on abortion in March, 1967, in which it advocated backing for the A.L.I. model law. As was customary in these woolly-headed little think-pieces in otherwise irredeemably frivolous magazines, "one recent poll" was cited—the source was not offered—indicating the questionable seventy-one percent of all Americans who were demanding some reform of the abortion laws. Further, to make NARAL's task ever so much easier in the coming days, the article declared: "Opposition to the easing of abortion laws centers in the Catholic church. . . ."

Plus ça change, plus c'est la meme chose. Rising again like Lazarus, *Life* ran an article on abortion in November, 1981, which was advertised with a four-color cover picture of a six week old fetus. The caption of the photo was: "When Does Life Really Begin?" The article in fact was an uneasy melange of the photographic odyssey of one Doria Sili which takes her through the Meadowbrook Woman's Clinic of Minneapolis and the sometimes laughably contradictory results of the Yankelovich poll. The photographs generally portray a grim-visaged Doria making her "difficult choice" in the clinic while Leonard Merck, described as the man with whom she lives, shepherds her tenderly through the putative ordeal. Leonard, complete with T-shirt, jeans, and beard and almost rigid with solicitude, weighs in with this profundity on the issue: "You don't call an acorn an oak. You don't call a seed a rose." You don't call two renegade cells a cancer, Leonard, but that's exactly what it is.

With more misdirection than is usual even for a feather-weight publication like *Life*, the magazine never comes close to discussing its cover question. There is not even a hint of the existence of a discipline known as fetology. The only reference to the question "When Does Life Really Begin?" is the response to this question: "When do you think a fetus becomes a human being?" That the plurality of respondents indicated life begins at conception and despite the fact that a clear majority of respondents answered that abortion is morally wrong, there is nothing but a crystalline pro-abortionism in the piece. Of the seven photographs of people holding opinions on the subject, four were of pro-abortionists and three were of the opposition. (The photograph accompanying my anti-abortion opinion was so sorry that one is tempted to accuse the editors of sabotage, but the picture of Uta Landy, executive director of the National Abortion Federation, is also a dreadful caricature of an attractive and charming woman. This is one *Life* we can trash with no regrets.) The article following the abortion piece, "Mick and the Stones Storm Again," may in fact be a more potent argument for abortion than anything adduced in the whole text.

(*Life* recently partially redeemed itself with a cover story on "Fetal Surgery." The photographs accompanying the article are spectacular, but the text is still faintly flavored with pro-abortion sentiment.)

Of the two national weekly newsmagazines, *Time* was the easier mark for us at NARAL. By 1970, Henry Luce, the conservative founder, publisher, and longtime editor-in-chief of the magazine, had been dead for three years and in fact had relinquished his editorial duties to Hedley Donovan six years earlier. The magazine had steadily taken on a more liberal coloration following Donovan's rise, though the reasons for the editorial shift to the left are not immediately apparent: Donovan was an exquisitely careful man with exquisitely careful politics—some said he had no discernible politics at all. But an examination of the editorial staff in mid-1970, the year in which *Time* flung aside all pretense at disinterested reporting on the social issues such as abortion, civil rights, and the like, is revealing.

The managing editor of the magazine was male, one Henry Anatole Grunwald, who today is the editor-in-chief. The assistant managing editors were both male—Edward L. Jamieson and Richard M. Seamon. The art editor was male—Louis R. Glessman. Of the twenty-one associate editors, twenty were male and one was female—Harriet Bachman. Of the thirty-seven contributing editors, only six were female. Thus, of the sixty-two journalists occupying the top editorial positions at *Time* only seven were female, and it is probably a safe guess that a majority of these females were in an older age group, had been with *Time* for some years during the conservative Luce regime, and were not generally in sympathy with the revolutionary fervor of the 1960s.

But in the lowest editorial echelon, those who were in the field seeking out the stories, there were sixty-five "researchers" *all* of whom were female and the vast majority of whom were young, college-educated, and thoroughly in sympathy with the feminist movement of the 1960s. Mere chance? No way. The most reasonable explanation for this clustering of females in steerage while the officers of the ship were virtually all male is that in a careful attempt to appear contemporary and responsive to what the editors at *Time* perceived to be their readership—the young college-educated crowd occupied with Vietnam protest and civil rights marches—they had made a conscious decision, and perhaps had even issued a directive, that women were to be given their chance on the magazine in other than girl-Friday duties but must be kept in steerage. The results of this affirmative action program for those women who would pursue a career in magazine journalism are, to be charitable, dubious. Currently, of the seventy-five people occupying the senior slots on the editorial staff of *Time*, only eleven are women; on the other hand, of the fifty-one "reporter-researchers" on *Time*, eleven are men.

In any case, the selling of the permissive abortion line to the group of females researching the story was about as difficult as persuading Harold Stassen to run for president. In NARAL, they became our "creatures," and the reportage could not have been more favorable for us at NARAL if we had written the story ourselves. Some of the material read as if they had run some of our press releases verbatim. For example, in the summer of 1970 following the passage of the new permissive New York statute, in New York City we were inundated with pregnant women from the eastern half of the United States and Canada seeking legal abortions. There were a few clinics operating, but most gynecologists were performing abortions in their hospitals; although hospitals attempted to cope with the emergency by devising ambulatory abortion in order not to clog the limited number of hospital beds available for acute care of medical and surgical ailments, nevertheless operating room time quickly became pre-empted by those who were performing abortions. This created serious disagreements among hospital staff members. Those who did not do abortions were railing against those who did because they couldn't secure operating room time for routine conventional gynecological surgery. Those who did abortions angrily accused the opposing faction of anti-feminism, obstructionism, and dark totalitarian motives. At the

St. Luke's hospital where I was doing the majority of my work, including abortions, each attending physician was assigned a quota, a certain number of abortions he could do each month. If he passed that number, then he would no longer be permitted to admit his patients for abortion until the next month's quota commenced. In July, 1970, I quickly exceeded my quota, and I was informed by the administration of the hospital that I would no longer be allowed to admit women for abortion after September 1. Outraged I called Larry Lader, and we swiftly decided to feed some of this good raw meat to the drooling beasts in the media. I rang up, among others, two young researchers at *Time* magazine. In my most aggrieved manner, I complained that we pro-abortionists were being discriminated against and, worse, that women were not being allowed to obtain safe legal hospital abortions. Both researchers soothed me, assuring me that something would be done.

And our faithful media apparatchiks came through as promised. The Medicine section of the September 7, 1970, edition of *Time* consisted of a three-column spread on the subject of abortion, largely devoted to a thorough airing of my grievances with the administration of St. Luke's Hospital. I was extensively quoted on the particular injustice, as I conceived it, of the "quota" system: "'The hospitals and the Establishment simply don't want to carry out the spirit of the law.'" They went on to repeat my charges that "'many hospitals have established arbitrary quotas for the number of abortions of different types (graded according to the length of pregnancy) and how many beds they will allot. Even worse . . . is that some hospitals will not take women who are more than twelve weeks pregnant. These . . . are the women who are really getting desperate, who need it most.'"

Later on in the same article, I was allowed to deliver a second broadside. "'The hospital's rationale for the quotas is that otherwise some doctors would flood them with abortion cases, leaving little room for other patients. That reasoning . . . is hypocritical . . . a vicious method of virtually shutting off abortions and curtailing those doctors who have the most patients from doing what the patients need and have a legal right to.'"

If there is any lingering doubt that these reporters were "our creatures," please note that the three hospitals cited in the second column of the piece, in which the abortion practices at the various hospitals in the New York metropolitan area are discussed, are the identical hospitals at which I was then working.

Given these two premises: That abortion had been legalized in New York State and that those reporting the story were white, middle-class, young, college-educated women, why did the officer corps of *Time* permit magazine policy to align itself so strongly with those of us on the far left of the issue? Permissive abortion was certainly not the national policy—that was three years away. Judith Blake, writing in *Science* magazine in February, 1971, an article entitled "Abortion and Public Opinion: The 1960–1970 Decade," used the results of a number of polls conducted in 1968 and 1969 to show that although a majority of men and women (Catholic *and* non-Catholic) throughout the United States supported abortion for reasons of mother's health and/or fetal deformity, a decided majority of these same respondents disapproved of abortion for economic reasons and/or birth control. Yet here was *Time* magazine—that paradigm of circumspection, that sterling example of Solomonic reticence—sending off a shower of sparks on the always-incendiary abortion issue like a runaway Catherine wheel. Why?

The reasons are to be found in the same issue of September 7. In a warm and generally sympathetic article on the Women's Strike for Equality in the section of the magazine called "The Nation," the Woman's Liberation movement was portrayed as militant but good-humored, dedicated but tolerant, impatient but persevering. Opponents of the latter-day suffragettes were characterized as hard-hats and far right nut cases. The People section of the magazine was dominated by a feature on the making of a move titled "The Trojan Women," and the photograph in the section was of Katherine Hepburn, Irene Papas, Vanessa Redgrave, and Genevieve Bujold, the stars of the production. Even the cover story of that issue fell readily into line. It featured Elliott Gould ("Star For An Uptight Age"), a slovenly hirsute mumbler well known for his laid-back liberalism and his equally fuzzy feminism.

Thus, there was intense sustained pressure both from without and within on the magazine. The Women's Movement was swirling around in the world at large, and it had everything a movement should have in order to be newsworthy: sex, violence, audacity, and humor. And from within, down in the ranks, were the sympathizers, vibrating in simple harmonic rhythm with the external dissonances. No wonder the senior male-dominated editorial staff cracked and crumbled.

Newsweek ran its first major abortion cover story on March 3, 1975, in the wake of the conviction of Dr. Kenneth Edelin in Boston on a charge of manslaughter. Its treatment of the case was unarguably sympathetic to Edelin and generally compatible with the pro-abortion line; it persisted in subtly characterizing pro-life people in religious terms. Calling them "anti-abortion missionaries" and "crusaders," the article described the activities of Jay and Cheri Bowman on behalf of the Georgia Right-to-Life Committee and covered an appearance of the Bowmans at the Corpus Christi Roman Catholic Church in Stone Mountain, Georgia. Bowman is not a cleric, as the article would lead one to believe in its lead paragraph, but is rather a systems manager at a local bank. Furthermore, he refused to reveal his religious affiliation, although the writer of the article, Joseph B. Cummings, the Atlanta Bureau chief of *Newsweek*, rather cheekily wrote: "I infer that he is Catholic." Cummings' own religious "affiliation" was unstated. Cummings goes on to portray Cheri Bowman as the owner of a "lullaby voice" and her physiognomy—"smiling, blond"—on the order of a cross between Eva Braun and one of the Sirens. The tone of the piece was waspish, strident, and fruity with indignation that any rational human could be opposed to the protocols of the abortion movement.

Now the dreary arithmetic: The editor was a man, Osborne Elliott; so was the managing editor, Edward Kosner; so too was the executive editor, Kenneth Auchincloss; and the art editor was one Alfred Lowry. Of the thirteen senior editors only one, Olga Barbi, was a woman. Of the six contributing editors only one, Shana Alexander, was a woman. Of the thirty-two general editors, the next echelon down, only five were women. That number included Linda Bird Francke who authored a pallid pro-abortion piece in 1978 entitled "The Ambivalence of Abortion." (The ambivalence expressed in the book was purely visceral; intellectually, politically, and morally Francke stoutly upheld the invincible orthodoxy that Orwell termed "defending the indefensible.") Thus, of the top fifty-five editorial positions, only seven were occupied by women. In contrast, of the assistant editors—those out in the field getting the story—nine were men and six were women, and on the bottom two levels—the senior editorial assistants and editorial assistants—there were thirty-six males and only twenty-one females. Although the domination of women in the news gathering ranks at *Newsweek* was not quite as pronounced as at *Time* (this may account for its slightly less strident pro-abortion tilt) the pressure from below was undeniably there.

THE TELEVISION NETWORKS

Television has, regrettably or otherwise, ascended to an inevitability in our lives on the order of, say, death and taxes. In 1950, when my family acquired its first black and white Magnavox television, a dark hulking monster which squatted forbiddingly in a corner of the living room with only its three-inch Cyclopian eye alive, it was considered a luxury, a mark of economic status. Now it occupies a position of central importance in American lives. It is the dominant wellspring of information, entertainment, culture, and education. The *Wall Street Journal* recently reported on an experiment in which a class of school-children in Ridgewood, New Jersey, were asked to eliminate television from their lives for a week, to go "cold turkey on TV." The resulting dislocation of these children's families deprived of television was not only amusing but chilling. The mother of a nine year old reportedly called the school to blister the author of such a "horrid idea," and indicated that the distraction of her son's attention from the television set was wreaking havoc on her life and time. He was harassing her with too many questions. Another parent turned up the volume of the television set so loud that the child had to leave the house. The agonies suffered by those participating in that experiment, children and parents alike, read like something out of "The Man With The Golden Arm." It appears that even affluent and well-educated families watch television an average of a little more than six hours a day, and several of the families owned four and five sets—two had seven sets—probably in some forlorn belief that perhaps one of the sets might somehow receive different, utterly marvelous programs from an extra-terrestrial source where all the sitcoms are indescribably funny, all the news unrelievedly good, and all the movies new, sexy, and thrilling.

There is no need to belabor the issue. Like it or not, television is remorselessly moving to the epicenter of our lives. Among other functions it serves, it is for most of us the primary source of education once we leave formal schooling behind. The serious reading public is a tough but declining garrison. Television has revolutionized the role of the print-press to the extent that the afternoon newspaper is a cachectic carcass owing to the omnipresent six o'clock news, and even those stalwart morning papers depend more and more upon the distance between the worker and his work—the commuter and his means of commutation be it bus, subway, train, or even plane—for their survival. Imagine if you will a society in which the industrial base is structured in such a way that no one is more than five minutes away from his place of work. Newspapers would be discarded virtually unread; by lunchtime the news would be cooling, and anyway most of us do not read the newspaper at lunch. The trip home, five minutes long, would equally discourage any serious examination of the paper. It is no surprise that morning newspapers have become increasingly bulky and consequently more spread out into the component sections of news, sports, entertainment, and business as the distance from home to work has increased in the past several decades. Morning newspapers shudder at the ultimate apocolyptic vision: An industrial society in which each worker sits at home with his work beamed to him through the television and through the multiple complex computers into which he is hooked.

Arguendo, television is forced kicking and screaming to deal occasionally with perplexing contemporary social issues. Sitcom characters may be the people of the opiates; old movies provide blessed hours of pain relief for television programmers; even the hard news is an island of respite, although there are the twin specters of news selection and time allocation to contend with; and soap operas, game shows, entertainment specials, and children's programming are comparative anodynes when compared with the documentary on the social issues (that bête noir, that nemesis of the networks).

For network television operates under two constraints that are not permitted to hobble the print press: the FCC license and the "Fairness Doctrine." Briefly, the license requirement includes, among other items, a demand for the service of the station in the public interest, A euphemism for "required reading," high-protein output, or medicinal television. And the "Fairness Doctrine," formulated in 1959 as a Congressional recommendation and amendment to the 1934 Communications Act, imposes the obligation on licensees of the FCC to "afford reasonable opportunity for the discussion of conflicting views on issues of public importance." The theory behind that amendment and its imposition only upon broadcasters, not on the print press, was that anyone can start a newspaper but that the airways are limited and in the public domain. In operation, the amendment forces the broadcasters to allot equal time to an opposing view whenever only one side of an issue is presented—or even where there is a reasonable, or sometimes unreasonable, perception of partiality or unilaterality of some controversial issue by an opposing camp.

The "Fairness Doctrine" has remained largely unaltered since its inception save for suspension of certain elements in recent presidential campaigns. Nevertheless, the theory upon which the doctrine was based collapsed with the arrival of the age of cable television. Now, with the number of television channels virtually unlimited and the diaspora of what was a solid constituency of television watchers into the untamed wilds of the cable country, it is now timely to admit that "anyone can start a television station" and that therefore either the fairness doctrine should be equally applied to the print press or else it should be withdrawn from its application to the broadcasters. In fact, it's not the air waves which are in the public domain any more than the pages of the daily newspaper. It is the public attention, the public *time* which is in the public domain. The only question which remains is: Shall we license those who would engage the public for commercial purposes?

From time to time, network television reluctantly confronts the social issues—abortion, gun control, bussing, euthanasia, capital punishment, nuclear power, and so forth—and manfully takes its lumps. Not only must it take care to present these issues periodically in order to maintain the license, not only must it conform to the "Fairness Doctrine," but it must also brace itself to meet the abuse, the impassioned fury of the opposing camps, each of which invariably conceives that the presentation has been skewed to the opposite side. Pressure groups, lobbies, boycotters, and demonstrators spring forth. The station *becomes* the news. The frequency of new documentaries on such divisive issues as abortion approaches the appearance rate of Halley's Comet, an apt metaphor considering the accompanying heat and fire.

The collective mind of the electronic medium is not especially distinguished for its subtlety. The "Fairness Doctrine" is generally carried out in the reporting of the social issues in its most brutish application—"balance." If one aspect of any of these perplexing issues is reported or explored, no matter how innocuous the reportage or how cool the content, the opposing camp must be given representation. The resulting fracas then serves several purposes admirably: "balance" is achieved, conflict and controversy reign—those overheated twins much beloved by the electronic mind—and the prevailing landscape of proletarian nescience remains undisturbed: don't burden the boobs with too much to think about. Giving Kermit the Frog an opportunity to comment on gun control is far more dangerous than giving Harold Bloom a guest spot on "Hollywood Squares."

I had encountered this drooling slavishness to "balance" on many occasions over the years, but it revealed itself to me in its most ludicrous form in my first appearance on the Phil Donahue show in November, 1979. *Aborting America* had been published in October to a deafening barrage of silence. John Miles, the astute editor at Doubleday who had conceived the idea for the book and with whom Dick Ostling, the co-author, and I had met on several occasions during the formative weeks of the contract talks, had fled Doubleday for southern California. We were then assigned to one Robert Heller, another editor at Doubleday who generally acted as if the book were radioactive. Struggling valiantly against a general hands-off policy and despite a meticulous attention to the non-marketing of the book, the company's publicity department had interested the Donahue organization in it, and I duly received an invitation to proceed to Chicago for a taping of Donahue, with all expenses paid and a magnificent room at the Ambassador East hotel for the night. I had been told by Donahue's functionaries that there would be someone else on the show representing the opposing camp, but the name of the person had not been disclosed to me by the afternoon I left for Chicago.

Now I had written a book which, at least by my lights, was a reasonable, dispassionate, and neutral examination of the abortion question. In order to keep the temperature at a noncombustible level, I had substituted the word "alpha" for all the combative, heavily loaded terms applied to the fetus from each camp ("pre-born" on the anti-abortion side, and "embryo" and "products of conception" on the pro-abortion side). I had been careful to list all the specious arguments each side had used in the promotion of their views, criticizing the anti-abortion forces as severely as the pro-abortion groups. I had treated the whole issue strictly from the perspective of the scientist, and the conclusions were founded on a purely secular ethic. Nevertheless, because the conclusion was inimical to the pro-abortion camp, the book was immediately branded as a fascist piece of anti-abortion propaganda, and as such was irresistible to the Donahue show, which dotes on naughtiness and controversy.

Donahue himself is a brilliant huckster, an alchemist of the electronic medium. He has raised the charming kitsch of the game show host to the rarified level of media populism with his intriguing boyish innocence and gray-haired maturity, gee-whiz enthusiasms and slick facility, surface neutrality, and deeply committed liberalism. But he is undeniably a consummate entertainer and a nonpareil seller of books. I accepted his invitation promptly. I was also aware that he is a media star unfettered by professional ethics and that no physician could ever be a match for him. He could make you look like a pompous ass.

Upon my arrival in Chicago, I was informed that the "balance" for the show next morning would be provided by Harriet Pilpel, Esq. Pilpel is a formidable name in the world of liberal litigation. What Marvin Mitchelson is to matrimonial litigation, what William Kunstler is to the radical underground, Pilpel is to liberal social causes. She had argued the Griswold v. Connecticut case in the United States Supreme Court—the question of the legality of selling contraceptives in the state of Connecticut—and had won. The victory had enshrined her in the valorous company which can do no wrong in the editorial columns of the mega-press and probably won her instant canonization in *Playboy's* Valhalla.

Pilpel is a tiny, grandmotherly woman with a deceptively mild façade and a silvery bouffant hairstyle reminiscent of a matron of honor at a 1956 cotillion. I had not had any previous confrontation with her and was utterly unprepared for the shrill ferocity with which she seized the microphone and held the entire program hostage to her fiercely pro-abortion line. I had come prepared to discuss the issue in the same cool, dispassionate light in which I felt the book had been written, and here was Pilpel shrieking her incessant and unremitting line of pro-abortionism into the Donahue microphone, not giving a damn for the opinions of anyone else. It was my baptism by fire with the new pro-abortion tactic: Grab the mike and drown 'em out. Too late I realized what had happened. If she had not won the day, she had at least dominated it.

I had a second confrontation with Pilpel a year later at the Union League Club in New York City. She and I had been invited to debate the constitutional merits of the abortion question for an evening's entertainment for the members of the club, many of whom are attorneys and jurists. Several days prior to the debate, she had called me with the assurance that she was looking forward to seeing me again, that she was making no special preparations for the debate and that she was merely going to "wing it." Playing by her rules, I accordingly prepared a lengthy, very carefully researched presentation on the question, many parts of which I checked with legal scholars of my acquaintance. We chatted amiably at the dinner preceding the presentation and, true to her word, she gave her presentation in eight of her allotted twenty minutes. It was a rambling, disjointed, and barely audible shambles, boring and repetitious enough to put a high glaze on the collective eyeballs of the audience. I then presented my arguments in what I felt was a compelling, confident, and forceful manner and even many pro-abortion members later conceded that I had quite overwhelmed Pilpel in this round.

The "balance," as it was euphemistically termed by the "administrative associate" (another amusing euphemism for secretary), of the Donahue bureaucracy, is in fact nothing more or less than network television's antidote to strong social medicine—its insurance policy with the FCC. Although I cannot document the charge, it is a reasonable probability that each producer of television shows has pasted up on his dashboard and his desk a list of issues which demand "balance." The "balance" to which the networks refer is in fact the great neutralizer, at once substituting the heat and drama of angry conflict for the more disturbing impact of a carefully researched, meticulously reasoned argument. In the former mode of presentation, there is something for everyone, with the viewer vicariously drained by the ferocity of his advocate's attack and the opponent's parry. With the latter, the unconvinced viewer is left muttering curses at the television set, and only two courses of action are available: either to place a heated call to the station excoriating all concerned as unspeakable beasts, fascists, communists, or hopeless idiots, or else to beat one's mate and/or children senseless. In extreme cases people have actually been known to shoot the television. The networks, at least in part, probably retain the "balance" mode in the mistaken belief that the level of violence will remain manageable.

The "balance" principle is applied with the same inequitable and arbitrary standards that are employed in other prickly areas in network affairs. Somehow "balance," or the supplying of the most vociferous liberal opposition, is necessary on such issues as abortion. However, when, for example, homosexuality is discussed on the air there is usually no "balance" supplied or else the "balance" is an artifactual one: The opposing sides in such a debate are usually homosexuality as an illness versus homosexuality as a valid and acceptable "life style" but *never* homosexuality as a sinful, wicked vice, or as a sexual perversion.

In November, 1972, and again in August, 1973, network television mounted an unprecedented probe into the menacing outland of abortion, avoiding "balance." Norman Lear, the creator of "All in the Family," "Sanford and Son," and similar paradigms of irredeemably tasteless schlock decided to have the lead character in another of his stunted litter, "Maude", become pregnant and opt for abortion. To fully comprehend the Herculean lengths to which Lear has gone to plumb the infinite depths of tastelessness on behalf of the television-viewing public, one must recall that on earlier occasions he had brought Archie Bunker's diarrhea, Mike's impotence, Gloria's miscarriage, and Edith's menopause to the rapt attention of his adoring audiences. Such discriminating critics as John O'Connor of the *New York Times* have compared Lear favorably to Molière, Shaw, and Sheridan. It is probably apocryphal that he is planning a series on the life and times of La Petomâne, the idol of the Parisian music halls of the 1890's who was reputed to be able, unaccompanied, to fart the tunes of no fewer than two hundred popular songs of the era, all in the key of B sharp.

In November, 1972, Maude, a forty-seven year old woman married to Walter, became pregnant through a malfunction of the condom method which they were using for birth control. I present the artful, elegantly structured dialogue for which the Lear shows are celebrated:

> MAUDE: "The gismo. Why weren't you using the gismo?"
> WALTER: "I was. It didn't work."

This was followed by a thunderclap of laughter. I'm not sure George Bernard Shaw would understand it, but Carl Jung very well might.

In the remainder of the two episodes, after what laughingly passes for introspection and responsible decision-making in a painful dilemma, Maude elects to have an abortion while Walter rejects both the vasectomy option and a cruel observation by the cretinous daughter of the pregnant woman that having an abortion "is like going to the dentist."

Now there is certainly nothing wrong with bringing the abortion issue out of the television closet within the framework of drama. But it is something else to drag the issue before a national audience within the context of a sitcom striving for cheap yuks with a canned laugh track, on a show whose producer thinks that toilet-training and suicide are irresistibly amusing subjects, in an anomalous situation, and with a forty-seven year old woman instead of the much more common—and therefore more valid—dilemma of the twenty-five year old single woman or the thirty-two year old married woman with several children. In the latter two instances, the complexity of the issue could be developed, even with some illuminating and gentle humor. It need not all be doom and dismay, but here Lear demeaned and denigrated the issue in an inelegant burlesque. When the expected avalanche of protest mail arrived and when at re-run time the following summer thirty-nine CBS affiliate stations refused to carry it and seven major sponsors withdrew their support, Lear struck the classic martyred pose and wailed on about engaging the feelings of people and artistic freedom. The *New York Times* adhering as always to the faithful liberal line, editorially castigated both the affiliate stations who dropped the re-runs and the sponsors who withdrew their support ("Those who did insult the public were the thirty-six CBS affiliates who bowed to pressure from the anti-abortion forces. . . .) and supported CBS for its determination to re-run the program. Aside from doctrinaire considerations, CBS and the *New York Times* have long been in bed together, what with their CBS-*New York Times* polls, and so forth.

But oh, how inconstant is that liberal love! How willing to overlook hypocrisy and inconsistency in the name of the larger adherence to the liberal dogma. In March, 1979, Kay Gardella, writer of the television critical column for the *New York Daily News* and whose integrity and clear vision I admire only one micron less than that of Beth Fallon, the political columnist for the same paper, wrote a piece entitled: "Black Pressure Kills Lear's CBS Series." She stated that Norman Lear, that exemplar of artistic integrity, had produced a comedy series called "Mr. Dugan," dealing with the trials and tribulations of a freshman black Congressman living it up in Washington and trying to cope with an all white staff. With his usual devil-may-care intrepidity and disdain of the Lilliputian minds around him, Lear arranged a private screening for the black congressional caucus, which found the show demeaning and foul. Representative William Clay, a Democrat from Missouri, was quoted as follows: "The disgust was unanimous among us." Representative Parren Mitchell, a Democrat from Maryland, reportedly left in the middle of the show, yelling: "It stinks." And, according to Alan Horn, president of T.A.T. Communications, Lear's production company, Lear had also taken the precaution of showing the series to a number of his black friends, all of whom had warned him to quash the whole enterprise and take a financial bath on it. R.I.P., Mr. Dugan.

Thus Lear bravely resisted the anti-abortion pressure and showed his vulgar "Maude" sewage, while cravenly collapsing in the face of black heat. And where was Mr. John O'Connor, the television critic of the *New York Times* at the collapse of Dugan? And somehow or other, the editorial boards of the *New York Times* and the rest of the mega-press sodality seemed to have conveniently overlooked the shameful surrender of the Lear organization in the matter of Dugan. Again, it depends upon whose Ochs is gored.

The three networks are also distinguished by their tapioca spines. In the era of the Maude mishap, CBS caved in to Jewish pressure groups which objected to a rather innocuous bit of fluff called "Bridget Loves Bernie," a sitcom valiantly attempting to extract a touch of humor from religious intermarriage, something which had been done with more artistry and good taste fifty years earlier in the radio series "Abie's Irish Rose." They withdrew the series when Jewish groups expressed fear that the series might encourage further inter-marriage, thus diluting the Jewish blood lines. And nothing makes the network pulses race like a little pressure from homosexual groups. When CBS News aired a program called "Gay Power, Gay Politics" examining the not inconsiderable political potency of the homosexual community in San Francisco and its queen-making role in the mayoral elections in 1979, the homosexuals filed a complaint alleging forty distortions in the story which were said to be inimical to the gay image. The complaints were referred to the National News Council for evaluation. Now the council is a toothless old beast composed of members of the press and the public who function as an ombudsman organization mediating differences between the press and those who fancy themselves injured by the press. After suitably grave ruminations on this matter, the council decided that CBS News had incorrectly inserted an applause track in a speech by Mayor Dianne Feinstein in an inappropriate place in the speech; CBS News ran an apology for that unspeakable incursion into gay rights.

That same cozy multiple standard (it's okay to trash Catholics and other anti-abortion groups while collapsing in the face of gay pressure) was again boldly practiced in 1974 when NBC had planned to televise a re-run of an episode of an otherwise eminently forgettable series called "Police Woman." The episode in question concerned a lesbian crime ring, but when gay groups registered a strong protest, not only did the network promise not to re-run the episode but also accepted a list of demands for fair treatment of homosexuals on television.

Note that when discussing the issue of abortion and the two offensive "Maude" programs, CBS's president Robert D. Wood indicated that to withhold the re-running of those programs would "suggest we made a mistake the first time around." He added that "if you start collapsing to one [pressure group] you're quickly going to have a long line of others outside your door." Evidently it's all right to collapse to black pressure, gay pressure, Jewish pressure, and for all we know Martian pressure, but there is something indefinably shameful about collapsing to pro-life pressure.

THE WIRE SERVICES

The great majority of newspapers, radio, and television stations cannot afford to maintain their own correspondents in every corner of the United States, let alone the world. Aside from the members of the mega-press, these newspapers and electronic media are dependent upon the wire services—Associated Press (AP) and United Press International (UPI)—for their news-gathering. The mega-press has not one but two of its own wire services, the *Los Angeles Times-Washington Post* News Service and the *New York Times* News Service, which serve not only those particular newspapers but increasingly other media as well. It would be foolish to think that these latter two services are uninfected with the liberal ideology of the parent organizations. Therefore, let us consider only the two leading non-affiliated wire services: the AP and the UPI.

The Associated Press, still the dominant force in the newsgathering business is a member-owned co-operative which serves 1,307 daily newspapers, 5,000 AM and FM radio stations, and 580 television stations and has sales of approximately 140 million dollars a year. It has a Board of Directors which includes Katherine Graham, chairman and chief executive officer of the *Washington Post* Company, and a corps of management officers which includes Keith Fuller, president and general manager, and James F. Tomlinson who serves as vice president, secretary and treasurer. The AP appears to be in no acute financial distress.

In contrast, United Press International, seventy-eight years old and owned since 1906 by the Scripps Company, has been in ill health financially for the past several years. UPI serves 1,040 daily newspapers and 3,500 broadcasters. Since it was privately owned (ninety-five per cent by Scripps and five per cent by the Hearst Corporation), there are no figures for its total sales yearly, but it was known to be losing an average of six million dollars annually from 1979 on. In early 1980, Scripps made an effort to sell the agency to the membership by peddling the ownership in forty-five separate units worth $280,000 each. Only sixty per cent of the offer was subscribed and Scripps terminated the sale in February, 1980. Subsequently, the Charter Media Company, a publishing concern in part owned and operated by an oil conglomerate, flirted with UPI for a short while but lost interest toward the end of 1980. In 1981 the giant London-based European news agency, Reuter's, expressed considerable interest in acquiring UPI, but by the year's end the courtship was broken off with no reason publically stated. Private interests have subsequently purchased it.

UPI and AP are difficult to characterize with respect to their handling of the reportage on social issues. They are difficult because of the far-flung decentralized nature of the operation in which the individual correspondent has little or no contact with editors, rewrite people, guilds, and financial officers; the correspondents are in the field mining the raw news and pumping it back to a central distributing operation. In turn, the central distributor moves the dispatches to the member media outlets which span the spectrum ideologically and politically. Some of the membership is strongly conservative, other members are militantly liberal, but most are in between. Thus, there is little or no tailoring of the news to conform to one central ideological focus as, for example, with the *New York Times* editorial policy. In effect, the news as pumped along by the wire services is unprocessed. The individual correspondents are generally less experienced and less skilled journalists. The "successful" ones gravitate to the mega-press newspapers and networks where the pay is better and the by-line visible. Because there is no newsroom, no guild meeting, no common lunchroom, or no mothership for these correspondents, they operate in relative journalistic quarantine, uninfected by a central doctrinaire line emanating from an editorial board or a publisher's penthouse.

On the other hand, events are observed, interpreted, and passed along by human agency. Inevitably some bias will appear, though it is kept to a minimum by the unaffiliated wire services. In short, the reportage from these sources is customarily as bland and as neutral as is journalistically possible.

One personal experience with the wire services occurred in an encounter with one Patricia McCormack in February, 1980. McCormack specialized in the handling of women's and social issues for the UPI. She interviewed me at my office in New York City in an effort to clarify the reasons for my "conversion" to anti-abortion attitudes, a matter which had been discussed both in innumerable other interviews in the media as well as in *Aborting America*. In a prologue to the interview, McCormack conceded that she had not read the book. The last thing she had read of mine was the 1974 article in the *New England Journal of Medicine*, "Deeper Into Abortion," although *Aborting America* had been published six months before the interview took place. When I queried her regarding what I considered a failure to do her homework, she countered that the working press doesn't have the time to read everything published by those who are in the news and in any case she liked to have it "fresh" for her readers.

In the course of hundreds of interviews, I have been given this same lame rationalization by the members of the media, and it never fails to puzzle me. If an interview is to be conducted, it would seem to me elementary that the interviewer should make some effort to acquaint himself with the background and publications of the subject. In this way, the interviewer would have to expend little time eliciting familiar material and instead could concentrate most of the available time plumbing the more complex depths of the interviewee and developing his opinions in a more searching manner. The failure to do so strikes me as symptomatic of the general indolence and laziness of the press in particular and reflects a not inconsiderable contempt on the part of the press for its consumers. All everyone wants, the thinking runs, is sordid revelation and shocking sensationalism, so why bother with attempts at serious journalism.

The substance of the interview then was about two-thirds rehash of what I had declared in the course of innumerable other interviews and on which I had elaborated at great length in *Aborting America*. The only new material that she elicited was the observation that my office was "a little dog-eared, the way a comfortable living room is." She obviously went home, read the book—or at least portions of it— and filed a story which was in part, quotations from the interview, large swatches from "Deeper Into Abortion," and whole, undigested chunks of *Aborting America*. There was also a contemporary photo of me sitting behind my desk hands outstretched and palms facing each other as if measuring some imaginary fish.

To give her her due, the interview as printed was nothing if not fair. It was entirely factual, composed largely of rather unusually accurate quotes, and uncontaminated by media attitude. Realistically, this may be all we can reasonably expect of the mega-press: An accurate exposition of one's views without analysis or interpretation.

The interview ran in a large number of daily newspapers. I picked it up in the *Bergen Record*, a medium-sized daily serving Bergen, Hudson, and Passaic counties in the state of New Jersey. It was head-lined "Why a Pro-Abortion M.D. Switched Sides." The headline in this case was as neutral and as bland as the substance of the article. I have seen headlines for articles dealing with the same material reading: "Turncoat Doc Tells Why He Defected On Abortion" and "Abortionist Confesses, Repents."

The wire services are grinding out copy in about as inspiring and dedicated a manner as General Foods turns out Puffed Wheat. The product here is news: it is as unseasoned, as impeccably neutral, and as wholesome and as immaculate as Puffed Wheat. And given the apparently irresistible penchant of the other members of the mega-press to affix their liberal print to the product, perhaps we should be grateful that the wire services at least adhere to a basic integrity in packaging, even with a minimal effort at interpretive and creative journalism.

Finally, I am not unaware that the neutral product pumped out to the member dailies and stations is often tempered with, tailored, altered, and generally reworked by the recipient media. An amusing case in point is a dispatch filed by the AP from Washington on February 11, 1982, and appearing on page ten of the *New York Daily News* of February 12, to wit:

> Say Support for Abortion Is Up
>
> An organization opposed to government restriction of abortion said yesterday that its membership has increased 50% thanks largely to the anti-abortion efforts of a "Gang of Four"—President Reagan, and Sens. Jesse Helms, Orrin Hatch and John East.

That is the entire story as it was printed in that worthy newspaper that day. No identification of the organization alluded to in the dispatch, no statement regarding the size of the membership to begin with, and no explication regarding the differing points of view of the various members of the "Gang of Four" with respect to regulation and restriction of abortion. Either the AP correspondent filed the dispatch while under a heavy load of Valium, or, more likely, the editorial staff of the *New York Daily News* truncated the story to nonsense. Try this on your imagination:

FOUR SHOT IN ASSASSINATION ATTEMPT

> *Washington* (API): The President and three other people were shot outside a Washington hotel today. The President was taken to a local hospital. He was suffering from bullet wounds. Three other men were badly hurt. They were thought to be suffering from bullet wounds too. Police say that someone shot them.

FINAL THOUGHTS

The free press is at the interface between events and the public perception of these events. Think of the press, if you will, as an active carrier membrane at which events collide on one side of the membrane and then are drawn across it. This is sometimes done by passive diffusion as in the case of the wire services, in which events emerge at the distal side of the membrane in virtually their crystalline form, uncolored and unaltered. Sometimes, it is done by active transport, as in the case of the newsmagazines, the giant newspaper complexes, and the electronic news in which events are pulled, shaped, colored, and styled in the membrane to emerge on the other side as almost unrecognizable polymers, permutations, and isomers of themselves. The membrane in the former instance is composed most entirely of the technology involved: the transcription of the event into symbols and the transport of the symbols through the appropriate electronic devices to the recipient outpost. In the latter instance, the membrane is largely composed of the human intelligence at once breaking down, filtering, and reconstituting events to conform to what the membrane itself perceives as the need of the body politic. By far the largest portion of the surface area of the membrane is the mega-press: the giant newspaper complexes, the newsmagazines, the three national television networks, the wire services, and in the particular issue in question, the *New England Journal of Medicine*.

To stretch the analogy to perhaps a perilous extreme, the function of the membrane must be committed to the public weal. If this is not the case—through accident or design—the product, the filtrate, will be defective and perhaps even poisonous. In ulcerative colitis, for example, in which the membrane of the intestinal tract is diseased and nutrients are either unabsorbed by the body or else absorbed in some valueless or even lethal form, the stricken patient will sicken and die. In short, the membrane must remain sound and vigilant in policing its healthful state. Necrotic cells and defective enzyme systems must be removed and replaced. Finally—bear with me, dear reader, just one moment longer on this inexcusably attenuated analogy—the cells, the units of the membrane, are the members of the press. Individually and collectively they tacitly pledge themselves to the public weal, recognize and defer to their fiduciary responsibility to the electorate, and carry out their duties to the electorate within the framework of a covenant with the republic. They must be allowed complete access to events, and they must observe, explain, and interpret these events honestly and impartially. They must be kept free of government interference.

The reporting of an event such as the eruption of a volcano or the shooting of a Pope, "hard news," is straightforward and requires little more than legwork, a modicum of enterprise, and a basic familiarity with the rudiments of the English language. It is in the reporting of the "soft news," that is, social issues, that the ability and integrity of the free press are strained to the limit and, regrettably, often beyond the limit. For it is here in the reporting of evolving ideas, changing standards, and social dislocations that the precepts of integrity and impartiality are repeatedly violated.

Nor is it enough simply to lump all the "soft news" into the category of "social issues." In order to understand more fully the shortcomings of the mega-press in the United States one must concede that the social issues can in turn be broken down into two main sub-categories: the issues of social disorder (for instance busing, gun control, voting rights, school prayer, women's rights, and gay rights) in which politically indoctrinated groups struggle for control of the community within the secular rules, and the issues of conscience (for example abortion, euthanasia, sex education, and capital punishment) in which the struggle takes place within the conscience of the individual and most often insists on transcending the secular rules. Concisely put, who shall live and who shall die? The issues of social disorder can be difficult to report fairly and impartially, but at least one has some data, statistics, and quantification on which to rely in reporting and interpreting: for example the costs of busing, the mounting rates of homicide with firearms, the changing patterns of voting and political control, and the emergence of women into the professions and the work force. But concerning the conscience issues, where data is exceedingly difficult to come by and quantification often quite literally impossible, great restraints are necessary on the part of the press to keep the reportage impartial and full. It is in this area that the press has failed us most lamentably, most particularly in the area of abortion reporting, unusually complex because it now straddles two areas: It is a social issue in that scientific data (fetology) have now accumulated and must be taken into account; it also remains a conscience issue since it raises the question of who shall live and who shall die. And it is precisely here that the temptation to abdicate conventional journalistic ethics for the deeply felt compulsions of the conscience is greatest; it is precisely here that the temptation must be most stoutly resisted. The public prurience in these issues of conscience is in a state of almost perpetual tumescence and, among other obligations, it is the duty of the press to report these issues in a manner designed to reduce the heat and to inform.

The media should have little difficulty with reporting the "hard news." Wars, turnover of political power, famine, and scientific achievement all call for a minimum of interpretive bias and subjective filtration. Yet within the past several years, we have had journalistic abuses of lamentable dimensions in the mega-press even in this relatively undemanding area of reportage. Michael Daly, a respected young columnist for the *New York Daily News*—the largest daily circulation in the United States save for the *Wall Street Journal*— was caught allegedly fabricating a story from Belfast in which he claimed to have witnessed British troops using real bullets instead of plastic ones on bands of young people throwing gasoline bombs at the troops. Daly, a graduate of Yale and a veteran of the *Village Voice*, resigned from the paper in disgrace. "The Ear," a gossip columnist for the *Washington Post*, once claimed that Jimmy Carter had Blair House bugged but was later forced to retract the item and apologize to the President. Raymond Bonner of the *New York Times* and Alma Guillermoprieto of the *Washington Post* at one time reported that several hundreds of civilians and non-combatants were massacred in a wanton attack by crack troops of the El Salvadoran army in a village known as Mozote. Assistant Secretary of State for Inter-American Affairs, Thomas O. Enders, denied the story, declaring only that a military operation had taken place in the vicinity of the village but no mass killing. In any case, the reporters had claimed that 926 people had been slaughtered in the operation, but the village only had a population of 300 to begin with. Christopher Jones, a twenty-four year old freelance writer who authored an article for the *New York Times Sunday Magazine* section of December 20, 1981, concerning a journey he had made and time he had spent with the Khmer Rouge guerilla forces in Cambodia, was forced to admit that he had fabricated the entire article. Donald Ramsay and Bob Reguly, reporters for the *Toronto Sun*, ran a story in that well-respected newspaper stating that John Munro, the Canadian Minister for Indian Affairs and Northern Development, capitalized on inside information he possessed regarding the Canadian government's purchase of Petrofina, an enormous oil company, in order to reap substantial gains for himself. The story recounted what was alleged to be Munro's exact role in the transaction, including the number of shares he bought and the dates upon which he bought them. Munro denied the story categorically, sued the *Toronto Sun* for libel, and the

Sun was forced to admit the story was fabricated. Ramsay was subsequently fired, and Reguly resigned. The catalogue of journalistic deceit and abuse of the public trust only begins with these melancholy tales. The true dimensions of the breaches of ethics, unprincipled distortions, and outright lies foisted on the poor public by the megapress will probably never be fully appreciated since it is axiomatic that the press controls the press.

Nor are the television networks any more responsible in the discharge of their duties in the reporting of the "hard news." Though there are fewer examples of obvious lying and fabrication—the networks after all operate more openly and with more immediacy than the print press—they too fail the public trust in the quality of reportage and the selection of news to be covered. For the networks to betray their trust in this regard is especially grievous in that Gallup polls have demonstrated that more than seventy per cent of people believe that network television is superior to any other branch of the media in the reporting of news (only fifty-seven per cent of respondents trusted the newspapers to do the job). But even the casual viewer of local newscasts has to be impressed, not to say paralyzed, by the frivolous *selection* of the news to be carried. In New York City it seems that tenement fires in Hackensack dominate the local television news, though by what perverse stretch of the imagination such insignificant—in the sense of impact on public policy—misfortunes qualify as news escapes the rational mind. Bank robberies, street crime, lurid trials, sensational divorces, comings and goings of celebrities, and assorted other fauna of the world of "show-business" are the heart and soul of the six o'clock news. Circuses and more circuses seem to be the theme of the day. Richard Nixon, who was never known to have conducted an extensive love affair with the press but was nonetheless a shrewd commentator on the political scene, once graded the preformance of the television networks thus: "Television is to news what bumper stickers are to philosophy."

This is, of course, not to exclude the networks from association with that unlovely band of brigands and liars who abuse the public trust. A trendy figure like Geraldo Rivera was awarded an Emmy for reportage on an arson-for-profit ring in Chicago, only to have the story severely questioned and largely discarded on its merits. Channel Seven (ABC) in New York had its Letterscam scandal in which bogus letters —supposedly from viewers but actually written by the staff of the station—were read and answered on a segment called "Air Mail Special." This shabby little deceit resulted in the firing or resignation of five staffers of the station. When Channel Seven's Joel Siegel authored a Broadway plastique called "The First," now mercifully defunct, and the critic assigned to review it for Channel Seven, Douglas Watt, drama critic of the *New York Daily News*, let it be known that his review was malodorous in the extreme, the review was quashed. And drearily on and on.

In justice one must concede that the newsmagazines, though shamelessly partisan on social and conscience issues, are generally reasonably trustworthy on "hard news" reportage, probably because of the time they have to digest the breaking news as well as the system of checks and reviews which they utilize on all news stories. And for precisely the opposite reason—their simply getting to the scene and reporting the facts with no time to compose or arrange the news—the wire services are generally trustworthy as well in this type of reportage.

But it is in the reportage of the social issues where the mega-press distinguishes itself by its liberal bias, its arrogant disregard of compelling data that is contrary to its tenaciously-held prejudices, and its adherence to democratic socialism—or to its chimeric cousin, social democracy. The coverage by the mega-press of the Vietnam War was in large part openly sympathetic to the Viet Cong from the start, and Vietnam is now writhing under one of the most repressive political regimes in the world. The coverage of the Sandinist guerilla uprising in Nicaragua was monolithically hostile to the Somoza regime, and ever since the Sandinist victory, Nicaragua suffers under a regime openly contemptuous of human rights in the finest Castro tradition. The mega-press despised the Shah of Iran and to a large extent goaded Jimmy Carter into abandoning him to the tender mercies of the Ayatollah Khomeini and his Islamic Revolution. This government is responsible for thousands of star-court proceedings, kangaroo executions, and the prodigal dissolution of the Iranian economy. Angolan rebels, South African agents provocateurs, Salvadoran guerillas, Filipino insurgents, Chilean marxists, Cambodian bandits —all lumped together as the "good guys" simply because they are challenging authority, whether benign or malevolent, and fomenting disorder—in other words, news.

The massive liberal blind spot from which the mega-press suffers is best anatomized in the squalid story of Janet and Jimmy. Janet

Cooke, a black female reporter on the *Washington Post*, concocted a story of a pseudonymous eight-year-old drug addict named Jimmy who lived in Washington, D.C. Cooke admitted fabricating all the academic credentials she listed in applying for the position on the *Post*, but the *Post*, evidently swept away by the affirmative action Zeitgeist, gratefully bestowed the position on her. She then proceeded to create the "Jimmy" story out of whole cloth. Now the affirmative action plot begins to boil: The story was nominated for a Pulitzer Prize in the local reporting category. Even loaded down with the gaudiest fictional embellishments, the story was clearly not good enough to win in that category. So without submitting either the question, or the story to its own jury, as is customary, the Board of the Pulitzer Prize arbitrarily shifted the story to the feature writing category and pressed this prize upon her. The story was subsequently proven a hoax, the prize was reclaimed by the hugely embarrassed Pulitzer Prize Board, and Cooke was forced to resign from the *Post*.

There are a number of instructions to be had from this example of the effect of the liberal plague on the mega-press. In its zeal to fill some self-imposed black quota on its editorial staff, the *Post* failed to check out Cooke's credentials and assess her ethical base, a serious blow to its credit. The Pulitzer Prize Board, in its zeal to get black representation in its prize selection, shamelessly manipulated the slotting of entries so that it could in fact make an award to a black female; it flouted its own rules by ignoring its own jury and virtually forcing the prize on Cooke. It demeaned the value and prestige of the Pulitzer Prize, making it a laughing stock in the public perception. And it may well have destroyed whatever chance Cooke had at a career in journalism. (Cooke later attempted to justify her *Post* scam by lamenting that she had had to make up the Jimmy story because she had invested two months in searching out such a child, and "if I did not produce a story, then how was I to justify my time?" The Cooke-Hearst Syndrome: Write the story first, then try to find the facts, and, if you can't, invent them.)

Here are the two flagships of the mega-press, each with impeccable liberal credentials, caught with their figurative pants down: the *Washington Post* with its Jimmy and Janet story, and the *New York Times* with its Cambodian Tales by Christopher Jones. What measures have been taken by these quasi-official newspapers (both enjoy unprecedented trust in the Federal bureaucracy, the Congress, and the Executive branch) to assure that such flagrant abuses do not happen again? Well, Benjamin Bradlee, the executive editor of the *Post*, fired Ms. Cooke and branded her a "pathological liar." The ombudsman of the *Post*, Mr. William Green, wrote a masterly 18,000 word report on the ordeal. The *New York Times*, in an orgy of self-abnegation worthy of Feodor Dostoevsky at his most elegiac, volunteered that such fabrications discredit publications, debase communication, and ultimately "may even debase democracy." Executive editor A. M. Rosenthal, head hanging, ruefully wrote: "I regret this whole sad episode and the lapse in our procedures that made it possible." If a scandalous episode of comparable magnitude had been uncovered by the mega-press in a governmental microcosm, Special Prosecutors would have been urged, watchdog committees convened, impeachment proceedings demanded, and the rattle of the tumbrils would have been heard across the land. But in the case of the mega-press, such monstrous abuses are largely either overlooked or excused as an excess of liberal well-intentioned zeal. Since it is the press that must indict the press, try the press, and judge the press, not a hell of a lot is going to get done. The offending reporter is fired, blackballed, or publically castigated; apoplectic letters to the editor are printed; and then the whole nastiness is swept under the rug which is already elevated thirty feet off the floor by the other accumulated nastiness underneath it.

The first step in the construction of a therapeutic regimen for the mega-press is to study its structure so as to understand the source of its failure. In this regard, S. Robert Lichter and Stanley Rothman, in a study conducted under the auspices of the Research Institute on International Change at Columbia University and published in the journal *Public Opinion*, have examined what they term the "Media Elite" with a clinical eye. The study is an unusually comprehensive one carried out in conformance with the most rigorous standards for work of this sort. Incidentally, Lichter's and Rothman's media elite corresponds almost exactly to the concept of mega-press set forth in the preceding pages: They studied backgrounds, vision of American society, and perception of the mega-press in interviews with 240 journalists and electronic media people working at the *New York Times;* the *Washington Post; Time; Newsweek;* the news departments at CBS, NBC, ABC, and PBS; the *Wall Street Journal;* and *U.S. News and World Report*. I have not included the latter two publications in my own concept of the mega-press, principally because they appeal to a rather limited segment of the economic and political cosmos—the decidedly more affluent and conservative upper middle class. Lichter and Rothman conducted hour-long interviews with reporters, columnists, bureau chiefs, editors, and executives in the print press as well as with correspondents, anchormen, producers, editors, and news executives in the electronic media. Their data:

Ninety-five per cent of the media elite were white and seventy-nine per cent male. Sixty-eight per cent were from the Northeast or North central states, ninety-three per cent were college graduates, and the vast majority were in their thirties and forties. Seventy-eight per cent had incomes over $30,000 a year, and one in three had salaries in excess of $50,000. Two-fifths of them came from New York, New Jersey, or Pennsylvania. Only an astonishingly small three per cent came from the Pacific Coast, including California, the most populous state in the union.

The origins of the media elite were of equal interest in attempting to understand the unrelievedly liberal bent of this group. Half of their fathers were college graduates, and a full forty per cent of their fathers were professionals; another forty per cent of their fathers were businessmen. Only one of five designated his or her father as belonging to the blue or white collar class. Almost half admitted that while growing up, the family income was certainly above average. On balance, this was a sheltered, privileged bunch. Lichter and Rothman include the following from this data:

> All these characteristics might be expected to predispose people toward the social liberalism of the cosmopolitan outsider. And indeed much of the media elite upholds the cosmopolitan or anti-bourgeois social perspective that Everett Ladd has termed the "new liberalism."

They went on to study the social and political attitudes of the group. Fifty per cent disdained any religious affiliation; fourteen per cent identified themselves as Jewish though twenty-three per cent were raised in a Jewish household. Twenty per cent were Protestant and twelve per cent Catholic. Only eight per cent attended religious services on a regular basis, and eighty-six per cent seldom or never did. Fifty-four per cent described themselves as "left of center" and only nineteen per cent as right of center. However these political solipsisms do not quite tally with the objective data: Examining the presidential voting record of the group we find that in 1972, eighty-one per cent of the group voted for George McGovern while only thirty-eight per cent of the general electorate supported him. All right, Nixon and the press loathed each other. In 1976, eighty-one per cent of the group voted for Jimmy Carter while only fifty-one per cent of the general electorate did. In fact, since 1964, less than twenty per cent of the group supported *any* Republican candidate. Eighty per cent of this group supports strong affirmative action for blacks; seventy-five per cent feel there is nothing wrong with homosexuality; and eighty-five per cent feel that homosexuals should be allowed to teach in schools. Fifty-four per cent felt there is nothing wrong with adultery, and a ringing ninety per cent uphold the right of women to decide on abortion—unregulated permissive abortion for all.

Now, when this predominantly affluent white male upper middle class faithfully and indiscriminately liberal company was queried as to who should rule American society, ranking the seven leadership groups in terms of the desired influence each should exert in American life, its expressed wish was as follows: The media should rule as the most influential group followed by (in order) consumer groups, intellectuals, blacks, businessmen, feminists, and unions.

The composite picture of the mega-press person is of a white male in his late thirties or early forties reared in a rather affluent and well-educated household in the Northeast or North Central area of the country, a college graduate now earning in excess of $30,000 a year. One in four is Jewish. In the general population twenty-five in every thousand persons are Jewish, but in the mega-press 230 out of every thousand are Jewish, a representation far out of proportion to their numbers in the census. This is clearly the source of the fulsome accusation from identifiably anti-Semitic sources that the media is dominated by the Jews (Lichter and Rothman are both Jewish, and so am I).

Thus, with respect to the social and political attitudes of people involved in the media, the composite picture is that of the committed liberal. But recall that Lichter's and Rothman's interview population included employees of the *Wall Street Journal* and *U.S. News and World Report*, publications which I did *not* include in my concept of the mega-press. So if we "subtract" these employees and their probably more conservative attitudes, we are left with a decidedly *more* liberal composite than the Lichter and Rothman portrait presents. Now we have placed the typical mega-press person even *more* strongly left of center, *more* committed to the customary liberal attitudes such as greater affirmative action for blacks and its corollaries, increased busing, larger quotas, additional welfare programs, and more money for remedial education; and a more dogged adherence to sexual permissiveness and its corollaries, more sex education, more abortion, more fractionation of the family through the granting of unrestricted sexual license for children unregulated by parents. And there is no hesitation about declaring that, with these avowedly liberal protocols dominating its thinking, the mega-press should be the decisive, the most powerful leadership force in United States society.

The composite picture of the typical mega-press person is important to determine with the conclusions arrived at from a *different* direction, for example the attitude of the mega-press toward abortion and specifically the manner in which abortion reporting has been carried out in the United States in the past fifteen years. The reporting of the abortion issue has been partisan, prejudiced, and consistently favorable to the liberal pro-abortion forces, and the reportage in the mega-press has been written by, processed by, and published by a cadre of strongly committed liberals persuaded to the pro-abortion side and who would view themselves as the most powerful influence on American life and society.

For those of us who insist on a standard of fairness in the reporting of the conscience issues such as abortion and the social issues as well, passivity and acceptance of the exalted status and self-proclaimed protection of the mega-press promise no relief. The abortion issue, along with capital punishment, crime, integration, gun control, euthanasia, school prayer, and the like, will continue to suffer from cruel distortion through the liberal prism. Without remedial action the conflict is stalemated. What is to be done?

Why not start with what cannot be done? we cannot insist that those who would enter the field of journalism pass a political "means" test. One cannot sanction testing of political attitude in the selection of candidates for positions in the schools of journalism or in the job area in the mega-press. Nor can one impose political attitude testing on those already working in the mega-press, with the view toward

correcting the political balance with appropriate conservative representation. This would be judged, let us say, on the proportion of
conservatives in the general population. The dangers inherent in the
imposition of such measures are obvious and chilling: Who would
make the judgments regarding the "proper political attitude?" How to
confirm the integrity of the attitude: Is it skin-deep, is the tested
person a crypto-liberal or a closet fascist? Why not impose political
attitude testing on the other professions such as medicine and the
law?

What we can do is insist on a reasonable standard of education and
competence from those who practice the profession of journalism. As
I have stated earlier, the journalist, like the physician or attorney,
functions in a fiduciary relationship with the American electorate. He
is in possession of facts and material which are essential to the public
welfare, and the unbiased forth-right transmission of these data to the
electorate is a sacred trust. To that end it is necessary that the schools
of journalism adhere to certain standards in the preparation of their
students for the practice of their profession. Just as Abraham Flexner
was commissioned by the American Medical Association to study the
state of medical education in the early twentieth century—and the
report born of this study effected sweeping changes in the quality of
medical education for decades to come—so too should a commission
be granted to a private responsible non-partisan body to study the
quality of journalistic education in the United States, establish
standards, and provide for watchdog organizations to maintain the
standards imposed.

Entry into the field of journalism should not be achieved through
nepotism, on-the-job training, or by lateral drift from other allied
occupations. The "administrative assistant" or "gofer" at a television
station should not qualify to write and read the news at six o'clock
merely by virtue of punctuality, diligence in the studio, and illness or
resignation of the regular. Journalism is not show-business, and the
ingenue stand-in hovering in the wings is not necessarily the most
competent replacement. We are long past the day when physicians
were trained in the art of healing by following the old family doctor
on his rounds for a year or when the young aspiring *Blackstone*
clerked in his preceptor's office for a year before putting up his
shingle as a country lawyer. Journalism is at once as complex, as

demanding, and as publically responsible a profession as medicine and law, and the education of the journalist must be made appropriate to these august responsibilities.

Again, mere graduation from medical school does not entitle one to practice medicine on the public. There are licensing examinations, certifying examinations for specialization, and now sub-specialty certifying examinations and recertifying exams. For attorneys, in addition to bar examinations after graduation from law school, there are in many states special examinations in the ethics of the legal profession. These licensing and certifying examinations for the journalist need not—in fact, *should* not—be under government auspices. This procedure would undoubtedly run afoul of the First Amendment guarantees, that "Congress shall make no law abridging . . . the freedom of the press," and government and the free press are by nature antithetical. Nevertheless there is nothing explicit or implicit in the Constitution to discourage the press from the establishing its own organizational instruments with the purpose of assuring a continuing high quality of journalism. I suspect the electorate would benefit from some badly-needed reassurance from such a self-policing force.

Apologists for the press, when not to be found cringing behind the First Amendment, do a good deal of swanning over the National News Council as a self-policing unit. The council, established in 1973 as a result of recommendations originating from a study of the press by a task force of the Twentieth Century Fund, is a private nongovernmental organization funded by private foundations on the model of the British Press Council. The latter is a watchdog group which has monitored the performance of the press in the United Kingdom since 1953 with considerable success owing to the general cooperation it has elicited from publishers and editorial staffs in England. The National News Council is composed of ten members from the general public and only eight from the media. This proportion prevents the media from dominating policy and throttling the chartered function of the council. (In actual fact, at present two-thirds of the council membership is from the media, contrary to the by-laws of the organization.) But the council is a paper dragon, which publishes impressive, thick paperback reports on all the complaints about the press that it has received and investigated but which have been rejected by all but two dozen of the 1,700 daily papers in the United States. The *New York Times* has steadfastly refused to acknowledge the existence of the council and regards it with the vast contempt it usually reserves for the "rich." (Its publisher, Arthur Ochs Sultzberger, is the scion of one of the wealthiest families in the United States.)

The working press is openly disdainful of the National News Council, and why not? Ninety-seven per cent of all American cities and towns with daily newspapers are monopoly towns. The newspaper or newspapers are owned by one publisher with no competition so that it's the only game in town.

Instead, let us take advantage of the open arena in which the press functions. Let us demand that the press set America an example by applying the liberal standards in employment that it demands of all other segments of business and society to itself. No longer should the press be dominated by white affluent liberal males from the Northeast. Let the press design and utilize a non-discriminatory test for employment on the same order it demands for the police department, the fire department, and the other organs of public and quasi-public functions. Let the press establish the same quotas in its ranks of employees that it demands from business, the professions, and government. Why shouldn't the mega-press have a ten per cent black representation? In fact, it is closer to four per cent: Why shouldn't it have a fifty per cent female representation, as it demands from law schools and medical schools? In fact, it has a twenty per cent female representation which is largely confined to the lower-paying slots. Why should a full forty per cent of the major-league journalists come from the three most populous Northeastern states, while only three per cent originate from the Pacific coast, including California, the most populous state in the union? With a press as heavily tilted toward the affluent northeast area, it's no wonder that the reportage is similarly tilted.

But these measures—widening the admission policies and procedures in schools of journalism to allow more minority representation in the ranks, re-evaluating the curriculum of schools of journalism with particular stress on the ethical aspects of reportage, forcing the profession to police itself by insisting on certifying and re-certifying examinations to assure quality journalism (spare us that old saw about how impossible it is to give an examination in journalism—the schools of journalism even now manage to do that quite nicely, thank you), applying the fair employment standards to this profession in which proportionate representation is critical both as an example to the other professions as well as a public assurance that elitist news will not continue to be the sole product of an elitist media (how many black or Hispanic couples have you seen in the society pages of the *New York Times* or the *Washington Post*), and private watchdog organizations like the National News Council—these measures are ineffectual little poultices on a giant suppurating carbuncle. We must devise an institution that is at once a watchdog, a standard of journalistic virtue, a press accessible to minority workers for employment opportunity, a neutral and hospitable bazaar for ideas of all shades and colorations, and above all a press accountable to the public and not to some unimaginably wealthy prince of the media interested only in power-brokering and empire-building. We need the public newspaper.

This is no reckless sally into murky constitutional waters. We have public television (the Federally financed Corporation for Public Broadcasting, aided by private donation) and we have public radio (National Public Radio, a little-known entity which nevertheless supports a substantial portion of its $14.5 million annual budget with Federal appropriation). Why can't we also have a Public Newspaper Corporation? This enterprise would be Federally financed to a large but possibly decreasing extent as private donations roll in and circulation flourishes, and it would be accountable to the legislative branch of the government. It would provide an alternate press in competition with privately owned newspapers in the ninety-seven per cent of all cities and towns in this country which are monopoly newspaper towns. It would provide reasonable access to its opinion pages for all bands of the political spectrum. No longer would that access be at the whim of a press lord. The performance of such a newspaper enterprise would be the public business and no longer the shadowy domain of a media elite. Here will be a press more concerned with local pollution problems than the winners of the Emmy awards; more interested in the local economy than in who is sleeping with whom in Beverly Hills. Here is a true alternate press pledged to the highest standards of journalism and not to the accountant's ledger. Here is a press that could bring us the print equivalent of *Brideshead Revisited* instead of *My Mother the*

Car and its print equivalent which we now receive from the un-challenged private monopoly newspaper system.

There is no First Amendment problem here. This public newspaper enterprise would function in parallel with the privately-owned press, just as the public television and public radio do. Nor would it crowd out the privately owned press; the private networks flourish with spiralling profits even as the public media offer us a different diet. But finally we would have a public print organ in every city and town which would offer access to all bands of the political and economic spectrum; it would not be afraid to report the difficult and wrenching social and conscience issues and would not worry about publisher profit or advertiser interest. And perhaps most importantly, it would not shrink at criticizing the performance of the private press in the public interest.

The Public Newspaper System is a democratically desirable, constitutionally acceptable, logical response to the increasing failure of the privately owned monopolistic press presently dominant in the United States. Because the press is perhaps the institution most essential for the continuing functioning of a democratic society, the failing health of the privately owned press must be acknowledged and acted upon. The time is now.

Part Two

Fetology for Pro-Life

I have spent a substantial portion of the past three years travelling the length and breadth of the North American continent, Europe, and Australia addressing pro-life organizations on the subject of abortion, with special regard to the bio-ethical aspects of the issue. Bio-ethics is a unique area of philosophy which concerns itself with the problems common to both biology (usually, though not always, medical sciences) and ethics (the science of moral duties). Bio-ethics is not a new field of philosophy, although the media, along with many bio-ethicists, would have us believe it is. Actually the first bio-ethicist was probably Hippocrates, who, writing in 400 or so B.C. laid down for physicians a remarkably prescient code of professional conduct including the following strictures:

> I will give no deadly medicine to anyone if asked, nor suggest any such counsel; and in like manner I will not give a pessary to a woman to produce abortion.

The oath, although written 2,400 years ago, is astonishingly contemporary: The first sentence in the excerpt quoted above forbids physicians to associate themselves with euthanasia, and incidentally prohibits organized medicine from participating in executions carried out by the state. (There is an increasingly popular move to execute criminals with drugs instead of electrocution, and physicians, no matter how tangentially, will necessarily be involved in such actions: the oath specifically forbids this.) With respect to the second sentence in the excerpt, a pessary is a ring-like device which is inserted into the vagina for a variety of purposes. Modern gynecologists use it to prop

111

up a sagging uterus ("prolapse") or to correct a retroversion of the uterus ("tipped womb"), and in fact the common diaphragm is more correctly referred to as a contraceptive pessary. In ancient times, the insertion of a pessary was thought to be effective in producing abortion. In broader terms, of course, the oath bars physicians from being a party to the process of abortion. I took that oath in the grassy quadrangle of McGill University on a misty June day in 1949, a gentler and more innocent time, and now to my sorrow the oath has been cast into desuetude; sometimes I think that today's graduates solemnly pledge their fealty to the Standard and Poor Index and swear by Bill Baird the Healer and Henry Morgenthaler the Surgeon.

Until the advent of the science of fetology, the abortion issue had been more frequently identified with pragmatically medical, medico-legal, and religious considerations than with bio-ethical ones. James C. Mohr, in *Abortion in America*, points out that the various abortion statutes in the United States, written for the most part in the nineteenth century, were formulated and passed in the state legislatures largely through the efforts of physicians alarmed by the toll of lives taken by abortionists plying their filthy and unscientific trade on trusting women in desperate circumstances. Combined then with the pronouncement of Pope Pius IX in 1869 that all abortion was anathema, these laws stiffened into unchallengeable commandments. They remained so until the 1960s when a combination of new abortion technology—the suction apparatus, refinements in anesthesia, and antibiotics—and an authority crisis conspired to strike down all those hitherto sacrosanct laws and endow us with the dubious benefits of mass-scale abortion.

For those of us in the 1960s who had no identifiable religious convictions and who were now convinced that technology had eliminated the surgical risks of abortion, why should we not then commence to advocate permissive abortion? Admittedly we had some dim, inchoate sense that something was being destroyed. It was something that could be seen on X-ray but not until the end of the fourth month of pregnancy, and it was something that we could hear with a special stethoscope but, again, not until the beginning of the fifth month. Indeed, even the mother herself could not verify that she was pregnant— that there was something human inside her—until she felt it move in the middle of the fifth month. So to believe that there was something demonstrably human in the uterus at the fourth, sixth, or eighth

week of pregnancy was quite simply an act of faith: You couldn't see
it, you couldn't hear it, and therefore you couldn't really know it.
Sure, some women would abort it, cast it out spontaneously, and
then the physician would see it as a meaty mass with a sac of fluid,
within which was a tiny, immobile, often disorganizing creature which
resembled nothing so much as a tadpole. Even though we accepted
intellectually that, undisturbed, this curious creature would ultimately
have gone on to become a human being, it was something *else* in
the early stages of pregnancy. It was as if the creature, more sea urchin
than human, dwelt in an ethical sanctuary: so mysterious, so exotic
in appearance, so silent in its uterine exile that it could not be a factor
in a consideration of the physician's duty to the living pregnant human
female.

It is an historical irony that physicians of antiquity and even into
the nineteenth century understood in a visceral way, lacking any of
the rudiments of embryology, that the fetus was human. Whether, as
some ancients would have it, the embryo was a homunculus (a tiny
person perfectly formed which, if held under a microscope, would
have the exact appearance of a mini-adult), or, as Hamilton stated in
his classic textbook *Midwifery* published in 1797, "The embryo in its
original state is entirely fibrous and nervous; and these primary parts
seem to contain in a small scale, all the others which afterwards are to
be progressively evolved." What was common to virtually all writers
on the subject was an implicit belief that the fetus was clearly a
human, in one form or another. Still, there *was* the Destructive
Operation.

The Destructive Operation in obstetrics has had a long and inglorious history and is seemingly at serious odds with the foregoing
statement concerning the historical acceptance of the fetus as a human
being. The Destructive Operation was reserved for those women who
had been in labor for excessive periods of time—in the eighteenth and
nineteenth centuries four or five day labors were not unusual—and
an excessively long labor would be defined as a period of over five
days. The baby was either too large or the pelvis too small to allow
vaginal delivery. In these circumstances it was accepted practice to
perforate and crush the skull of the baby and thus allow the head to
deliver. Occasionally, when a tumor of the fetal body made delivery
impossible, a hole would be made in the abdomen of the baby and the
viscera pulled out; the baby was literally disemboweled. The crushing

of the skull was called a craniotomy, and to that end there were numerous quite repulsive instruments devised such as the Cranioclast which resembled nothing so much as a giant garden shears with numerous ominous-looking screws and locks on it, and the Tarnier Basiotribe, an unimaginably complex, evil-seeming instrument consisting of three separate stout metal bars, two of which were shaped into shallow curves at their ends and these cradling a long sharp spear between them.

To put the Destructive Operation into its proper historical context, we must remember that until 1882 Caesarean section carried with it a mortality rate for the mother of seventy-five per cent: three out of every four women on whom Caesarean section was done would die, usually from uncontrollable hemorrhage or infection. From 1882, when a man named Sanger figured out that suturing the raw bleeding edges of the uterus after the child had been extracted from the uterus would cut down on the bleeding, up until 1920, the mortality rate still ran at about ten to fifteen percent. It was only toward the close of the Second World War with remarkable advances in anesthesia techniques, blood replacement, and antibiotics that the mortality rate became significantly lowered, and Destructive Operations finally were relegated to the obstetrical junkyard.

Thus, prior to the mid-twentieth century, Caesarean section was such a dangerous operation that the obstetrician would, in the circumstances of an obstructed labor with no prospect of vaginal delivery, choose to destroy the baby rather than risk losing the mother *and* the baby. This was no tacit recognition of the unborn as a second-class human, but the unavoidable reality that the mother frequently had other children at home who needed her and therefore the painful choice had to be made. Still, the Destructive Operation was performed on a mute, invisible human being and was carried out in the silent shadowed recesses of the birth canal; it was not as if the infant was stretched out in the crib. Thus the choice was an uncomfortable, but tolerable one—to all but Catholic obstetricians.

For the Catholic obstetrician there was no choice to be made. In Catholic doctrine the unborn was not only equally human but perhaps even more so. It was unsullied by sin, it was the ineffably innocent human, and was therefore untouchable. No Destructive Operations were permitted to the Catholic obstetrician and the laboring woman had to die undelivered—usually from sepsis, or from a rupture of the uterus with massive internal hemorrhage. Understandably there arose a fear among women, both non-Catholic and Catholic, of Catholic obstetricians. Although there has probably not been a Destructive Operation on a healthy unborn child in thirty years, that now unreasonable fear of Catholic obstetricians still lingers like a particularly odious spectre over the pregnant population. It continues to have an irresistible appeal to abortion advocates, who convert it to political gold in the abortion controversy.

So the unborn child *was* a human being, hidden, unknowable, but expendable in the extremity. Until the mid-twentieth century, the teaching and practice of obstetrics emphasized maternal health and safety, and well it should have: Consider the following figures in order to understand how dangerous child-bearing was up until the end of the Second World War.

The current generally accepted maternal mortality rate (women dying from the outset of pregnancy until four weeks following the delivery of the baby) is ten per one hundred thousand births. Ten pregnant women in every hundred thousand will die during the course of their pregnancy, labor, or delivery, or during the first four weeks following delivery. In 1930, the rate was almost 700 per 100,000. It was seventy times as dangerous to have a baby then as it is now. Infection accounted for 250 of those deaths, toxemias 180, hemorrhage 70, and miscellaneous causes (clots from the legs to the lung, cancer in pregnant women, pneumonia, anesthesia deaths, or tuberculosis) another 200 or so. Is it any wonder that obstetricians viewed pregnant women as suffering from a potentially lethal disorder, concentrated their attention on the pregnant woman, and regarded the child with a mixture of awe and curiosity but mostly as a mischievous interloper responsible for a "whole hell of a lot of trouble," as one of my obstetrical instructors once told me in 1946, in medical school.

By the end of the Second World War, the mortality rate had been halved. Abortion had not even been declared legal yet; pro-abortionists are fond of attributing the massive reductions in maternal mortality to legalization of abortion, but the fact is that the most dramatic reductions in the death rate preceded legalization by thirty years. By 1945 the rate was 300 per 100,000 and dropping fast due to antibiotics, improved anesthesia techniques, blood banks, better diagnostic methods, large-scale immunization programs for diseases like poliomyelitis, a higher standard of living and more jobs with better nutrition for the pregnant population, better and more available pre-natal care, and better training of specialists in the field. By 1960 the toll had dropped to thirty per 100,000, one-tenth of what it had been only fifteen years before.

By the mid-1960s, concern for the mother's health and safety was no longer the all-consuming matter it had once been. The mortality rate had been reduced so sharply that it was almost taken for granted that pregnant women would survive their pregnancies, and attention could be turned to a consideration of the child. For the first time, we began to discuss *fetal* mortality rates. The maternal mortality committees of the various state and county medical organizations, committees which would review and analyze all maternal deaths, gradually disbanded for want of work, and perinatal mortality committees made their appearance. These were groups of obstetricians and pediatricians who would convene periodically to review *fetal* deaths. Obstetricians began to discuss fetal health, fetal well-being, and the quality of obstetrical care—up to that point measured only by what happened to the mother—in terms of maternal well-being and the fetal "outcome," that is, how good a baby did we get?

The scientific mind is a restless beast. As our attention swung from the visible—the pregnant woman—to the invisible—the fetus—the challenge became irresistible. How could we know more of this creature bricked in, as it were, behind what seemed an impenetrable wall of flesh, muscle, bone, and blood? I well recall my frustration as a resident when women were admitted to my hospital and I was required to estimate the weight of the child using only my hands and my eyes. I would pontificate before my junior residents and my medical students ("oh, this one is seven and a half pounds, definitely") and to my chagrin be proven wildly wrong when the baby was weighed in the nursery (nine and a half pounds—where was she hiding it all?). There was a story making the rounds in those days— perhaps it was apocryphal—that an experiment was run at the Harvard Medical School in which every laboring woman admitted had the fetal weight estimated by the Professor of Obstetrics, by the Resident in Obstetrics, and finally by the lowly medical student assigned to Obstetrics: The professor and the resident each spent a good deal of time poking and prodding the abdomen learnedly and muttering to themselves while laboriously performing some unimaginably complex calculation in their heads; they would then gravely enter the figure in a notebook kept for the results of the experiment. The medical student, on the other hand, would simply say "seven pounds" for every woman who came in regardless of her size, shape, pre-natal history, or anything else. You guessed it: the student was, on the whole, closer in his estimate than the other two were.

We gynecologists would try any formula, any incantation to try to know more about the intra-uterine exile. I recall McDonald's rule: measure the height of the uterine fundus with a tape, subtract thirteen, and divide by three. This is about as scientific and reliable as counting the fetal heartbeat and deciding whether it is a boy or a girl. I recall theorizing then that perhaps passing an electrical current of low voltage through the uterus could in some way or other be used to calculate the fetal weight, on the not very sound premise that the larger the baby the more resistance the current would encounter and the slower its passage. I even went so far as to consult one electrical engineer friend of mine who, upon hearing my pathetically simplistic scheme, cocked an eyebrow and allowed as how there were a hundred or more variables that one would have to deal with in even beginning to consider such a method, and besides how did I think women would take it upon hearing that I proposed to electrocute their babies? As it has turned out, we now use another form of physical energy (high frequency sound waves) and their passage through the uterus and the child allows us to calculate the weight to within a few grams. I suppose that same friend, if he had been consulted in the 1950s with a proposal to pass sound waves through the uterus to estimate fetal weight, might have bridled at that idea and made some acid comment about making babies deaf.

I suppose one could say that modern means of communication with the unborn up until very recently was one-sided; now with our beaming various types of physical energy at it—X-ray and ultrasound—and prodding it with needles—electrodes screwed into its head during internal fetal heart monitoring—that communication can be said to be bilateral though clearly not always mutually comforting.

Fetal communication began with the discovery of the fetal heart sounds by a French physician named Kegaradec. Kegaradec was persuaded that in splashing around in the amniotic fluid the child made discernible sounds which should be audible through the maternal abdomen. He convinced a number of pregnant women to allow him to press his scientific ear to their abdomens, through the requisite layers of corsets and crinolines of course, and instead of perceiving the sounds of intra-uterine aquatics he heard what he described as a double sound resembling the ticking of a pocket watch under a pillow. Kagaradec published his information in a small monograph in Paris in 1822; it is astonishing that even 150 years later we find that he was remarkably thorough in his description of the fetal heart sounds. Obstetricians in the 1920s and 30s occupied themselves with fashioning innumerable variations on the stethoscope in order to hear the fetal heart more clearly. When I was a student, and in fact until the advent of electronic fetal heart monitoring, the Hillis DeLee fetoscope was the rage. It was a gadget that made the wearer look like a refugee from a cheap B Grade space movie. It had a shiny steel head piece flexible enough to conform snugly to the contours of the physician's head from forehead to occiput, and mounted on the front of this headpiece and sticking out like a unicorn's horn was a metallic hollow bell. From the sides of the bell and attached to it were the usual rubber tubings which in turn were plugged into the conventional metallic ear pieces of the average stethoscope. The received wisdom was that this was not just a stethoscope when it was applied to the mother's abdomen but was an amplifying apparatus in that the central metallic headpiece, when rested against the physician's forehead, would allow bony conduction of the sound through the physician's skull to his ears. DeLee, a prominent obstetrician in Chicago and the co-inventor of the device, made a series of grainy films to illustrate the use of the apparatus, and it appears that his hands were used to keep count of the fetal heart for some other observer: He would flick his forefingers up and down in exact rhythm with the heart, and the nurse would make the count watching his fingers. Even as a student, I felt not a little foolish flicking my fingers up and down like a man in the grip of a seizure, and early on I dispensed with using the head-piece entirely and simply pressed the hollow bell to the mother's abdomen and plugged the ear pieces into my skull (I found no difference in acuity with that method).

Another method of primitive communication with the child was the perception of movements. This of course depended largely on the mother and her reporting of the event: were the movements frequent, forceful, persistent? The obstetrician, if patient, could discern the movements merely by placing his hand on the pregnant abdomen and waiting. He would be rewarded with a light tapping and sometimes a slow rolling under the wall; once in a while there was an impatient thump. But this communication, like the perception of the fetal heart, was only accessible after the fifth month of pregnancy, and therefore the certainty of a human presence in the uterus before the fifth month was still a matter of faith during that obstetrical Stone Age. It's not surprising then that common law permitted abortion without penalty before quickening, that is, before the fifth month; it was simply that one could not even be sure a woman was pregnant until that event. What is surprising is that the Stone Age thinking—the division of pregnancy into the trimesters, wherein the first trimester connotes no human presence at all and the second trimester does—still pervades thinking in the abortion arena (more of this later). We now know through ultra-sound and electronic heart monitoring that the heart begins to beat at four weeks, and the child begins to move at five weeks. We may even find these milestone statements to be on the late side as our technology becomes more refined.

The caste system—unknowable and invisible in the first three months, confirmable and unassailably visible in the second three months—was advanced with the use of the X-ray. As if to confirm the invisible status of the child in the first trimester of pregnancy, the X-ray was unable to identify the presence of the child before four and a half months, when the skeleton calcifies sufficiently to be visible on the X-ray film. There are kidney stones which are termed radiolucent because they are not visible to X-ray examination: the failure to demonstrate them on the X-ray does not invalidate the existence of the stone any more than the failure to photograph the child on the X-ray film denied its existence.

These relatively primitive modes of communication from the little aquanaut to the world outside should have sufficed. We should not have doubted that the failure of communication before the fifth month was our failure, caused by inadequate technology, insufficient attention, and inexcusable impatience. If we were to receive on our huge radio telescopes a beat repeating itself over and over at a recognizable rate of one hundred and forty-four per minute, the sound arching across the vault of the universe to be neatly trapped in that dish, how excited we would be, how quick to acknowledge some sort of life out there somewhere in the universe. Like a steady unacknowledged love, this life has been there all the time, but we were unmoved in its presence.

In the early 1960s, curiosity about the child began to mount and became in a sense unrestrainable. Reports began to appear in the journals of obstetrics recounting insertion of long needles into the pregnant uterus to study the fluid within, the sea in which the unborn child incubated. We were not then performing amniocentesis to search out the defective children and destroying them.

I recall a series of amniocenteses I did to study the changes in that fluid during pre-eclampsia (toxemia); the clinical experiment came to nothing at all. There were, in fact, no consistent significant changes in the amniotic fluid to be found in that condition, but one day while I was doing an amniocentesis, the membranes suddenly ruptured, and the woman began losing large amounts of fluid from the vagina. An instant after the membranes ruptured I noted the needle jumping furiously in the abdominal wall, and I wondered why the fetus had reacted so violently to the bag of water breaking. Was it the imposition of the unrelenting and ubiquitous force of gravity upon it? Floating in its internal sea the child had never experienced the insistent pull of gravitational forces before. Previously weightless, it now felt itself in its physical relationship to the universe around it.

We continued using the Hillis-DeLee stethoscope (it was also referred to as a "headscope" or "fetoscope") until well into the mid-1960s. This was the threshold of the era of ultrasound: Suddenly the almost limitless uses of ultrasound in medicine became evident. The first contribution of ultrasound technology to obstetrical technology was in the invention and employment on a wide scale of the Doppler machine for hearing the fetal heart. This machine relied on the principle that if one pulsed high-frequency sound waves at a moving object—the walls of the fetal heart, for example—the sound waves would echo back in a pattern reflecting the motion, and the pattern could then be translated from sound to electrical energy and put through a special speaker system to emerge as sound again. Now we could put the Doppler instrument on the mother's abdomen and the fetal heart could be heard loud and clear by all—the doctor, the mother, the father, the sibling or siblings who were present, and even—who knows?—the child himself.

The use of the Doppler apparatus for listening to the fetal heart in a sense revolutionized the practice of obstetrics. Heretofore only the doctor could hear the fetal heart, and pregnancy was a closed and secret matter, discernible in some major part only to the doctor's ear. Consider what pregnant women experienced at each pre-natal visit. The blood pressure was taken. What pregnant woman could read that shiny column of silvery liquid bouncing up and down in the glass compartment? And anyway, the doctor was bent over her elbow with his stethoscope listening with his private little horn to her artery pounding in his ear. The urine specimen was tested with some paper stick which had a variety of colors on it, and the doctor stuck it into the urine and murmured over it like an alchemist. He would then bend over her abdomen with his fetoscope, listen for fifteen seconds, and straighten up with a satisfied smile. The pregnant woman heard not a thing and was totally excluded from the communication with her own child. She herself was privy to only the most humiliating part of the visit, the ritual weighing and the obligatory scolding if she had gained one gram over the prescribed limit. As shut out as she was during the pre-natal visits, this systematic exclusionary process continued during the labor: heavy medication to make her drowsy and amnesiac, anesthesia for the delivery, and forceps to the head as if to emphasize how insignificant a part she played in the whole childbirth experience. As a final fillip, the baby was shut away in the nursery for long periods of time, and breast feeding was discouraged and even sneered at. It's little wonder that one of the early targets of the radical feminist wrath was the male obstetrician. (In fairness, female obstetricians behaved no differently toward their parturient sisters, and it *was* male obstetricians such as Grantly Dick Read, Fernand LaMaze, and Frederick LeBoyer who led the way to wider family participation in the rites of childbirth.)

The Doppler machine, a small seemingly innocent apparatus no bigger than a pack of cigarettes, put everyone into the middle of the pregnancy tableau. The little instrument was placed over the pregnant uterus, and everyone in the room could hear that little heart thumping away at an incredible 144 beats a minute ("Why is it so fast, Doctor?" "It's supposed to be, that's normal."). Increasingly, husbands began edging their way into the examining room during the pre-natal visit. There was something to hear; communication had been established with the child. At first, fathers would timidly ask the nurse if the doctor would mind if they sneaked into the examining room and heard the heart; later they would become bolder and simply *be* there standing by the head of the table when the doctor walked into the room. Now siblings, mothers, and mothers-in-law all claim the right to be there, to listen to the signals from inner space.

It couldn't have been more timely. The mid-1960s saw the move to natural childbirth and family participation in delivery. Husbands were first in the labor rooms coaching their wives, breathing deeply with them, and sweating and groaning in unison. In an instant they were in the delivery room with us. Now they are even in the operating room with us during a Caesarean. And it was all inevitable: With the burgeoning notion of consumer participation in health care and with the increasing focus of obstetrical care on the child came the means to communicate safely with the child on a mass scale. This was no X-ray or fluoroscopy where the hazards of communication far outweighed any benefits. Obstetrics would never be the same again!

Ultrasound, or sonography, is a medical success story of the 1970s, ranking with transplant immunology and CAT scanning. It is a diagnostic method which relies on the use of high frequency sound waves passing through the body and giving off echoes as the sound waves hit various tissues of different densities. The echoes are collected by a very sensitive device called a transducer (from which the sound waves originally emanated) and the echoes are then arranged by a computer into a black and white pattern which forms a recognizable picture of the tissue being examined. Something of a similar technology was used to transmit the pictures of Saturn back to earth: The photographic images which the cameras on the Explorer satellite captured were converted into electronic messages, flashed through the heavens and collected by a radiotelescopic device, and then reconverted into photographic images at this end. The sound waves used here are at an inaudibly high frequency. We do not know whether the child can hear them or, if it can, what the message is, but because the waves are given off in a pulsed pattern—like Morse code at an impossibly high scream—instead of in a continuous barrage, they are thought to be harmless.

The history of ultrasound is not a chronicle of unbroken successes. Francis Galton, the restless Victorian genius whose intellectual prurience led him from researches in the hereditary patterns of intelligence to the invention of a rotatory engine and a workable periscope, devised a hydrogen whistle capable of producing sound vibrations as high as 25,000 per second. The human ear perceives sound at a range of 100 to 10,000 cycles per second, and Kirsten Flagstad broke the glass at about 11,000 cycles per second. Galton published his work in *Nature* in 1883, but it was ignored and forgotten.

During World War I, an enterprising Frenchman named Langevin devised a method of transmitting high frequency sound waves through water, using a quartz crystal as a source. It appears that all fish swimming in those waters were instantly killed, and it is unclear as to whether Langevin considered this biologic effect of his invention salutary or simply a pesky side-effect. Sokolov in 1929 invented an ultrasonic machine with which he could pass the high frequency sound through metal and detect flaws in the structural integrity of the metal. It was in World War II, however, that ultrasound came into its own as Sonar, the device employing sound waves to track submarines. Following World War II, a number of researchers in Europe and Scotland began applying the technology to medical science and diagnostics.

The application of ultrasonic technology to obstetrics and fetology has been an especially fruitful enterprise. Now, for the very first time, that mysterious squirming occupant of the uterine capsule could be photographed, measured, and examined. X-rays, hot and dangerous, were able to show us the fetal bones and skull but not the vital soft tissues. Ultrasound, cool and safe, allowed us to measure the ventricles of the brain, the diameter of the great vessels, and the chambers of the heart of the child. And finally in the early 1970s, the refinement known as realtime ultrasound, the continuous projection of the ultrasonic images as a motion picture, revealed the tiny heart coiling and thrusting, the lungs and chest wall expanding and contracting in the familiar kinetics of breathing, and even the eyes moving about in their jerky rhythms.

In the film *Close Encounters of the Third Kind*, the climactic scene depicts the hero ascending into the mother ship surrounded by the elfin aliens (who, by the way, resemble human unborn rather alarmingly); the aliens were photographed in a blurred and tantalizing manner. As we strain to see more of them, we will the camera to approach them and eyeball them. Alas, we never see them close up, and the film succeeds in leaving us happily frustrated, wanting more but respecting Spielberg's elliptical statement. With realtime ultrasound, obstetricians and fetologists have floodlit the mother ship and the alien is pinned in its blaze. Or: we have met the alien, and he is us.

But this was not yet fetology. This was still classical obstetrics, with the focus subtly shifting to the family-centered experience we are familiar with now. In the epicenter of that family, the child was figuratively pushing and shoving the mother to one side, demanding equal or more time. With the Doppler instrument having been perfected, two generational lines of technology budded forth. One line was electronic fetal heart monitoring, a clever marriage between the Doppler instrument for listening to the fetal heart and the computer (more about this later). The other line was ultrasonic imaging.

Imaging began in the early 1950s, with the machine known as the A-scanner which was fairly crude by our present standards: The patient had to stand in contact with a column of water, and the picture obtained by this machine was one-dimensional. The interpretation of the picture was anyone's guess half the time. A Scottish obstetrician named Ian Donald tinkered with the instrument, made some imaginative improvements in it eliminating the column of water, and first applied it to pregnant women in 1958. By the early 1960s, the B-scanner had been developed, a machine which would afford us two-dimensional pictures with considerably more diagnostic precision.

In 1962, I was a young attending obstetrician at the Woman's Hospital in New York City. Although it seems unimaginable at this time, ultrasound was then virtually unheard of in the practice of obstetrics. Conjure up the year 1900, think how the practice of medicine must have been without the X-ray machine, and you have some idea of what the practice of obstetrics was in 1962 without ultrasound. A rotund, florid Hungarian, Dr. Lajos von Micsky, joined our staff in that year and was touting the virtues of ultrasound. Von Micsky had fled the communist regime in Hungary in 1946 and had emigrated to the United States via employment with the United States Army in Munich with the ninety-eighth General Hospital, then practiced obstetrics in Mayaguez in Puerto Rico for several years. During his time in Puerto Rico, he became involved with the research arm of the National Aeronautics and Space Agency (NASA) which was then experimenting with ultrasound. He picked up the technology and became quite literally obsessed with it. When he joined us at Woman's Hospital he owned an A-scanner and was trying to convince us that it was the technology of the future. We scoffed: the pictures he produced for us of the fetus were of uniformly poor quality, so poor that many of us, myself included, accused him of guessing out the results. We used to tease him by withholding the patient's history while he was interpreting his pictures and trying to piece together a result (if he didn't have any information about the patient then his guesses would be more wildly wrong than usual). Though his diagnoses were often wrong, his prophecy regarding the use of ultrasound in obstetrics was eerily correct.

Contrary to what the public may think, physicians, especially those who have been in practice a while and have evolved a comfortable pattern of practice based on the state of the art at the time of their residency training in hospital, are loathe to accept new technology. They fight it by scoffing at it, denigrating it, accusing it of financial waste and potential harm—anything which will beat back the inexorable march of progress and relieve them of the necessity of learning a significant portion of their specialty all over again. So it was with the early ultrasound machinery. With von Micsky and his Model-T, we at Woman's Hospital were one of the very first obstetrical institutions to have this technology, yet all we did was poke fun at him and deride the apparatus. Poor von Micsky (he died in 1975 at the age of only fifty-seven) has been vindicated a thousand times over.

But even the two-dimensional B-scanners and later the so-called "gray-scale" machine—a refinement which allowed us to see the picture better because it was no longer simply stark black on white but of intermediate shades of gray—were to the realtime instrument as the daguerrotype was to the motion picture camera. Realtime ultrasound allows us to see the picture instantaneously and in motion, and it is this improvement which has rung up the curtain on the science of fetology. The difference between the "antique" machinery of the past, along with the impact of that difference—the A-scanner and the B-scanner—and the realtime ultrasound is best illustrated by a personal memory spanning forty-five years.

I attended the Columbia Grammar School in New York City, and one of my classmates was a boy named Tom Sarnoff, the son of General David Sarnoff, the long-time president and chairman of RCA Corporation. In the seventh grade, Tom and I were close friends and invited each other back and forth to our respective homes. On one of my visits to his home, a palatial apartment on New York's East Side and several cuts above our considerably more modest digs on the less fashionable West Side, Tom asked me if I wanted to watch "television." There was nothing astonishing in that simple question except that it was 1938, I was twelve years old, and I didn't even know the meaning of the word "television" (nor did anyone else). We sat down in his living room in front of a giant mahogany box in the center of which was a tiny screen perhaps two inches square. We watched some rather blurred, indistinct flickerings accompanied by a sound track explaining that what we were seeing were films of the burning of the zeppelin in "Hindenburg." I recall being less than impressed by what appeared to be such an imperfect tiny movie, and privately I wondered what all the excitement was about. My father, who had arrived to take me home, stopped for a moment to watch that miniature movie. He scoffed, saying that it would never get off the ground or something to that effect. Well, it's only revolutionized the twentieth century; similarly realtime ultrasound has only revolutionized our perception of the fetus, and modern obstetrics.

No more images frozen on a polaroid film, as we had with the old-style scanners; instead we had realtime, with immediacy and motion, and the child was now moving in *our* continuum of time. If you doubt the importance of motion, watch a television program which features nothing but still photographs with a voice overlay; you find yourself yearning for the figures in the photographs to move, to become animate beings in this moment of time. For want of a better term, I will call what is lacking the "dimension of time" (not an original formulation with me; relativists such as Einstein spoke of the dimension of time with a fine disregard for gadgets such as motion pictures and televisions way back at the turn of the twentieth century). Simply put, life *is* motion although motion is not necessarily life: planets move, and light spurts out in unimaginably speedy waves.

So realtime ultrasound added two essential elements to the old static black-and-white pictures of the A and B-scanners: motion and contemporaneity. Watching the fetus move was exciting enough, but of course we could have constructed time lapse films of the fetus using the static images of the old B-scanner just as biologists do when they wish to study how a flower unfolds. That would have been interesting but always an artifact, a trick. We not only had motion but contemporaneity: The motion of the child was in *our* time frame, and this realization catapulted us into the world of the unborn, the Era of Prenatality. Communication back and forth was finally a reality.

The first scientific papers based upon the use of realtime ultrasound began appearing in 1976, and logically concerned themselves with the movements of the child. Amazingly, these early investigations disclosed that the child begins moving at six weeks and the movements, feeble at that stage, are not perceived by the mother. Not until ten weeks following the beginning of fetal movement does the mother begin to perceive the movements herself. And when she finally does begin to perceive them, she only feels one third of them. Two out of three movements, even in advanced pregnancy, are not felt by the mother. Watching that realtime ultrasound screen we quickly became aware that the child is virtually always in motion during its waking periods. Through the use of electronic heart monitoring in combination with the imaging of the child with realtime ultrasound, we divined that the child has a fairly well defined sleep-wake cycle of about twenty minutes: it's awake for twenty minutes and then sleeps for twenty minutes.

By 1976, researchers in England, using realtime ultrasound, had demonstrated conclusively that the human unborn actually makes breathing movements in the uterus. This observation had been made many years earlier in animals such as fetal lambs, and many investigators hypothesized that the human unborn also breathed. However, the breathing had never been shown on an imaging apparatus before. Not only that, but the technology in 1976 became sharp enough for us to ascertain that the human unborn breathed on an average of from thirty to ninety times a minute depending on its physical—and perhaps even its emotional—state. In the undisturbed state, the breathing pattern was regular, shallow, and even, but if stress were placed on the fetus, such as a sudden sharp deprivation of the oxygen supply or even a loud noise or a rude jolt to the abdomen of the mother, the breathing became more of an irregular nervous gasp, identical to the respiratory pattern that you or I would adopt if we were suddenly badly frightened, or if someone were trying to strangle us. Of course the unborn doesn't breathe air; it takes amniotic fluid in and out of its lungs, but the movements of the chest and diaphragm and the various patterns of the breathing are in all essential ways indistinguishable from ours.

Machinery fine enough to detect and even quantify breathing movements certainly was up to the task of watching the heart beat. Training that realtime ultrasound apparatus on the chest of the child allowed us first to appreciate that the heart begins to beat far earlier than our old stethoscopes indicated at seventeen weeks. The realtime machine was even better than the Doppler apparatus which could pick up heartbeats at ten or eleven weeks. The realtime machine saw the tiny heart fluttering at *four* weeks. This solved a serious problem in the practice of obstetrics: Sometimes we suspected that an early child had died, but we could not prove this one way or another since pregnancy tests do not turn negative until almost two weeks following its death; now we could look directly at the heart and tell at a glance whether it was beating. From there it was only a short step to beginning a careful study of the heart of the unborn child in order to diagnose disorders. In both children and adults, echocardiography (ultrasound) is now widely used to image the heart and discover structural or functional disorders. In the same way, realtime ultrasound could now be trained on the unborn child heart; suddenly we were diagnosing congenital defects of the heart. The next step will inevitably be intrauterine cardiac surgery, of such delicacy that it may have to be done with lasers or some similar fine surgical technique. But rest assured—it will be with us soon.

No organ system is hidden from the relentless probing and pulsing beam of the ultrasound machine. Study of the urinary tract of the unborn child has shown that it is in all ways identical to ours, and complex and demanding surgery has been already performed on the unborn child during pregnancy for obstructions and similar disorders of the urinary tract. The brain, the blood vessels, the bones, and the joints have all been studied, probed, and evaluated. The brain itself has even been operated upon in pregnancy: In cases of congenital hydrocephalus (water on the brain resulting from faulty formation of the drainage system of fluid which normally surrounds the brain and spinal cord) fetal surgeons, using realtime ultrasound imaging, have inserted tubes into the brain in order to drain off the excess fluid. Thus the brain is spared the accumulating pressure which would ultimately flatten and severely compromise it if unrelieved.

With increasing refinement of the machinery, we are seeing more and more of the unborn child and translating the information we obtain into clinically useful concepts. For example, the ability to watch it move and breathe has allowed us to construct a "biophysical profile" similar in many ways to an annual check-up examination. By observing the frequency of breathing movements, the pattern of gross movements of the body, the muscular tone, the volume of the surrounding amniotic fluid (we can see the fluid with realtime ultrasound and can fairly accurately estimate the actual amount), and, with the aid of the electronic heart monitoring apparatus, the patterns of the heart rate in response to rest and movement. With these five observations a formula has been worked out to assess quite accurately the health of the child. Thus, in a woman whose baby is overdue or who has some other condition which may threaten her child, ultrasound has now allowed us to give the baby a "check-up" at appropriate intervals and to deliver the baby in good condition when the check-up examination indicates that we should do so.

The machinery gets more and more refined and delicate. We can even observe the rapid eye movements of the baby beginning at the twentieth week of pregnancy; we can predict how healthy its nervous system will be ten or twenty years from now based upon these observations. Think how fine and exquisitely precise this machinery must be to allow us to make such sensitive determinations!

Recently we have been able to see the sexual organs of the male on the ultrasound screen as early as fourteen weeks. The sexual organs are identifiable at ten weeks if you could see the baby directly. Now we can predict sex *without* the amniocentesis procedure. This knowledge has limited medical value: Some male babies are afflicted with diseases such as hemophilia whereas female babies never are; thus, in a family in which there is hemophilia and we know this particular baby is a male, we can make the appropriate preparations for this baby in terms of its medical needs after birth (hemophilia does not affect the baby until after birth and indeed usually not until nine months to a year later). But it's a reasonable probability that with the advances in genetic engineering—the ability to insert a healthy gene into the body to replace an unhealthy one such as the one which fails to manufacture the Factor VIII, the missing item in these hemophiliac babies—we shall be able within a relatively short period to correct such a defect before the baby is born.

But there is an even more valuable reason to know the sex of the baby before its birth. In other years, much of the mystique of birth, and therefore the mistaken belief that life begins at birth, was the reality that we knew virtually nothing about the baby before birth, not even such a seemingly simple and certainly fundamental fact as its sex. Now with the masses of information we have of the baby before it is born, especially the certain knowledge of its sex, the mystery of prenatality is dispelled, and once and for all the myth of life beginning at birth should be entombed forever.

Incidentally, not only can we now ascertain the sex of the baby prenatally with ultrasound, but we now have positive information that female babies can *ovulate* while still in the uterus. Though it is not a common phenomenon, even the notion that it can happen while the female baby is still unborn is astonishing. It is yet another piece in the increasingly undeniable picture of the unborn child as one of us.

As long ago as 1906 a physician named Cremer was able to pick up the electrocardiogram of the unborn child with the most primitive machinery. Nothing further was done in this area until the early 1960s when there was again a flurry of interest in the fetal EKG, now utilizing infinitely more sensitive and more precise instrumentation. Even so, it was an interesting though essentially fairly esoteric matter. After all, the unborn child does not have heart attacks or hardening of the arteries while still in-utero. Edward Hon, an obstetrician in California, then devised a method of continuous EKG fetal monitoring by means of a computer which could calculate with the lightening speed characteristic of such technology the instantaneous fetal heart rate from one moment to the next. Consider: If you take your own pulse and you want to calculate your pulse rate per minute, you would have to keep taking it every ten or fifteen seconds in order to know what the rate is four or five times a minute. To know what the rate is sixty times a minute would be quite simply impossible for you or me. But if we had an EKG machine from which a computer could calculate the interval of time between one heartbeat and the next, then the computer could also instantly calculate the heart rate from one second to the next. This is the principle of the electronic fetal heart monitor. In fact, most of the machines now use the ultrasound machine instead of the EKG to pick up the heart action that the computer calculates from. Before electronic fetal heart monitoring we used to think that the heart rate of the healthy unborn child was pretty well fixed in a relatively narrow range between 140 and 160 (remember the old wives tale about girls' heart rates being faster than boys'!). Now we know that the fetal heart rate changes from moment to moment. Indeed, if it doesn't we suspect serious illness. We now know that the fetal heart rate undergoes obvious and drastic changes in response to everything, from being pushed externally through the mother's abdomen, reacting to a loud sound, to being deprived of oxygen. Recognizable patterns have been worked out which permit us to identify sick babies, knowing only the heart rate patterns; we either treat these babies or deliver them.

The ability to monitor the heart rate of the child from moment to moment has opened the door to studying the reactions of the child to various stimuli other than those which pertain directly to labor and delivery. And of course this machinery is used at present primarily to monitor the baby during the stressful time of birth. Remember, you and I respond to external influences by a change in our heart rate: danger speeds up the heart, pleasure may restore the usual slower rate, and sleep slows it down further. Similarly, we now know that the baby responds to the movements of its own limbs or trunk by speeding up its heart; this is the basis of the so-called nonstress test. We consider that the child is sick if the monitor fails to show the acceleration of the fetal heart rate in response to its own movements. The child must either be treated promptly or delivered quickly. But we also know that the healthy baby will respond to such annoyances as an automobile horn by speeding up its heart. Dr. Marcello Zugaib in St. Louis devised a test in which an automobile horn is honked next to the baby, and if it is healthy, it will speed up its heart rate by ten to fifteen beats per minute. Other investigators believe that the unborn child can distinguish between individual sounds, such as music or voices. We know that it perceives the sound of the blood periodically rushing through the mother's major blood vessels; years ago some imaginative person devised a tiny toy which simulates the sound of the maternal heartbeat and is useful for calming fretful babies in their cribs. They seem to remember the sound from their prenatality period.

Electronic heart monitoring has enabled us to precisely identify the sleep-wake cycle of the unborn child. Because the sleep state dulls the reaction pattern of the human, the heart rate remains constant and does not accelerate in response to external noise. The unborn child has a rather constant twenty minute sleep-wake cycle, and in the twenty minutes during which he is asleep, the heart rate does not vary in response to stimuli. But if you doubt that he is asleep, you merely have to prod him either externally through the mother's abdomen or push on his head during a vaginal examination. Immediately you will see the heart rate speed up and the body movements resume. It is probably not too far-fetched to postulate that the unborn child dreams during these sleep periods. Rapid eye movements characteristic of our own deep sleep periods can be identified in the unborn child, and these eye movements are said to be typical of the dream state. Electroencephalograms (brain-wave technology) seems to confirm that the unborn child dreams during these rapid eye movement periods. To find out the content of the dream, we must await better technology in the near future.

Another piece of new technology that is now in rather restricted use but has enormous potential is the procedure of fetoscopy. Here an exquisitely fine optical instrument is inserted into the uterus through the mother's abdomen, and the child can be viewed directly. No more highlights and shifting shadows as with the ultrasound machine, which for all of its miraculous abilities is still an indirect picture much like a fluoroscopy. With fetoscopy we are looking at the child eyeball to eyeball, seeing it in living color. The instrument itself is about a foot long, and is about one-twelfth of an inch in diameter. There is a light at the far end and an eyepiece at the observer's end. The instrument is pushed through the abdominal wall and then through the wall of the uterus, carefully avoiding the afterbirth, and literally confronts the child. Sometimes the light is so strong that the child flinches when the light is switched on. Most of the research with this instrument has been done at such centers as Yale University, the University of Toronto, and in Tokyo, but as the instrument itself becomes more refined and obstetricians become more experienced with the technique there is no doubt that it will become in time a rather standard procedure for hospital fetologists. At the present time there is risk of precipitating premature labor or miscarriage with it, and the actual figure for this risk runs about five per cent—not an acceptable figure for casual inquisitive viewing of the unborn child but certainly acceptable where the technique is necessary for the diagnosis of fetal illness.

What can we do with fetoscopy and where is it applicable in fetology? One obvious use for it is in studying the limbs, extremities, eyes, face, and other fine features which ultrasound is simply not able to do at present. The skin can be observed, and skin diseases have been diagnosed in utero. But the main advantage of this technology is the ability to thread two devices through the instrument. First of all, we can thread a fine needle which we can insert into a blood vessel of the unborn child and actually carry out blood tests on it, even as we can in adult patients. Thus we can diagnose hemophilia, clotting disorders, sickle cell disease, anemia, and a host of other blood disorders. We can also thread through the length of the instrument a biopsy forcep, an instrument which can take a piece of tissue for analysis. In this way, we have been able to actually take a biopsy of the liver of the unborn child and study that organ with its enzymes and complicated chemistry. We have been able to take biopsies of the skin and diagnose congenital skin diseases. We can even take biopsies of the afterbirth itself to determine its health, and whether it will be able to serve and support the child through the entire length of the pregnancy.

But exciting as this instrument is for diagnostic purposes, think how fantastically useful the fetoscope will be in the future! For treatment of those unborn children with vitamin deficiencies or infections and for those with growth disorders or endocrine disturbances, medications could be given directly into the mouth or even injected right into the skin. For those unborn children with conditions requiring surgery, the instrument could be used to visualize the area to be operated on (a fused set of fingers, a palate which is not developing properly and threatens to become cleft if allowed to continue untreated), and surgery could be carried out via a laser beam or an ultra fine cautery threaded through the instrument. After all, we routinely perform complicated surgery on the female reproductive organs through the laparoscope, an optical instrument inserted through the naval, and it's not too visionary to believe that in the very near future we will be able to do complex and demanding surgery on the unborn child through the fetoscope.

Amniocentesis is a technique which has also been of great help to the fetologist. It currently has an undeserved bad name because it is often used for search-and-destroy missions on handicapped unborn. However, it has allowed us to identify those babies severely affected with Rh disease and either to transfuse them with blood while still in utero or else to deliver them in a timely manner. It has permitted us to identify those children who have passed the due date for delivery and are in jeopardy from "post-maturity," a condition which occurs when the due date is passed by two weeks and the afterbirth begins to fail in its many vital functions. We can identify those children with "neural-tube defects," conditions such as spina bifida in which coverings over the spinal cord are imperfectly formed or missing. In the future, fetal surgery and fetal medicine will be able either to reverse these conditions at their onset or to prevent them entirely.

The amniotic fluid is the environment in which the unborn child lives, very much like our air. We have been able to take samples of that fluid for analysis to determine the health of the fetal environment, as well as to understand better how the unborn child eliminates its waste products, how it manufactures and controls its fluid environment, and a great many other vital functions including the regulation of the quantity and density of the fluid. The fluid is an important protective device for the baby as it shields him from the effects of a direct blow and prevents squeezing or compressing forces from harming him. For example, we know from analysis of dissolved sodium in the fluid that the unborn child replaces the entire volume of its fluid environment about eight times a day. In short, far from being only a lottery basket for selecting out those handicapped unborn doomed to die by the abortionist's hand, the amniotic fluid is the repository of a wealth of important data which has allowed us to arrive at an increasingly sophisticated view of our state of prenatality.

Another technology which has allowed us to perceive the unborn child directly is hysteroscopy. A hysteroscope is a long slender optical instrument, similar to the fetoscope or even the laparoscope, with a light at the far end and an optical eyepiece at the observer's end. But instead of being thrust directly through the abdominal wall later on in pregnancy, this instrument is pushed up through the cervix in *early* pregnancy at four, five, or six weeks. Peering through the eyepiece with the light on at the opposite end, one can see the six week old infant clearly. We can even study the face, fingers, and toes—in fact, the entire young child. *Life* magazine, belatedly coming to the conviction that the unborn child is an identifiable human being both anatomically and ethically, has published a series of startlingly clear, dramatic photos of the unborn child taken through the contact hysteroscope. One can see the eyes, count the fingers and the toes, and even see the blood vessels of the child through its incredibly fine, translucent skin!

Leaving aside for the moment the individual technologies, let's look at the unborn child as a whole—holistic fetology, as it were. There is a book published in 1982 by Drs. Ernst Niedermeyer and Fernando Lopes Da Silva entitled *Electroencephalography*—a long tongue-twister for brain-waveology. The book is published by Urban and Schwarzenberg, and Chapter Nine deals with the development of the brain and the appearance of brain-waves in the unborn child. The authors go on to state that there is unquestionable brain-wave activity at the level of the pons (mid-brain) at ten weeks gestation, and cortical (higher brain) activity at twelve weeks. Actually, brain-waves have been recorded from the unborn child as early as six weeks in other publications. In an amusing and enlightening article published in the prestigious *British Medical Journal* on January 26, 1980, Drs. H. B. Valman and J. F. Pearson make the following statement: "The fetus's environment is disturbed by sounds, light, and touch, and he responds to these disturbances by moving." The article is entitled "What the Fetus Feels," and it goes on to detail how the fetus responds to loud noises such as the slamming of a door or loud music, how the ultrasound machine used for monitoring the fetus will often provoke the fetus to increased activity, and how the fetus may be able to perceive sound frequencies too high and too low for the adult ear. The authors go on to state that the repeated and frequent flashing of a light will often quiet an active fetus, that the fetus makes facial expressions and even smiles at eleven weeks, and that it signals its reaction to pain by increasing its heart rate and movements.

Fetology is a science only ten years old. Still, the volume of scientific information and vital data proceeding from it is an unrelievedly massive flow. This book would literally be four or five times its projected length if we were to discuss in detail all the information we have concerning the unborn child. As an example: The Cumulated Index Medicus is an enormous book brought out annually and can be found in *any* medical library. It lists every scientific article published throughout the world by subject. In 1981, the Index listed approximately *two thousand* articles concerning the fetus, on a wide variety of subjects. In contrast, in that same year, 1981, there were only four hundred scientific articles published on the subject of abortion: a ratio of five serious scientific articles on fetology to one on abortion. (I suspect that the large majority of articles on abortion were not published in reputable scientific journals such as the ones encompassed by the Cumulative Index Medicus but in such magazines as *Mother Jones* and *Hustler*.)

The accumulating weight of evidence for the scientific certainty of the unborn child as a human being and a legitimate member of the human community has created increasing fissures in the monolithic resistance of the pro-abortion groups. The *New England Journal of Medicine*, a stoutly liberal medical publication but undeniably one of the most prestigious medical publications in the world, finally yielded some precious editorial space to two investigators who expressed in other terms the same doubts about the continued exile of the unborn child from the human community that I had expressed in that very same journal eight years earlier. John C. Fletcher, from the National Institutes of Health in Washington, D.C., and Dr. Mark I. Evans reported their experiences in interviewing women in the early part of pregnancy who were privileged to watch their infants on the realtime ultrasound screen. The women were asked if they would still entertain the thought of abortion after having seen their babies move, breathe, and do all those inexpressibly endearing things that all babies do, born or unborn. Both women categorically rejected the abortion option, one stating it thus: "I feel that it is human. It belongs to me. I couldn't have an abortion now."

What sets this article apart from the general run of medical publications is first, its provenance: Fletcher is an ethicist of unimpeachable credentials from the universally respected nonpolitical governmental agency known as the National Institutes of Health. Unlike the Center for Disease Control in Atlanta, a long-time breeding ground for abortion advocates such as Grimes, Tyler, and Cates, the N.I.H. has attempted to preserve a reasonable objectivity in its medical pronouncements. Further, as I stated above *The New England Journal of Medicine* has been anything but neutral in the abortion conflict. Thus, for the *Journal* to have accorded editorial space to this article which undermines the most powerful argument the pro-abortion forces have historically leaned upon—that the unborn child is a sub-human, a creature of lesser worth—is a signal development. The article also suggests strongly that we have missed the ontological point: that there is a phase of our lives spent in a curious sort of imprisonment for a period of nine months which is comparable to other passages in our lives and which the authors term "prenatality". Recall if you will that in my editorial piece in the *Journal* eight years earlier I had stated that: "Life . . . is a continuous spectrum that begins in utero and ends at death—the bands of the spectrum are designated by words such as fetus, infant, child, adolescent, and adult." Fletcher and Evans have suggested that that first nine months of life—the first band of the spectrum—be called "prenatality."

Fletcher and Evans relied exclusively on the technology of realtime ultrasound in assessing their patients change of mind on the question of the humanity of the unborn child and the acceptability of abortion following the viewing of the unborn child on the screen. I should remind the reader here that I have been advocating for many years that a realtime ultrasound examination should be a mandatory part of the informed consent for abortion: that every pregnant woman seeking abortion should be required to submit to a realtime ultra-sound examination before signing the consent for abortion, with the screen turned in full view for the woman. Pro-abortionists, and even Fletcher and Evans, suggest that this might be ". . . a potent (and unfair?) maneuver in the hands of those who represented the interests of the fetus in a dispute over proposed fetal therapy" and by extension an unfair device in the struggle for the unborn. I say that no abortionist could legitimately object to the requirement for such a pre-abortion examination. It fixes precisely the size of the uterus, the presence of a pregnancy, eliminates any lingering doubt about the validity of the pregnancy test or the estimation of the length of the pregnancy by the doctor's examination, and even allows the abortionist to pin-point the location of the child to facilitate the abortion procedure. Mind, I am not advocating the use of ultrasound to make abortion easier. I am merely countering in advance objections pro-abortionists would have to the proposal that all women requesting abortion have a mandatory preliminary realtime ultrasound examination, and stating that, if anything, such an examination would be of enormous technical advantage to the abortionist who carries out the procedure.

Correctly, Fletcher and Evans suggest that just as it took centuries for humanity to understand that children were not sub-human crea-tures, that childhood was a clear and distinct "differentiated stage of life," prenatality is similarly a sui generis, a stage of life all its own. Recall please that even as late in human history as the beginning of the nineteenth century, cotton mills were worked largely by boys and girls aged seven to twelve and that even by 1832 children aged seven to sixteen comprised forty per cent of the factory workers in New England. Modern labor legislation protecting children under sixteen years of age from exploitation did not exist until 1903. In fact, the laws regulating child labor are all statutes emanating from *state* legislation. Even up until recently the Federal government has been unsuccessful in passing legislation concerning child labor, despite an attempt in 1924 to amend the Constitution. And it wasn't so very long ago, in the late 1960s and early 70s, that children were finally recognized as legal entities in their own right and were granted legal privilege and status, for example representation in court by their own attorneys and legal standing to sue for violation of civil rights.

We know proportionately as little now about the state of prenatality as medieval men and women knew about childhood; in that dark and distant time, once children had been weaned and set free from their mothers, usually by age seven, they were cast into the adult world as little adults. Universal education for children in an organized communal sense was unknown, life was shorter and more uncertain, farm labor was a valuable commodity, and the biology of growth and the psychology of development were centuries away. Even the great sage Montaigne denigrated childhood, complaining: "I cannot abide that passion for caressing new born children, which have neither mental activities nor recognizable body shape by which to make themselves lovable, and I have never willingly suffered them to be fed in my presence." He probably would not have taken too well to the notion of prenatal bonding either.

So now we propose prenatality as a separate and distinct period in our lives. It is a period of rapid growth far more pronounced than at any other time in our lives, in that if we grew through prenatality at the same velocity we grow between four and eight weeks we would each weigh 28,000 pounds at birth. It is a time of testing body function, gathering sensory impressions for storage and future retrieval, establishing emotional ties with parents through the kicking movements and heart sounds echoing through the obstetrician's examining room, and planning the infinitely complex preparations for the passage through the birth canal to the outside world. No prisoner of war ever planned his escape more fastidiously than this prenatal person does. There are fascinating features to contemplate about prenatality. For example, the amniotic fluid environment in which the child floats not only provides nourishment—the child swallows the fluid from time to time—and protection, but, as stated earlier, it also serves to spare the child the devastating effects of gravity. A person floating freely in a fluid environment is weightless, as free of gravity as any astronaut in space orbit. The development of muscle function, the formation of the facial features, the working out of the various organ systems can all be accomplished in this physiologically ideal environment, without the insistent destructive force of gravity pulling him down. Think however what a sudden startling shock he is subjected to when the bag of waters is broken in labor and he feels the pull of gravity for the first time, like an astronaut re-entering the earth's relentless embrace. No wonder women report a flurry of excited movements from the baby when the bag of waters breaks.

Old hands in the pro-life movement, those who have *known* with the power of faith and the certainty of intuition that there has always been bonding between the pregnant woman and the tiny creature within her, will understandably stand back and say, with a knowing smile: "But Doctors, we've known this all along. It's no surprise to us." True, but consider that there is a great uncommitted mass out there who refuse to accept anything on faith, who sneer at intuition and who believe only what appears on the television screen at six o'clock in the evening, what they can read in *Time*, *Life*, *People*, and in the daily newspaper, and what they are taught by their largely liberal teachers and professors in college and graduate school. Fletcher and Evans are telling that group that prenatality is on that television screen *now*, that it is in your magazines and newspapers and soon will be in your college and graduate school books. Prenatality is reality.

Still other observers have chronicled bonding between fathers and the unborn during ultrasound viewing, and more recently Dr. Wulf Utian working in an in vitro fertilization program at the Mount Sinai Medical Center in Cleveland has documented bonding between the prospective mother and the dividing fertilized egg. When informed that the division of the egg had ceased, that the egg was no longer viable and therefore unsuitable for implantation into her uterus, one mother stated that she felt as if she had: "just suffered a stillbirth." Even more astonishing is Utian's entirely unsolicited observation that the medical team conducting the in vitro fertilization program—the physicians, nurses, laboratory technicians, and sonographers—became caught up emotionally in the work to the extent that they experienced a bonding to the developing unborn themselves. He states it thus:

> As eggs are collected and fertilization is attempted in the laboratory, there are strong feelings by the team toward the early cleaving embryo. . . .
>
> My experience with an in vitro fertilization program, although also anecdotal, would confirm that "bonding" may occur even before the embryo is placed in the mother's uterus.

Not even the stoutest advocates of permissive abortion will deny that the science of fetology is here, that it is a rapidly expanding universe of ideas and information, and that its potential is virtually limitless. Think for a moment of the advances in understanding of the basic processes of life we will possess when we understand more of our biologic beginnings. Just as the leap into space in the 1960s and 1970s accelerated the development of the most dazzling technology in computers, guidance systems, metallurgical research, astronomy, and a host of other disciplines, so the journey backwards into prenatality will allow us to understand the regulation of growth—the secrets of cancer are locked up there, the development of memory—the key to more capable computers with artificial intelligence is hidden there, and the genesis of the personality. We are only at the threshold of the world of prenatality, but already we know an infinity more about the prenatal person than we did ten years ago when the infamous Roe v. Wade decision burst out of the Supreme Court.

Fletcher and Evans were being unnecessarily circumspect when they confined the limits of their evidence for prenatality as a separate passage in our lives merely to realtime ultrasound imaging of the unborn child. I suspect that they had to rein in their enthusiasm for this new (to them) perception of the unborn child for fear the *New England Journal of Medicine*, not to mention their bureaucratic superiors in the Federal health care system and their fellow scientists, might perceive the article to be a provocative, inflammatory, pro-life polemic. Hence the couching of the conclusions of the article with a little artful waffling, "*Perhaps* a new stage of human existence, prenatality . . . will be as real to our descendants as childhood is to us," and visionary speculation, "Of such stuff are many human dreams made." Still, the pro-lifer must welcome new scientific discoveries and ethical perceptions which support the pro-life cause regardless of their provenance and the carefully qualifying disclaimers which may accompany them.

Like Copernicus, Fletcher and Evans (and Utian too) have demonstrated a truth beautiful in its simplicity but explosive in its political and ethical implications, sure to be unspeakably invidious to the liberal proabortion establishment. I am not necessarily equating the discoveries of Fletcher and Evans and Utian with that of Copernicus, but Copernicus had altered our understanding of the physical universe by demonstrating that the sun, not the earth, was the center of our universe, and Fletcher and Evans have made a similarly significant contribution to our understanding of our socio-biologic system. Unlike Copernicus, however, Fletcher and Evans were unwilling to carry their discovery to its logical end: that if prenatality is in fact nothing more or less than another stage in our lives as human beings, then all those who dwell in the state of prenatality are human beings and indistinguishable morally, ethically, and politically from any of us. And therefore abortion, the capricious destruction of those humans passing through their prenatality, is categorically unacceptable.

Fletcher and Evans needed encouragement. More, they needed a moral engine to be installed into their lovely intellectual vehicle. They had propounded with great eloquence and irresistible logic the existence of the state of prenatality, but they shied away from its ineluctable ethical implications. I wrote the following letter to the editor of the *New England Journal of Medicine:*

March 2, 1983

To the Editor:

Re: *Maternal Bonding in Early Fetal Ultrasound Examinations*

Drs. Fletcher and Evans have provided graphic examples of a phenomenon which many obstetricians have observed in this era of high-tech fetology: the establishment of a significant emotional nexus between the mother (and the father as well) and the fetus during real-time ultrasound examinations in the first and second trimesters of pregnancy.

Of equal interest perhaps is the undeniable emergence of *physician* bonding during these ultrasound examinations. With more numerous and more efficient methods of communication with the fetus (e.g., electronic heart monitoring and fetoscopy in addition to realtime ultrasound) the obstetrician now cannot help but conceive of the fetus as his/her patient. Obstetricians are not only physicians but often parents as well and the impact of this burgeoning communication gives rise ineluctably to sobering second thoughts concerning the destruction of the intra-uterine patient for less than compelling medical reasons.

Ruddick and Wilcox have pointed out the disturbing antinomy developing on Ob-Gyn services throughout this country: on one hospital floor we have the intra-uterine patient being subjected to intricate diagnostic testing, medication, transfusion, and even surgery—while one floor below that same patient's life is being extinguished without valid medical indication. This is creating a subtle but insistent moral tension in health institutions which can only worsen as the technological means for communicating with the patient improve—and improve they will.

Sloganeering, politicking, stultifying bickering about rights will not suffice. Science is hurling us forward at a frightening velocity into the Huxleyan future and all we can rely upon is a sound, decent, and timeless ethic based upon a profound respect for all the manifestations of human life.

Sincerely,
BERNARD N. NATHANSON, M.D.

The letter of course was rejected by the *Journal*. In the rejection there was the usual mumbo-jumbo about the lack of space to print all the worthy letters and the editors would be sending the letter on to Fletcher and Evans for a personal reply, but the truth is that my letter posed embarrassing and unanswerable questions to the medical community at large. The central question of course was: How can we continue to sanction permissive abortion?

Scarcely six weeks following publication of the Fletcher and Evans article, Dr. Sherman Elias of the Department of Obstetrics and Gynecology at the Northwestern University Medical School and George J. Annas, an attorney working at the Hastings Center Institute of Society, Ethics, and the Life Sciences co-authored a piece in the April 1, 1983, issue of the *American Journal of Obstetrics and Gynecology* entitled "Perspectives on Fetal Surgery." The first half of the article is a consideration of the many technological challenges and possibilities posed by the rapidly developing specialty of fetal surgery, and the second half is a thoughtful and, to abortion advocates, deeply troubling reflection on the many perplexing ethical issues raised by this new discipline. Annas, who probably authored the ethico-legal portion of the article and has long been a discreet but devoted abortion advocate, commences with this statement: "Developments in fetal therapy will enhance the status of the fetus, and raise new ethical and legal issues." Could anyone be more forthright than that in proclaiming a "New Deal" for the fetus? He goes on to query the reader: "If both [mother and fetus] are really patients, do both need their own physicians?" After all, one can easily envision the following situation in the very near future when fetal surgery becomes more commonplace and when many more physicians are trained in the specialty of fetal surgery and are therefore more anxious to ply their skills: An intra-uterine diagnostic team has established that an unborn child is ill with a disorder which requires surgery, and the fetal surgical team moves in only to be met with the refusal of the mother to submit herself and her unborn child to the indicated procedure. Two logical consequences flow from this dilemma. One is that a court order would have to be sought compelling the mother to allow surgery to proceed (we assume here that there is no major risk to the mother herself in the surgery—a reasonable assumption). With the present law, a parent cannot reasonably withhold permission for treatment of a desperately ill child, and if a parent does withhold permission, then a court order can usually be obtained. Secondly, if a court order were sought, necessarily the unborn child would have an advocate to speak for it in such a hearing. It follows then that if the unborn child is legitimately a patient and if it has an advocate in a legal hearing, then the unborn child must be a person with legal standing in the community. In truth, whether or not the court order was issued to proceed with the surgery is almost moot in this particular context: the mere fact that the unborn child has standing to seek a court order for treatment and that it has a full-fledged officer of the court for representation is ipso facto indisputable proof of its status as a person in the law.

Abortion advocates may argue that fetal surgery is confined to the unborn in the late stages of prenatality, a time at which even the Blackmun "gang of seven" accorded some grudging recognition, and therefore does not materially alter the status of the abortion argument in that abortions are rarely, if ever, performed on those children who would properly be candidates for fetal surgery. We must then remind them that the search for afflicted or handicapped children commences in Blackmun's *second* trimester—and a revoltingly large number of second trimester abortions are still being done—increasing by the so-called D. and E. (dismemberment and evisceration) method. And it is a reasonable probability that in a startlingly short time fetal surgery will have evolved into a technical specialty applicable even to the first trimester fetus. Therefore, the validity of the arguments flowing logically from the reality of fetal surgery are not in the slightest diluted or altered by a consideration of the length of the pregnancy.

To take the argument one step further: If a judge, over the objections of the mother, issues a court order to proceed with vital life-saving intra-uterine surgery on the fetus in, let us say, the second trimester of pregnancy, then it follows that an advocate for a healthy infant (an attorney or even the father) could logically obtain a court order prohibiting the same mother from damaging, that is aborting, her unborn. After all, if a judge concludes that a mother may not interfere with the preservation and restoration of the health of her unborn child, how could that same judge allow the mother to purposefully conspire to destroy that child?

In this regard, a March 9, 1983, decision of the Appellate Division of the Second Department, New York State, touches briefly upon these issues. In the case brought to the judges, a drug had been prescribed for a pregnant woman, and the risks of the drug had been explained to her only with respect to the risks incurred by her own body. The physicians failed to inform her of the risks to the child from this drug, and therefore there was no properly informed consent elicited from the child, as represented by the guardian mother. The *New York Law Journal* reported thus:

"In a ruling described as one of apparent first impression on the appellate level, the Appellate Division Second Department has permitted an infant to have an independent cause of action for prenatal injuries suffered because of an obstetrician's alleged failure to obtain the informed consent of the mother before rendering treatment."

They affirmed that the infant had a "viable and independent" basis for claims and that there was an independent duty flowing between the doctor and the infant in utero. It is also interesting to note that this distinguished court did not dither about with euphemisms such as "potential life," did not even call the injured party a "fetus," and made no distinction or even statement in the body of the opinion concerning the stage of the pregnancy at which the tortuous action occurred. Although I do not have further details of the obstetrical aspects of the case, I am of course aware that adverse drug action on the unborn child generally occurs during organogenesis, that period of the first fourteen weeks of the pregnancy when the organs of the unborn child are being formed. Therefore, this judicial body has in effect granted personhood in the law to the very young unborn.

At the present time, we have unimaginably sophisticated methods of communication with the very young infant in utero: an array of instrumentation to diagnose its ills and disorders, even at very early stages of pregnancy; perceptible bonding between the unborn child and the mother, father, and even doctor in the earliest stages of pregnancy; a newly defined stage of our lives, known as prenatality; a new surgical specialty, surgery on the unborn and fetal medicine, that branch of fetology in which we diagnose and treat the unborn child with medications and blood transfusions; and the unborn child asserting its rights as a patient requiring a separate physician and a separate legal advocate for its rights in the law. What shall we do with this fantastic farrago of explosive technology and rapidly evolving ethical perceptions unknown of a short ten years ago?

The current constitutional status (or lack thereof) of the unborn child is to be found in the text of the Roe v. Wade decision, and most especially in the Amicus Curiae brief filed by the American College of Obstetricians and Gynecologists; the American Medical Women's Association; the American Psychiatric Association; the New York Academy of Medicine; and, in the words of the brief, one hundred and seventy medical school deans, departmental chairmen of various specialties in the medical schools, and professors of obstetrics and gynecology and other branches of medicine. The brief was filed on behalf of Doe in Doe v. Bolton, the twin case of Roe v. Wade, this one having as its provenance the abortion laws of the state of Georgia. The brief itself consists of ninety-six pages of text, followed by an appendix which contains various copies of letters from the Joint Commission on Accreditation of Hospitals, as well as a number of maps purporting to illustrate the claims set forth in the text.

Of considerable interest are many of the names which crop up in this brief, submitted to enable the United States Supreme Court to examine the medical issues in this case fairly and knowledgeably in order to arrive at an informed and just decision. To begin with, the entire brief is submitted over the signature of that old abortophile stalwart, Roy Lucas. The ubiquitous Roy, in those days styling his legal factory with the grandiose title of the James Madison Constitutional Law Institute Inc., had early on in the late 1960s smelled a meal ticket in the abortion arena and had insinuated himself into virtually every important legal conflict in the nation over abortion. (To his chagrin he did not get to argue the Roe v. Wade matter in the Court; Sarah Weddington had that dubious honor and of course has parlayed it into a lucrative legal and political career.) But it was constantly astonishing to me how Roy Lucas could smell out an abortion case and turn up in the most unlikely places.

In 1979, the Medic-Management Corporation based in Miami and operating a string of abortion clinics across the South and Southwest opened another one in Beaumont, Texas, despite the fact that there were already nine such abbatoirs operating in Houston, a scant one hundred miles away. The Roman Catholic Bishop of Beaumont, Bernard J. Ganter, took a public stance against the issuing of a Certificate of Need for the clinic by filing as a party to the Texas Health Facilities Commission's review of the clinic's application. At that time, there were federally appointed commissions in every part of the United States functioning under the overall aegis of the Health Systems Agencies, empowered to allocate health resources throughout the nation. If one wished to open a clinic, build a new hospital, or even expand the facilities in an old one, one had to make application to the HSA before going ahead with the proposed project. In essence Bishop Ganter declared himself and the Diocese of Beaumont as opposed to the opening of this first abortion clinic in Beaumont and engaged George Brown Jr. and his law firm to fight the clinic at the Commission's review of the application. Brown, a delightful gentleman and a brilliant attorney, in turn engaged me to testify on technical matters regarding the operation of an abortion clinic, the standards involved, and whether one hundred miles of travelling for an abortion was an undue burden on a woman who wished one. The hearing was held in Austin, Texas, on a gray and unpromising Tuesday morning, March 25, 1980. I had no idea who our adversaries were, but, I had done my homework on the case, acquainting myself with the history of that clinic, the nature of the proceeding, and the standards and requirements of the Health Systems Agencies. Actually the workings of the Health Systems Agency were not unknown to me;

when I had taken over the Center for Reproductive and Sexual Health as Director in February, 1971, one of my earliest duties had been to attend a hearing of the agency in order to obtain a Certificate of Need for *our* clinic so that it could continue to operate legally. That hearing was almost pro forma, and we were in fact granted the certificate quickly.

The members of the Greater East Texas Health Systems Agency filed in just after George Brown, Bishop Ganter, and I had taken our seats at a table facing the commission. The attorneys representing the clinic were a little late. We all sat waiting patiently, and in walked my old colleague and comrade-at-arms from those dim and distant NARAL days, the ubiquitous Roy Lucas. Roy's chin dropped to the floor. It was clear that he had anticipated a quick pro forma run-through at this hearing with no formidable opposition; instead, here was Nathanson, the keeper of the keys and the man who knew where all the skeletons in the abortion closet were located. The hearing proceeded in a perfectly satisfactory manner as far as we were concerned, and Lucas's cross-examination of me was timid and perfunctory. It was obvious to all of us that he had been taken completely by surprise, had not foreseen any serious resistance to the granting of the certificate, and was seemingly utterly unprepared for it. The commission denied the certificate, and a bitter court fight followed. But it was an immensely satisfying victory for me personally, and it did tie up that corporation for a long time in an expensive and lengthy litigation.

Another familiar name attached to the brief was that of Alan F. Guttmacher, M.D., at that time president of the Planned Parenthood empire and a dedicated advocate of the abortion ethic. Still another familiar name in the list of sponsors of the brief was that of Jane E. Hodgson, M.D., at the time assistant clinical professor of obstetrics and gynecology at the University of Minnesota Medical School and later to become director of PreTerm, the well-known abortion mill in Washington, D.C. Make no mistake, though, it was a list of distinguished names which sponsored this document. Eighty-eight obstetricians and gynecologists signed the document, as well as twenty-eight pediatricians. Given the general state of ignorance of the discipline of fetology at the time—1972—I can indeed almost exonerate the obstetricians on the list. Indeed, had I then been asked to sign the document, I probably would have. However I find it difficult to exonerate the pediatricians on the list. After all, where did they think their patients came from? And how Dr. Frank Bowman, medical director of the Southern California Edison Corporation, got on the list, I'll never understand. Being conservative, I'd say that as physician to a major energy corporation in Los Angeles, his expertise in the area of abortion and medical ethics was somewhat restricted, although in Los Angeles I suppose, anything is possible.

Now let's examine the document itself, since it was a major instrument upon which the court relied in formulating its opinions in Roe v. Wade and Doe v. Bolton. The brief commences by attempting to define the word abortion and goes on to quote the Fourteenth Edition of William's *Obstetrics* to the effect that:

> Abortion is the termination of pregnancy at any time before the fetus has attained a stage of viability. Interpretations of the word "viability" have varied between fetal weights of 400 grams (about twenty weeks of gestation) and 1000 grams (about twenty-eight weeks of gestation). . . . Although our smallest surviving infant weighed 540 grams at birth, survival even at 700 or 800 grams is unusual. [In San Diego, an infant weighing 448 grams—less than a pound—is now, in 1983, not only surviving but flourishing with no detectable physical flaws.]

That was the state of the art in 1971, when this text was published. In fact, "viability" is a term which is, according to most ethicists writing on the issue, slippery and unreliable. What "viability" is depends upon where one is speaking from. Viability of an infant in inland Zaire is significantly different from that of an infant in Houston or Manhattan. Furthermore, it depends upon the time of definition: In 1971 "viability" was widely considered to be at 1000 grams but today with the immense advances in the technology of life support systems, in the training of neonatologists, and in the generally better brand of obstetrics practiced across the nation resulting in better and healthier newborns, the word "viability" is no longer used. The velocity of the advances in the field of neonatology has virtually ridden the word into obsolescence. (Do we any longer seriously discuss the immediate survival rate following blood transfusions, as was customary and de rigeur in my father's days of practice sixty years ago?) And of course survival of an infant with a birth weight of

750–1000 grams today is not unusual. The actual survival rate for such infants at this writing is eighty per cent and improving all the time.

The brief dithers on about the tiny human embryo having "a conspicuous tail," as if somehow that appendage were a badge of inhumanity. Yet when an infant was born in Boston in 1982 with an identifiable tail, it was treated as an interesting occurrence with evolutionary consequences. The tail was removed, and the infant was returned to the nursery following the operation. It was *not* consigned a stall in the nearest menagerie.

The Amicus Curiae brief is shot full of anachronisms, misstatements, and flagrant deceptions. Take for example the table listed on its page thirteen which purported to compare the mortality rate of women who died from childbirth in 1967 vis-a-vis deaths from legal abortion in 1967. This of course is still a classic statistical tactic of the Abortion People in fighting off any incursion into their bloody domain. The eminent justices were then treated to a comparison of deaths from legal abortion in Hungary with deaths from childbirth in the United States. To begin with, as I warned in an early paper of my own on abortion technique and as most honest observers have agreed for many years, abortion figures from Eastern European countries have always been suspect owing to the intense political pressures on physicians in those countries. The figure quoted, 1.2 per 100,000 abortions, is even better than our figures in the United States in 1983, with our extensive resources, our healthier population, better techniques, and more skilled physicians. Thus the figure is quite simply a fiction. More important, why was the comparison not made with maternal mortality *in Hungary* in 1967? Probably because the figures for maternal mortality in Hungary in 1967 were verifiable and quite probably so terrible that they were embarrassing. It simply would not do for the abortion advocates to produce figures on the safety of obstetrical and gynecological procedures which were so bad and so embarrassing that they would discredit the entire thesis. Based upon this brazenly fallacious comparison, the brief concludes:

> In sum, the medical procedure of induced abortion, which is severely restricted by the [abortion] statute involved in this case, is potentially 23.3 (28.5) times as safe as the process of going through ordinary childbirth.

This conclusion, concurred in by eighty-eight professors of obstetrics and gynecology over the United States and offered as a statement of fact to the United States Supreme Court, is so patently dishonest, so politically engineered by Lucas and Co., so offensive to the integrity of my chosen profession, that I am moved to blush for these feckless, manipulated fools. Incidentally the figure of twenty-eight maternal deaths from childbirth per 100,000 deliveries is now closer to ten per 100,000, one-third of what it was only twelve short years ago.

One continues reading the brief with sinking heart. Not one word of the child and its life in the uterus in the stage of prenatality that marks the lives of all of us. Where are the references to ultrasound, fetoscopy, electronic heart monitoring, fetal diagnostic medicine, fetal surgery, in vitro fertilization? The brief is silent on these matters—indeed, it had to be. These are creatures of the technological revolution in medicine known as fetology.

I am often asked—usually by those uncommitted in the controversy over abortion, sometimes by abortion advocates themselves who are still uneasy with the issue—of what value is it to *see* the human unborn child, to know how its metabolism works, to know how it perceives sensation, and what those sensations are. This data, they maintain, does not in and of itself make a creature a human being, and a legally protectable, fully privileged human being at that. In other words, they say, your mass of data in the field of fetology is very interesting, indeed fascinating, but of what value is it, how is it to be applied to the abortion question? What is that creature to me?

I have countered the old pro-abortion slogan, "It's a woman's right to control her own body," by pointing out that the modern science of immunology has shown us that the unborn child is *not* a part of a woman's body in the same sense that her kidney or her heart is. Immunologic studies have demonstrated beyond cavil that when a pregnancy implants itself into the wall of the uterus at the eighth day following conception the defense mechanisms of the body, principally the white blood cells, sense that this creature now settling down for a lengthy stay is an intruder, an alien, and must be expelled. Therefore an intense immunological attack is mounted on the pregnancy by the white blood cell elements, and through an ingenious and extraordinarily efficient defense system the unborn child succeeds in repelling the attack. In ten per cent or so of cases the defensive system fails and the pregnancy is lost as a spontaneous abortion or miscarriage. Think how fundamental a lesson there is for us here: Even on the most minute microscopic scale the body has trained itself, or somehow in some inchoate way *knows*, how to recognize *self* from *non-self*. Scientists still do not understand precisely how the individual white cells of the body recognize self and differentiate it from non-self. But it is this mysterious ability that keeps the body from destroying itself. For if that ability were not part of our most basic biologic equipment, our own white blood cells would simply destroy all our own organs, and human survival would of course be an impossibility. Indeed, there are certain diseases in which the capacity of the body to recognize and distinguish self from non-self fails, and our own organs are destroyed. An example of this phenomenon, called auto-immune disease, is disseminated lupus erythematosus, in which the white blood cells of the body systematically attack and destroy the kidneys. Alternately, if the white blood cells, charged with the defense of the body from an alien invasion, failed to perform their function because they were unable to distinguish self from non-self, then bacteria would have free and easy access to our bodies and organ systems with nothing to fight them off, and we would all perish from bacterial infections.

Hence, even on this tiny but impressive scale it is clear that we recognize self from non-self. Incidentally, the ability and the necessity of creatures throughout nature to recognize their own is basic and requires no extended comment. How one wolf or one lobster recognizes another one is not known precisely to scientists, but these creatures unarguably do. Within an organized societal framework, excluding fights over territory, animals of the same species seem to be able to recognize their own and do not attack each other as aliens.

Accepting, then, that it is essential in nature for any organism to recognize and distinguish self from non-self, how are we to recognize our fellow humans? After all, we are the most developed form, the creatures which think at the highest level, and therefore we should be able to bring to bear the most efficient means to accomplish this most important biologic duty. But we have still only limited methods with which to recognize our own. One of course is to examine the genetic structure of a creature whose exact nature we are unsure of; another method is to test it immunologically. If we can transplant tissue and organs from one creature to ourselves successfully, then the creature must be of our species. The heart of a pig transplanted to a human will simply not survive for more than a few days despite all the immunosuppressant drugs and serums we use. Another way is to study the creature's reproductive compatibility with us. If we can successfully mate with it, (pigs do not mate successfully with horses) then it must be self. Another valuable way is to study its form and function. If the suspect creature looks like us, if it has the same metabolism we do, using oxygen and throwing off carbon dioxide, if it responds to the same stimuli, if its organs are identical to ours, then there is a reasonable probability that it is one of us. Fetology has been of immense value in not only identifying the intra-uterine creature as self but also has enabled us to understand that we humans may have a somewhat different appearance at various stages of our lives, in the journey from prenatality to old age, but we are ever and always humans. A quadruple amputee, or a two week old unborn, may not appear human on superficial inspection, but after applying those various tests to each of them, we would be forced to conclude that each is as human as you or I.

To put it another way, the data of fetology cannot and must not be accepted in an intellectual and moral vacuum. It is not enough to accept that the unborn child is biologically and demonstrably human but that because it is not *recognizable* as a human, therefore it is permissible to destroy it. Suppose for example that the Martians were preparing to come down to Earth and had been instructed by their leaders that they were not to attack or hurt human beings but that it was all right to kill other life forms for food. And assume that in their pre-flight briefings they were shown pictures of men and women and were cautioned that these were the creatures which they could not harm. The Martians then would descend to Earth in their great machines, take over our planet, and allow all men and women to go about their business. Unfortunately, they are unable to communicate with us in our languages, and so seeing newborn babies they kill them without a single thought. Newborns are tiny, red, and plump without discernible characteristics of form to qualify them as adult humans, and the Martians in their ignorance would unhesitatingly slaughter them. Those who continue to advocate slaughter of the newborn are the moral Martians in our midst. They are uninstructed as to what a human being is and how to identify one, and thus they are unable—I recoil at asserting that they are unwilling

—to distinguish species self from non-self. The data of fetology and of the allied sciences, genetics and immunology, are the instructional material they need, just as those Martians needed to be *shown* pictures of infants and taught their status as humans before they invaded Earth and killed off our newborns out of ignorance.

Let us now turn to the document itself: the text of the Roe v. Wade decision. The text occupies thirty-four pages in the Supreme Court Reporter and has a curiously dry and rustling quality, as if one were leafing through an old book. Although it was written only ten years ago, it is the ten-year hiatus on the order of 1939 to 1949 (conventional warfare and nuclear nightmare) or 1955 to 1965 (earthbound voyaging and space travel). It is a marvellously skilled boxer alone in the ring; it is a Picasso painting without a surface to be painted on, a Zen masterpiece. There is an air of anachronistic unreality to it. Even the terms used now seem quaint and almost endearingly antiquated. The first page of the opinion which asserts the decision of the Court goes on endlessly about "trimesters" of pregnancy, which in fact was a term we were still using in 1972, but the word "trimester" is virtually obsolescent now. In other more innocent, less informed times, we obstetricians arbitrarily divided pregnancy into three trimesters—the first twelve weeks, the second sixteen weeks, and the last twelve weeks—in the implicit belief that there were distinguishing characteristics and sharp differences between the child in those various trimesters. Today, of course, with the widespread use of realtime ultrasound, we understand that pregnancy is a smooth and uninterrupted continuum in which the unborn of one week merges and changes into the unborn of the next week in the same imperceptible way that childhood proceeds to puberty, puberty to adolescence, young adulthood to middle age, and indeed, on to old age. I am now middle-aged, or so I think, but again I am at a loss to know in precisely what category I fall; I can't recall, except with a sigh, exactly when it happened. Obstetricians no longer speak in trimesters. We now speak in terms of weeks since we can precisely identify the week of gestation by ultrasound, and in our stage of prenatality the weeks are to the unborn child as the years are to the born, one merging gradually and insensibly into another with changes in form and function proceeding inexorably. The old discarded concept of trimesters had implicit within it a belief that something magical, something immensely significant, occurred in the jump from one trimester to another, in the leap from the twelfth to the thirteenth week. Wiser now by virtue of ultrasound and fetoscopy, we now know that this is nonsense; from the moment we are set in motion with the penetration of the egg by the sperm we are an unstoppable continuum.

Blackmun skates quickly by the term "viability" in Section Fourteen of the opinion, where he asserts:

> If the state is interested in protecting fetal life after viability, it may go so far as to proscribe abortion after that period except when necessary to preserve the life or the health of the mother.

Cleverly preserving his own legal life and health, he touched ever so briefly on the term "viability," juggled it momentarily, and let it fall where it may. And if, in the Huxleyan future of the day after tomorrow, viability is three weeks of gestation, so be it.

The gut of the opinion rests in two main areas: the historical reasons for the banning of abortion in the United States and the inapplicability of those reasons in 1972 medical practice, and the Right to Privacy in the Constitution. I shall leave to legal scholars a consideration of the mining of a Right to Privacy in that document— John Noonan has broken many a bit on *that* particular rock—and instead confine myself to the former area.

Blackmun stated that there were three historical reasons for the banning of abortion in the United States in the nineteenth century: the imposition of such laws would discourage illicit sexual conduct; the abortion procedure was so hazardous that it involved unacceptable medical risk for women, and thus the state had to act to protect women against the unskilled and unscrupulous practitioners of the procedure; and the interest of the state in protecting prenatal life. With respect to the first reason, it appears almost frivolous in 1983 in the aftermath of the sexual revolution, and really requires or deserves no comment from fetologists and physicians. But the second reason is intriguing as a scaffolding for the abortion liberty: If a medical procedure or practice previously banned because of its danger to those who have it practiced upon them, or who practice it themselves, should we then condone it when it becomes technically safer for the practitioner or the patient?

The Harrison Narcotics Act of 1914, superseded by the Comprehensive Drug Abuse and Control Act of 1970, banned the possession or use of narcotics except by licensed physicians on the shaky premise that such drugs were injurious to the health of the user, the person to whom they were prescribed or sold. Yet we have known for years that if a person were to be given unlimited access to a narcotic such as Demerol or Morphine and had independent means of financial support so that he could just "drop out" early every morning and stay high with the narcotics all day long for years, a physician would be unable to demonstrate any specific lesion, disease, syndrome, or illness specifically attributable to the prolonged unrestrained use of the drug. (This is unlike alcohol which, paradoxically, we do not ban.) Because the "safety" of such drugs has been demonstrated today, should we now move, in a social and moral vacuum, to legalize the sale and use of these drugs in an unlicensed manner? Society has answered this question with a resounding *no*. The list of drugs encompassed by the Federal Controlled Substances Act grows lengthier year by year.

The argument that a medical or surgical practice, previously banned because of its danger, should be legalized because of its increasing safety is demonstrably fallacious since it ignores other considerations which, while they may not lend themselves to neat statistical analysis, nevertheless have important social and moral consequences inimical to society at large, such as the practice of permissive abortion. That a physically dangerous and morally unacceptable practice has been made less dangerous—even safe—does not make it any less morally repugnant.

The heart of the heart of the opinion—indeed, the core issue in the entire abortion controversy—rests on the definition of the nature of the unborn child. The opinion states it fairly when it says:

> The third reason is the State's interest—some phrase it in terms of duty—in protecting prenatal life. Some of the argument for this justification rests on the theory that a new human life is present from the moment of conception. The State's interest and general obligation to protect life then extends, it is argued, to prenatal life. Only when the life of the pregnant woman herself is at stake, balanced against the life she carries within her, should the interest of the embryo or fetus not prevail.

A few lines farther down the opinion defines the alternative:

> In assessing the State's interest, recognition may be given to the less rigid claim that as long as at least *potential life* is involved, the State may assert interests beyond the protection of the pregnant woman alone.

The opinion then goes on to deny, albeit a trifle reluctantly, that the original abortion laws in the United States formulated between 1821 and 1841 were designed to protect fetal life. Furthermore, the statement is made:

> . . . adoption of the quickening distinction through received common law and state statutes tacitly recognizes the greater health hazards and impliedly reputes the theory that life begins at conception.

Or, in other words, even where state laws made abortion after quickening a crime considerably more serious than before quickening, it was not because quickening proved beyond doubt that there was a person of value in the womb but because quickening occurred at a later stage of pregnancy, and therefore the abortion procedure would be proportionately more dangerous.

But consider that in the early nineteenth century when these abortion laws were written there were no pregnancy tests, no ultrasound examinations, and indeed vaginal examinations were never done in early pregnancy. Women shrank from discussing their pregnancies with anyone, they did not seek prenatal care as it was then unknown, and they were frequently ignorant of their pregnancy until the baby moved. Malnutrition was common in the female population in the United States in the nineteenth century, and amenorrhea was not at all unusual, especially in women doing heavy manual labor on farms. Missed menstrual periods meant little or nothing then. Ignorance concerning sexual matters was massive, and many women who had missed three or four periods did not even suspect they were pregnant. Thus with no pregnancy testing as we know it today, the only way a woman could be sure she was pregnant was by perceiving fetal movement. In other words, quickening *was* the pregnancy test, and to attempt to define abortion before pregnancy could be established was an untenable notion.

The perception of fetal movement, or quickening, was in practical terms in the nineteenth century when the original abortion laws were written, the beginning of legally provable pregnancy. I would venture to say that if by some temporal dislocation, a realtime ultrasound machine had appeared, H. G. Wells-like, in America in the nineteenth century and movement of the child was seen with the heart beating at five weeks, then these original laws would have been formulated quite differently. The laws would have defined pregnancy as commencing at scientifically observable animation at five weeks, instead of at the movement perceived by the mother at quickening at eighteen weeks. And therefore the laws regulating abortion would have required equal penalties at seven weeks, twelve weeks, or eighteen weeks; fundamentally, the value of the intra-uterine person would have been granted from that scientifically perceptible movement onward.

Later in the opinion, the Court once more fixes the fulcrum of the argument, this time without any cavil:

> If this suggestion of personhood is established the appellant's case of course collapses, for the fetus' right to life would then be guaranteed specifically by the [Fourteenth] amendment.

But we now know, based on all the data we have and all the perceptions we have acquired of the unborn child over the last ten years, that the human unborn is *self*, in a species sense. It is definably human biologically and scientifically by every sophisticated and refined measure we now possess, and it is as assuredly *self* as you are or I am. Ask me to define beyond what I can see and hear and touch of you, that you are *self*, one of my species, and I would probably blurt out something like "I don't know, but I *know*." Recall Potter Stewart's reply to a challenge that he define pornography; he said that he couldn't define it, but he knew it when he saw it. Beyond all the scientifically validating tests, measurements, and observations we have that the human unborn is *self* in the species sense, is the growing visceral certainty that it is also *self* in the social and emotional sense. I don't know, *but* I know. Prove it to me that you are of my species if you're so smart.

The opinion dithers on a little more to this effect:

> The pregnant woman cannot be isolated in her privacy. She carries an embryo, and later a fetus if one accepts the medical definitions of the developing young in the human uterus.

But, as I indicated earlier, realtime ultrasound technology has obliterated all those neat partitions we used as late as ten years ago. We know that prenatality is a continuum, that dividing it into factitious developmental compartments is incompatible with science today. No more trimesters, no more embryo or fetus, just as there are no junior children or senior children, no major adolescents and minor adolescents; it is simply one seamless continuum of prenatality, with no Bar Mitzvahs in the uterus.

Now let us turn to perhaps the most provocative statement in the entire opinion, one which has turned otherwise pacific legal scholars into rampaging juggernauts, and unexceptionably reasonable scientists into raving maniacs. To wit:

> We need not resolve the difficult question of when life begins. When those trained in the respective disciplines of medicine, philosophy, and theology are unable to arrive at any concensus, the judiciary, at this point in the development of man's knowledge, is not in a position to speculate as to the answer.

In 1972 this statement had to be conceded a place as one of the artful legal evasions of all time, a world-class circumlocution. This assertion, this paradigm of legal humility, sweeps us back with dizzying speed to the state of the biologic arts in the eighteenth century in Bologna. In the middle of that century, the Age of Enlightenment, Lazzaro Spallanzani took issue with the prevailing theory of spontaneous generation, that animals of all sorts can develop de novo in putrefying matter, and published his landmark work *Saggio Di Osservazioni Microscopiche Relative Al Sistema Della Generazione Dei Signori Needham E Buffon.* In this work he proved, studying fertilization in frogs and toads, that fertilization could not occur without direct contact between the male spermatozoon and the female ovum. In fact, he was the first to effect artificial fertilization by injecting dog's sperm into the uterus of a bitch. Spallanzani's work had thereafter not been seriously challenged until Roe v. Wade when the Magnificent Seven seemed to disavow it. I suppose that if one sees a gigantic fire roaring through a city block in the South Bronx, one could theorize that it probably started from one single ignition, but not having seen that particular event that caused the ignition, one would be justified in a purely phenomenological sense to doubt the origin of the fire. Maybe it just happened spontaneously.

Fortunately for us, for old Spallanzani, and for those United States Supreme Court justices who will be compelled in the near future to review Roe v. Wade in the light of fetology, we have now seen the moment of ignition. Steptoe and Edwards, in their monumental work on in vitro fertilization, have allowed us to be present at that moment and to see that divine continuum set in motion. Not only have we witnessed it, we have been the agents of the ignition. For any sentient human to deny that life begins when sperm penetrates egg is to deny that the earth is round or that blood circulates.

But legal scholars will still cavil, indulging themselves in that most delicious of legal divertissements: pilpul, the Talmudic hair-splitting, the Hebrew equivalent of the medieval theological conundrum of how many angels can dance on the head of a pin. Admittedly, carp the scholars, you have started human life in motion, but when does that human life become a recognizable person, a being of worth and value?

Now through the work of Steptoe and Edwards, we have been able to set the divine continuum into motion and observe the first few divisions of the new life as it proceeds to organize itself and prepare for the passages from prenatality to infancy to childhood to maturity. And, thanks to Utian and his group, we know that that fertilized ovum is a significant person, socially and emotionally. However, at this writing, the earliest stages of human prenatality are still hidden from us, in the sense that we have still only seen the shadows. We can follow the new life from its transfer from the Petri dish at eight cells into the uterus, but from that point on, its progress can only be marked by the flickering images of the ultrasound screen. Dramatic they are, and thoroughly convincing to fetologists, obstetricians, and ultrasonographers. However, they are shadowed enough so that obstinate Abortion People persist in clinging to the notion that at some theoretically-defined points thereafter, the embryo becomes a fetus, the fetus becomes a viable fetus, and the viable fetus becomes a human being.

We can now keep the human being alive outside the uterus for observation, study, or treatment, at the two opposite ends of prenatality: at the beginning for a period of several days and in the middle of the prenatal stage when the baby may be expelled from the uterus at twenty-two or twenty-three weeks. Between those two extremes, our understanding of prenatality is limited by the definition of the ultrasound shadows. But very soon, probably by the time this matter is returned to the High Court for review, we will have the technology to keep that dividing and organizing human being in its early stages of prenatality in a life support system, an artificial uterus, and *not* have to implant it into a human maternal organism. Now, in this Huxleyan world, we will watch the tiny human being proceed through prenatality out of the shadows, in the strong sunlight of direct scientific observation. Consider this: As we watch that person developing moment by moment and day by day we will surely be entirely unable to speculate as to which exact moment it becomes an

"embryo," a "fetus," or a "baby." The development and maturation
will progress before our very eyes in that slow miraculous continuum
I spoke of earlier; at certain points we will discontinue the intravenous
infusions, we will reduce the oxygen supply, we will administer drugs
and medications, and we will feed it by mouth, but when will it be a
baby? Don't forget that this child of the Huxleyan future will never
undergo birth; on some morning five or six or seven months into
prenatality it will be held by a nurse, cuddled by an adopting mother,
and eventually taken home. Just as we will have to sit down, scratch
our heads, and rethink such questions as when to call it a baby, so we
will have to discard antiquated terms such as embryo and fetus. I
suppose that the best answer is that it is a baby when it is bonded to
another human being and when it can be touched and seen and
talked to by another person; in that Huxleyan future, right around
the corner, those of us in prenatality will be visible, palpable, and
audible to those who care for us. Nurses refer even now to tiny
prematures at twenty-two and twenty-three weeks—some the pathetic
survivors of botched abortions—as babies even though they are
unimaginably small, red, plugged into a myriad of tubes and monitors.
A prenatal person, a human being in prenatality, is a baby when it is
bonded in the most universal sense of the word, to someone else,
whether it be physician, nurse, social worker, or mother. That raging
conflagration in the South Bronx was also a fire when it was a Zippo
lighter touched to a gasoline-soaked rag lying in a dim corridor in
some obscure tenement.

In that technology there is no such thing as "potential life"; not
when it lies in front of you in an artificial uterus, a fantastically
complex isolette, or a quiet bassinett in a corner of a nursery. Not
when it responds to your voice, your touch, your concern. Dr. Lyndon
Hill, working with ultrasound at the Mayo Clinic, reminds us that at
five weeks after conception one can stroke the region around the
mouth and the unborn will reflexivly pull away its head and neck. By
virtue of this new technology, when the human unborn child in its stage
of prenatality finally emerges from the ultrasound shadows—convincing enough for most of us in science but apparently still not sufficiently
convincing for abortion advocates—and lies in front of us in its life
support system in our full view, then I am certain that this destructive
medieval disputation on the exact nature of the prenatal human will
cease and with it the inexpressible horror of the abortion madness.

One final word on the opinion. Doe v. Bolton was the sister case to

Roe v. Wade and concerned itself with the constitutionality of the Georgia abortion statute which was modelled on the American Law Institute Model Penal Code statute allowing abortion for fetal defect, maternal health and life, or pregnancies resulting from rape. Doe v. Bolton evades the substantive issue of Roe v. Wade, that is, the legal status of the unborn child, and confines itself to finding unconstitutional the following provisions in the Georgia statute: the requirement that abortions must be performed in a hospital accredited by the Joint Commission for the Accreditation of Hospitals, that the abortion must be approved by a hospital abortion committee, that the abortion decision must be supported by an independent examination of the pregnant woman by two other physicians in addition to the woman's own physician, and that abortion facilities must be restricted to residents of the state of Georgia. There is still however the same heavy reliance on the terminology of embryo, fetus, and trimesters—concepts which, as I have indicated above, are discarded in 1983-style obstetrics and fetology and are now only of use in discussing and analyzing statistics on abortion. These partitions are useful to the statistician in the same way that studies on the treatment of cancer rely upon the division of any given cancer into stages. The division is a statistical artifice designed to allow us to study the effectiveness of treatment at various way-stations in the natural history of a cancer. In gynecology, we divide cancer of the uterine cervix into four stages depending on the extent of spread: In stage one there is no spread, in stage two the cancer has spread to the upper portion of the uterus or to the surrounding tissues immediately adjacent to the uterus, stage three involves spread to the adjacent organs such as the rectum or the bladder, and stage four involves spread to distant organs such as the liver or lung. Yet we know that cancer of the cervix is a continuum, a process which once set in motion will proceed unchecked to the death of the patient. Nevertheless, for purposes of study and data collection regarding the efficacy of treatment at a given stage, it is useful to deal with factitious partitioning of the disease into stages. So it is with "trimesters." And if we did not have permissive abortion, the concept of trimester would long ago have been relegated to the obstetrical antique closet.

Given the massive amount of data already available to the obstetrician-fetologist and the convincing, seemingly unanswerable arguments which flow from these data demonstrating the personhood and human life of the baby in prenatality, how is it that obstetrician-fetologists are still practicing abortion? Is there some fatal defect in the data which renders them unacceptable? Are the data and the various conclusions which emerge from them so unpalatable and unsettling as to require mindless rejection out-of-hand by those very physicians who have special access to the modern means of communication with the unborn? And leaving aside for the moment the individual practitioners of obstetrics-fetology, why has organized medicine in general chosen to ignore ethical imperatives flowing from the science of fetology and, in so doing, endorsed the wholesale casual destruction of the unborn?

There are a number of explanations—not excuses—for the large number of obstetrician-fetologists who actively participate in the abortion cataclysm. To begin with, abortion is now a major industry. In 1980, the last year for which we have complete figures, there were 1.55 million abortions. Although it is concededly difficult to set a precise figure on the Gross National Abortion Product (GNAP), an estimate of perhaps three hundred dollars per abortion would not be egregiously out of line, and the GNAP would approximate five hundred million dollars annually, a not inconsiderable figure, placing it firmly in the Fortune Five Hundred largest industries in the nation. A substantial portion of these funds are siphoned off by hospitals, abortion clinics, and laboratories; still, a reasonable estimate for the physician's cut of this loot would be fifty to sixty per cent, or perhaps $250 to $300 million a year. Most of this blood money is flowing into the pockets of the younger members of the obstetrical discipline, those who have just entered practice after having completed a long period of training and who are anxious to begin supporting themselves in the style to which they would like to become accustomed. Many of them complain that those long years of training have been spent in relative penury, that hospitals pay them poorly, and that the work burden during residency is enormous. In fact, the current salary in the New York City area for a resident in the first year of an accredited training program in obstetrics and gynecology approximates $21,000 while a chief resident (fourth year) makes almost $30,000. In contrast, in 1950 when I was a first year resident in obstetrics and gynecology at the old Women's Hospital in New York City, I was paid the princely sum of $75 a month with room, board, and as my father often reminded me "all the water you can drink." I worked a schedule of thirty-six hours on and twelve hours off, with every other week-end for myself (week-ends began on Saturday at noon). Today's residents work every third night and have three week-ends of every four off. Now I am not deploring reforms in what ad-mittedly were exhausting workloads and unfair labor practices, but on the other hand wages and working conditions today provide no excuse for the graduating obstetrician to immediately prostitute his talents and education in the service of the GNAP. In the words of that old drinking song which resounded through the halls of dear old Michael Reese Hospital in Chicago where I interned:

> There's a fortune in abortion
> Just a twist of the wrist, and
> you're through.
> The population of the nation
> Won't grow if it's left up to
> you. . . .

In all modesty, I know a little about money and abortion clinics. The Center for Reproductive Health, the giant abortion clinic in New York City of which I was director for almost two years, was a $4.5 million dollar a year business. I had upgraded the medical staff when I took it over by discharging a covey of drunkards, sex deviates, mafia satellites, FBI fugitives, sadists, and assorted incompetents, and by luring well-qualified gynecologists to the staff with exorbitant pay scales. I had a number of physicians working for me who made more in the two or three eight-hour weekly shifts in my clinic than they had ever made, or ever would make, in private practice.

Yet another reason for the apparently inexplicable paradox of young obstetricians trained in the arts and science of fetology cheer-fully participating in the wholesale destruction of their patients, is the ethical training, or more precisely the lack thereof, in the various medical schools and residency programs in the United States. All emphasis is now on instant disposition of the patient. There is little or no time for listening to sick people, for offering sympathy, counsel, or compassion and caring. Instead the most expeditious disposition of the patient consistent with assembly-line diagnostics and high-tech treatment is the order of the day. It is far easier to see a woman who suspects she is pregnant with an unplanned child, make the diagnosis, and in fifteen seconds jerk the thumb toward the abortion clinic down the street while baring the other palm for the fee and, with what seems to be a third hand, buzz for the next patient than it is to sit with the un-happy woman, counsel her, offer her solace and encouragement, and remind her of the wonderful advances in modern obstetrics which have conspired to give us the happiest, healthiest, and most long-lived babies we have ever known in Western society.

What of organized medicine and its attitude toward permissive abortion? In May, 1857, the American Medical Association appointed a Committee on Criminal Abortion which presented its report to the twelfth annual meeting of that organization in 1859. In stark contrast to the arrogant assertions of the Amicus Curiae brief to the Supreme Court from the American College of Obstetrics and Gynecology and its fulsome allies, all of whom cling to the notion that the only reason for the passage of statutes against abortion in the nineteenth century was to protect the pregnant against unscrupulous and unskilled abortionists, the A.M.A. report states that three major considerations in advocating, as it did, suppression of abortion were:

> a widespread popular belief of the true character of the crime—a belief, even among mothers themselves, that the fetus is not alive till after the period of quickening. . . .

> the profession themselves are frequently supposed careless of fetal life. . . .

> the third reason for the frightful extent of this crime is found in the grave defects of our laws, both common and statute, as regards the independent and actual existence of the child before birth as a living being . . . with strange inconsistency the law fully acknowledges the fetus in utero and its inherent rights for civil purposes; while personally and as criminally affected it fails to recognize it and to its life as yet denies all protection.

Following the presentation of its report, the committee offered a resolution protesting against such "unwarrantable destruction of human life," and importuned state legislatures and medical societies to endorse and act upon these views. The A.M.A. adopted the committee's recommendations without significant dissent. Another special committee of the A.M.A. in 1871 expressed virtually identical sentiments.

It is an irony which perhaps only a serious observer of the abortion scene can appreciate that the above quotations from the reports of the special committees of the American Medical Association, emphasizing as they do the value and the undeniable presence of prenatal

life, can be found in the Roe v. Wade decision of the United States
Supreme Court, while such putatively authoritative statements such
as the Amicus Curiae brief mentions them not at all and the otherwise
impeccably scholarly tome by James C. Mohr, *Abortion in America*,
mentions the reports and resolutions of the American Medical Association in the nineteenth century but never acknowledges that the
primary reason for the recommendations of the committees was the
certainty of the value of prenatal life. Presumably keeping his liberal
credentials intact, Mohr skirts around the fetal-value aspects of the
reports, refrains from quoting the reports at any length, and leaves
the reader with the mistaken impression that the A.M.A. committees
acted as they did only with an eye to maternal safety.

Bowing to increasing pressure from liberal trendies and militant
females in the membership in the turbulent year of 1967, the A.M.A.
adopted a resolution endorsing the American Law Institute model
abortion statute and finally in 1970 knuckled under completely and
ratified permissive abortion.

The American Medical Association recently sent me a card in
response to my payment of my annual dues which certifies that I am a
member in good standing of that redoubtable sodality, and on the
other side of that card reprints for me its Principle of Medical Ethics,
which includes among other head scratchers:

III. A physician shall respect the law and also recognize a responsibility
to seek changes in those requirements which are contrary to the best
interests of the patient.

IV. A physician shall respect the rights of patients, of colleagues and of
other health professionals and shall safeguard patient confi-
dences. . . .

V. A physician shall continue to study, apply and advance scientific
knowledge, make relevant information available to patients, colleagues and the public. . . .

Now how does a conscientious physician square these sententious
sonorities, along with the A.M.A.'s stated policy on abortion which
indicates that

The Principles of Medical Ethics of the A.M.A. do not prohibit a
physician from performing an abortion in accordance with good
medical practice and under circumstances which do not violate the
law. . . .

with the new science of fetology? How can this high-sounding flatulence be compatible with explicit permission to eradicate the "patient"? Let the moguls of the A.M.A. review the Preface of the Sixteenth Edition of *Williams' Obstetrics*, a textbook universally acknowledged to be nonpolitical, current, and authoritative in many areas. It states the following:

> Happily we have entered an era in which the fetus can be rightfully considered and treated as our *second patient* . . . Who would have dreamed—even a few years ago—that we could serve the fetus as physician?

So we have the baffling, monstrous paradox of the new science of fetology proving beyond dispute that the fetus is a human being, a valued protectible life, and indeed *our patient* referred to so piously in Principles III, IV, and V, while the A.M.A. moves inexorably backward into the medical Ice Age.

If anything, the American College of Obstetricians and Gynecologists (ACOG) is more inexcusably, unconscionably political and more wrong-headed than the A.M.A. Here is an organization which has the most direct and enduring contact with the unborn; which is responsible for the standards of research and teaching in the discipline of fetology; which should be the strongest, most outspoken advocate for its *patient* (I would venture to guess that virtually one hundred per cent of the membership of the ACOG has studied from *William's Obstetrics* either through purchase of the book or through library reading); and which in many of its publications and technical bulletins to the membership repeatedly refers to the unborn child as the *patient*. Yet it too endorses selective destruction of this patient, though if one were to suggest that a certain arbitrarily chosen number of pregnant women, also *patients*, should be destroyed merely because they are not as intelligent as the physician would like or they failed to pay their bill for the last delivery, the ACOG would undoubtedly refer one to one's friendly family psychiatrist.

Here is the ACOG in late 1982 submitting to the United States Supreme Court an Amicus Curiae brief in affiliation with the A.M.A., the American Academy of Pediatrics, and the Nurse's Association of the American College of Obstetricians and Gynecologists opposing the Akron abortion law. That proposed law, which adheres faithfully to Principle V. of the A.M.A.'s code of medical ethics, to wit, "A physician shall . . . make relevant information available to patients, colleagues, and the public. . . ." simply would require physicians eliciting informed consent from their abortion patients to apprise such women of the fact that the child may be viable after only twenty-two weeks gestation (true), that abortion is a major surgical procedure (malpractice insurance companies require gynecologists who perform abortions to carry *major* malpractice insurance at the same rates they would have if they did hysterectomies), that the operation can result in sterility (it most certainly can if it is followed by infection, a not uncommon post-operative problem), and that the unborn is a human life from the moment of conception. Well, if it's not, then what is fetology all about? What is the Sixteenth Edition of *Williams' Obstetrics* talking about when it refers to the prenatal person as *the patient*?

The ACOG, along with the American Academy of Pediatrics, has also placed itself on record as opposing restrictions on fetal research included in an amendment to the National Institute of Health authorization bill. In general, these restrictions would prohibit experimentation on a living human unborn child or infant unless such experimentation was done for the purpose of insuring the survival of that person. The ACOG took the curious position that this perfectly reasonable restriction, compatible in every way with current standards set up by hospital ethics committees throughout the United States, would "stifle the freedom of science. It would interfere with genetic amniocentesis as well as many other important areas of research."

Just how these restrictions would interfere with amniocentesis for genetic purposes in the practice of obstetrics and gynecology, Dr. Pearse, spokesman for the ACOG, never satisfactorily explained; furthermore, he never elaborated on what other "important areas of research" he included in that sweeping generalization. Hospital ethics committees and research review committees do not sanction experimentation on patients unless that experimentation is directly related to the treatment and survival of the patient. Why should it be any different for the prenatal person, unless of course you are of that mind-set that persists in regarding that person as a second-rate citizen.

The ACOG betrays itself constantly with its confusion of purpose and its muddled perceptions with respect to its charge. Regard, if you will, its Statement of Policy as issued by its Executive Board in December, 1977, and amended in April, 1978:

> The ACOG supports the right of the pregnant woman to informed consent, while recognizing that at the same time the woman assumes responsibility for decisions she makes in the interest of her own health, and the health and welfare of her *infant*. [The italics are mine. Please note that the ACOG did not waffle about the nature of the person in the uterus. It came bravely out and called it an infant.]

The ACOG has published a series of "Ethical Considerations in the Practice of Obstetrics and Gynecology," which were approved by its Executive Board. Among these considerations is the following:

> These obligations [on the part of a Fellow of the ACOG who seeks to pursue a high ethical standard] include recognition of the patients' right to be fully informed and to decide to participate in or withdraw from medical research without jeopardizing the quality of her medical care.

If the unborn child is a patient, and we have concessions not only from the Williams' textbook but also from the ACOG itself when it uses the all-inclusive term "infant" for the intra-uterine person, then who speaks for the child when it comes to research and experimentation? Does the child have a chance to withdraw from frivolous experiments designed more to add to the bibliography of the researcher rather than further its health and well-being? One Dr. Joe Leigh Simpson, a professor of obstetrics and gynecology at the Northwestern Medical School in Chicago, adhered faithfully to the ACOG party line, complaining that good alternatives to fetal research "do not exist." He went on to say that the way to learn how to do fetal surgery was to: "practice on pregnancies that will be terminated anyway. You don't want to make your mistakes on ongoing pregnancies." Quite apart from the observation that abortions are the most egregious medical mistakes of all, experimental procedures in medicine have classically been worked out and perfected in *animal* laboratories; we do not utilize humans for that purpose. Or was Simpson suggesting that the prenatal person is nothing more or less than a laboratory animal, to be tinkered with by every hare-brained sadist who has a new gadget in mind? There was no research on *human beings* before the artificial heart was placed in Dr. Barney Clark. Is Clark to be regarded as nothing more than a laboratory animal to be experimented upon?

Although the new science of fetology so far seems to have little impact on organizational policy in medicine and less on national politics, what effect has it had on the average practitioner of obstetrics and gynecology? Or, perhaps more to the point, how has it affected those practitioners who had been most active in abortion advocacy and abortioneering? Clearly it is impossible to interview every one of the eighteen thousand or so members of the ACOG; most members, I would venture, are still resisting the data on the pragmatic—as they see it—ground that if we illegalized abortion again what shall we do with the women who are pregnant with unwanted pregnancies?

Well, it is now legal to smoke cigarettes, but if further data with respect to smoking point to an undeniable cause and effect link between cigarette smoke and cancer of the breast in women, it may then become necessary to ban smoking. What will we do with those smokers who are really addicted to smoking and simply refuse to give up the habit, claiming freedom of choice? Shall we refuse to act on the data simply because some smokers will obtain cigarettes illegally in the underground, thus exposing themselves not only to legal action but also to inferior black market cigarettes which will harm them even more? And if we refuse to act on the rather fragile basis of freedom of choice for the smoker, suppose further data emerges that provides an absolute link between the mere presence of cigarette smoke in the air and breast cancer for non-smoking women who inhale that air, eat food contaminated by the smoke, and drink water polluted by the smoke? Shall we still cling to the fatuous notion that freedom of choice, skulking around somewhere in the Fourteenth Amendment to the Constitution, is to remain the over-riding moral principle of twentieth century life in the United States? Those people whose lives are touched by abortion—husbands, lovers, parents of women who choose abortion, other children in the family—suffer the effects of abortion in a moral sense as surely as the women on whom the operation is performed, yet these sufferers have been disenfranchised.

And what is one to say of the Nurse's Association of the American College of Obstetricians and Gynecologists? This is a group of women trained in the nursing arts and in constant communication with the intra-uterine patient. Many of these women have borne children themselves and are no strangers to that heart-stopping jolt, that warm suffusion of hope and pride that a woman feels when her pregnancy is first confirmed. For these women to have pledged their hearts and minds to this joyless purge of the unlucky unborn is equivalent to watching nursing-home attendants starve the inconvenient and disabled elderly or orderlies in a home for the mentally retarded tormenting the mattoids in their charge.

I accuse the policy-making bodies of the American Medical Association; the American College of Obstetricians and Gynecologists; the American Medical Women's Association; the American Psychiatric Association; the New York Academy of Medicine; the American Academy of Pediatrics; the Nurse's Association of the American College of Obstetricians and Gynecologists; and the 170 medical school deans, departmental chairmen and professors of obstetrics and gynecology throughout the nation of a willful and conscious disregard of the massive and still-growing data identifying the prenatal person as a living, valuable, and fully protectible human being. I accuse them of abandoning the canons and principles which lent legitimacy to their organizations, and caving in to trendy political fashions of the moment. I accuse them of a heinous abuse of their professional trust in failing to protect this unborn patient in their charge. I accuse them of voluntary collaboration in an unprecedented surgical holocaust against these mute and defenseless victims, and I accuse all physician members of these organizations who fail to speak up against this unspeakable crime of complicity in that crime.

History will not forgive them.

* * * *

Adamandia Panayotopoulos is a sixty-six year old obstetrician and gynecologist practicing in New York City. She changed her name to A. Panay several years ago, claiming that her patients could never remember it or spell it; even with the change, she still prefers to be called Tulla. She was born in Greece in a little town called Xylokastron near Corinth on the Peloponnesian peninsula in 1917. Her father was a priest in the Greek Orthodox Church, married with six children. She attended the University of Athens until 1941, and with the German occupation of Greece in 1941 she was forced to interrupt her education and worked in a medical laboratory throughout the war. She obtained her medical degree in 1947, in the face of her father's objections: he warned her that if she became a doctor and did abortions—they were of course illegal in Greece—he would place a curse on her for the rest of her life.

She married immediately after graduation and completed a year of residency in general surgery at the University of Athens hospital. Her husband was a lawyer-businessman who travelled a great deal, and the marriage soon fizzled. They separated when she accompanied her brother, ill with tuberculosis, to Zurich in 1949. She had no license to practice medicine in Switzerland and the licensing procedure was a lengthy and exacting one, so she supported herself for the next year working as a domestic, cleaning houses for affluent Swiss. Once she obtained her medical license, she eked out a living by filling in for practicing physicians who were on holiday, covering their practices.

She emigrated to the United States in 1956 ("Dolling, there was simply no future for a tall ugly Greek female physician in Europe then") with no English and lots of hope. She spent a year at the Lebanon Hospital in New York City in a residency program in obstetrics and gynecology and then went on to a hospital in Woonsocket, Rhode Island, where she took a residency in general practice for a year and a half. She returned to New York City to a residency at the Jewish Memorial Hospital in obstetrics and gynecology for two years and then joined our staff at the Woman's Hospital as resident for three more years in ob-gyn. By the time she finished her residency at Woman's Hospital, she had spent a total of seven and a half years in residencies, living in airless little hospital rooms on a salary ranging from $50 to $150 a month, and perfecting her skills. When I first met her at the Woman's Hospital in 1961, she was already an excellent obstetrician and a skillful and resourceful surgeon, and by the end of her residency three years later she was without question one of the most competent practitioners I had ever met.

She was, however, discouraged at the prospect of opening an office in New York City (her English was still not Churchillian, to be charitable) and having received an attractive offer to return to Zurich (she spoke flawless German) she took a position as pathologist in a large hospital in that city. Things, however, did not work out. The Swiss attitude toward female physicians had not perceptibly changed, and she returned to the United States in 1966. She was forced to take still another year of residency before she could obtain her license to practice in New York, and she finally opened her private office in 1968.

She was now fifty-one years old, tall, rangy, large-boned with a strong deeply-seamed face. Today she bears a remarkable resemblance to the late Golda Meier, although she will take a playful swipe at anyone who tells her that. She developed a small practice in ob-gyn and was simultaneously trying to send money back to her family in Greece for the education of her various relatives there. Even now she regards this as almost a sacred duty, and has put one nephew through the University of Pennsylvania's Wharton School of Business single-handedly, and is presently supporting another one at New York University.

She needed the money, and I needed the talent. So when I approached her in February, 1971, to join by clinic staff at the Center for Reproductive and Sexual Health, she assented and took on four or five shifts a week. We were then paying ninety dollars an hour. She was a careful and quick surgeon who could be counted upon to do her eighteen or twenty abortions on her shift, carrying her own workload and helping slower physicians with theirs. She estimates that in the two years she remained at the clinic she did ten thousand abortions and earned an average of $150,000 annually. She was still carrying on her private practice as best she could and was doing second-trimester saline abortions, albeit reluctantly, in the hospital for those patients who required it. She did feel, she relates, a certain repugnance for that procedure—"My God, dolling, those are babies you know"—but felt that it was part of abortion practice and "in for a penny, in for a pound."

She quit the clinic in mid-1973 to return to private practice on a full-time basis. I had left in September, 1972, and, loyally, she felt the working conditions had deteriorated following my departure. At this time she also stopped doing second-trimester salting-out; she did not feel the money was worth the offense to her sensibilities. Incidentally, like me, she did not leave the clinic for any ethical reasons but felt that her practice was suffering as a result of the work demands at the clinic; in addition she had developed hypertension in 1973 and was told to decrease the strains in her life. She did, however, continue to perform early abortions in her private practice until 1978, coincidentally the same year in which I did my last "therapeutic abortion." I had stopped doing unindicated *permissive* abortions a year earlier.

Tulla has always been religious and a more or less regular church goer. When in 1978 she discovered that she had cancer of the breast she felt that she was being dealt divine retribution, not only for the abortions she had undergone herself—there were several earlier in her life—but also for the ten thousand human lives she had destroyed at the clinic. This was no mindless superstition on her part. She believes as a matter of faith that a human being exists from the moment of conception, and now that science has demonstrated this conclusively, she no longer feels any conflict between the values she learned as a youngster in the Orthodox Church and the information she has been privileged to receive as a practicing obstetrician. She likens abortion to infanticide and reminds me that in ancient Greece the practice of infanticide was acceptable and widespread, calling it one of the less commendable aspects of the Hellenic culture. She also cautions me that in the Greece of her youth the practice of infanticide was *still* going on in the mountains and rural areas of the country, and she remembers her father railing against it at home. It is going on in the United States too, she says ruefully.

Tulla declares that by 1978 the data and information we had regarding the unborn child were sufficient to establish the fetus's personhood and protectibility and that even without her religious beliefs and her ill health she would still have stopped doing abortions. Moreover, she also believes that "abortion destroys women"; it violates their spirit and their souls, and equally important it damages the reproductive tract to the extent that she believes gynecologists are seeing more problems with infertility and pelvic infections than ever before. In her practice, she has her secretary inform patients that she does not do abortions before the patients appear for their first appointment. But for those women who are pregnant and have sought her counsel, she has convinced a number of them of the inviolable humanity of the unborn and has persuaded them to keep the pregnancy. Her face lights up when she tells me this.

Tulla is a forceful, aggressive woman who has been outspoken all her life. She has held her own in what she conceives to be the hostile world of the male physician and now has a thriving ob-gyn practice in this city. She has never been a political activist or a joiner of causes. But she believes that in the case of abortion, political action is necessary. And, as I do, she finds it impossible to understand how the various prestigious medical organizations such as the A.M.A. and the ACOG can continue to pander to the slaughterous ideology of the

1960s, when medical science knows so much more now. She wonders how the ACOG can reconcile its sanctimonious pledges to care equally well for mother and baby with its continued endorsement of abortion on demand.

* * * *

Fetology, the New Science, is expanding at an astonishing rate. Even now it has spun off its first sub-specialists, the fetal surgeons and fetal diagnosticians. Soon we will have fetal neurologists to monitor, diagnose, and treat neurological abnormalities of the prenatal person. These doctors will be able to increase the intelligence potential of that person, correct those flaws which ultimately lead in the adult to near-sightedness and far-sightedness, and successfully treat Tay-Sachs disease before it blossoms into the obscene flower which kills our loveliest children. We shall have fetal hematologists who will diagnose and treat sickle-cell disease in the unborn, find the fatal gene which triggers leukemia and substitute another for it, and winnow out the clotting defect in the hemophiliac unborn child and correct it before it begins to express itself. There will be fetal cardiologists, fetal endocrinologists, and even fetal psychiatrists—don't laugh, nothing is out of the reach of human ingenuity—who will unearth the disordered neurochemistry culminating in schizophrenia and correct it before it ever takes root.

Fantastic? Rubbish. When I was a child I recall my father telling me over and over again that the great Sir William Osler had taught him at McGill: "Pneumonia is the captain of the men of death." When I became ill with pneumonia at the age of eight, before any antibiotics had been discovered or developed, it was a desperate time for my parents. I have a dim recollection of the tears and the long deep sighs when I passed my "crisis" on the seventh day of the illness, after the fever broke and I was on the mend. The treatment of pneumonia then consisted of lots of fluids, quinine, digitalis, and prayerful vigilance. Now pneumonia is so simple to treat with antibiotics that the current joke goes: Don't get a cold, get pneumonia so at least we can treat it.

My father is now eighty-nine years old and has been practicing medicine for sixty-three years. As he puts it: from the era of the darkening cave and the knobby club right into the nuclear dawn.

Though he styles himself an agnostic, he maintains his sense of a cosmic mysterium tremendum, an inchoate awe before the universe. He dismisses no possibility when it comes to the unlimited potential of scientific technology. When I pose for him the real probability that in five or so years we will have the ability to remove the human fetus from its burrow in the uterus and transfer it to another uterus or to an entirely artificial life support system (the technology of surgical embryo transfer is already in use in Australia), he purses his lips, stares out the window, then nods and says:

> Yes, but who'll pay for it? It will surely solve the current controversy on abortion—everyone's rights will be respected—but it will raise a host of other equally difficult questions. If a woman wanting an abortion consents to this procedure does she also relinquish her rights to that baby? Or does the state own it? And how about the child—to whom will it owe its loyalty?

Advances in technology not only create new specialties, new techniques, and new ethical questions but they also create new constituencies. When fetal medicine becomes a full-fledged field of medical endeavor with specialists and even sub-specialists within it, those physicians themselves will become the loudest, most aggressive advocates for the unborn. (I note, with perhaps a smug satisfaction, that the September, 1983, newsletter of the ACOG cites the following item: "Joseph D. Shulman, M.D., has been elected the first president of the new international organization called the Fetal Medicine and Surgery Society.") They will be vying for Federal funds, for the positions within the universities, for their place in the medical pecking order—all in the name of their client, the human unborn. This will be bitter vindication indeed for those of us who are pleading this lonely cause in 1983 in the name of decency and simple humanity. Still, if it saves one unborn life, let it be.

Part Three

Catholics

The major opposition to abortion law repeal comes from the Roman Catholic Church and groups like the Right to Life Committee, organized and funded by the Catholic Church. All present had seen evidence of opposition tactics in the form of election campaigns against proponents of abortion law change, pastoral letters, etc. Suggested ways to contend with this opposition were to support actively those Catholics who support abortion law repeal, to emphasize the minority opinion within the church (Daniel Callahan, "Abortion: Law, Choice and Morality") and separation of religious conviction from legislative judgement as proposed by such notables as Robert Drinan S. J. and Richard Cardinal Cushing. The opposition argument of abortion law repeal promoting promiscuity can be exploited to expose the immorality of the "pregnancy as punishment" philosophy.

This paragraph appears in the transcribed minutes of a national high-level strategy meeting held at the Marriott Hotel at Chicago's O'Hare airport on January 9, 1971. The meeting had been called by Lawrence Lader, then chairman of the Executive Committee of the NARAL, in order to counter what he perceived to be a serious threat to abortion advocacy: the increasing number of live-born infants emerging from second-trimester saline abortions. Lader saw these abortion survivors as an embarrassment to NARAL and was concerned that the press had made much of them and that the opposition elements were seizing upon them as a tactic in the abortion wars.

At the time of this meeting I was chairman of the Medical Committee of NARAL as well as a member of the Executive Committee. In characteristic fashion Lader brought me along not only to reassure

177

the General Staff of NARAL that if a late saline abortion is done properly it should not result in a surviving infant (which is true) but in so doing to provide him with the opportunity to deliver himself of another splenetic anti-Catholic harangue. The paragraph articulates clearly the "Catholic strategy" which he and I had agreed upon several years earlier as one of the most fruitful tactics to be pursued in the abortion wars. Consider the following statement issued by NARAL (the chairman of its policy-making executive committee was Lawrence Lader) at the National Symposium on Legislative Breakthroughs on May 12, 1972:

> We meet at the end of a week when insanity seems to be engulfing the country. In two incredible steps only a few days apart President Nixon [another favorite Lader whipping boy] has plunged us into a confrontation with Russia and China and brought us close to a constitutional crisis. With similar recklessness Mr. Nixon injected himself into the New York legislative struggle over abortion and allied himself, obviously in the delusion of picking up a few votes, with Cardinal Cooke and the Catholic hierarchy. At the same time he has threatened abortion rights in Michigan with its upcoming referendum [though where Lader found these "rights" is a mystery since Michigan had a restrictive abortion law at the time and this was pre-Roe v. Wade], and ruthlessly employed Federal authority in a state issue to bludgeon the courts and electorates everywhere.
>
> With Mr. Nixon's bungling assistance the Catholic hierarchy has proved in the last month that it is bent on a frightening course: to turn the abortion issue into a religious war. When almost twenty state legislatures have liberalized their abortion laws and a dozen major court decisions increasingly guaranteed that no woman shall be forced to bear a child against her will, why has a fanatical minority of one religious faith suddenly determined to impose its dogma on the majority? Why has it endlessly screamed "murderer" even at clergymen and legislators? Why has it harnessed its vast finances, even sheltering the so-called Right to Life Committee in its tax-free chancery office in New York, in this drive to overcome the most humanitarian legislation of our time? "Heaven forbid that Albany should become a Dublin or Buffalo a Belfast to prove the ruthless power of any religious organization," the Rev. Jesse Lyons of the Riverside Church warned recently.
>
> Only one conclusion can be made: that the Catholic hierarchy is determined to bend the country to its will over abortion. What happens to all human rights in the next few years depends on what happens to abortion. If the Bill of Rights is to survive, we must never allow

Cardinal Cooke to rule our bedrooms. We must never allow Catholic dogma to take over a legislature as it has just done in New York, and try to force every woman to bear a child against her choice.

We have learned a terrible lesson: the Catholic drive is unrelenting, and this is only the beginning. We must start next week to match the most powerful lobby in the nation with equal force and similar tactics. We must match money with money in Michigan, our two points of concentration. We must match them with professional political staff and skilled organizers. The Catholic lobby succeeded in New York by concentrating a massive attack on a carefully chosen list of spineless legislators and terrorizing them with the votes of controlled Catholic blocs. . . .

It is worthwhile examining this document closely since it anatomizes the fundamentals of NARAL's Catholic strategy. One is immediately struck by the fury, the pure vitriol of the text. Substitute the word "Jewish" for "Catholic" in that exhortation and it would stand as one of the more poisonous anti-Semitic outbursts in recent memory, worthy of a place alongside the works of Alfred Rosenberg or Arthur Gobineau. Substitute the word "black" for "Catholic" and it emerges as a fulminating racist tirade one might hear at a Ku Klux Klan gathering. It's no wonder that such material does not appear in the account Lader has written of the abortion wars (*Abortion II: Making the Revolution*), nor in any of the other pro-abortion literature such as that paradigm of abortion advocacy *Enemies of Choice* by Andrew Merton which similarly purports to trace the history of the abortion conflict. The American Civil Liberties Union had been drawn into the conflict on the side of NARAL as far back as 1969 when it represented us in Federal court in an effort to force Washington D.C.'s General Hospital to perform abortions on indigent women after the Vuitch decision had come down; yet the ACLU failed to disavow itself of the decidedly anti-Catholic taint of the NARAL and it is difficult to believe that it was unaware of it.

But examine if you will the premises of the statement. It is implied that any state legislator who voted against abortion law repeal in New York State was "spineless" in the sense that he was knuckling under to some massive conspiracy having its roots in Rome and its agents scattered across the United States, skulking in the shadows of all the churches in the nation. That a legislator might be voting his conscience, or might be voting what he perceived to be the will of his constituency is simply ruled out. NARAL was quite as effective in terrorizing elected officials as it imputed the church to be.

Aside from its venomous tone the statement is also remarkable for the sweep of its indictments against the Catholic Church. The church stands accused of promoting religious warfare in the United States, of flouting the tax-exemption laws for religious organizations, of attempting to repeal the Bill of Rights, and of intimidating legislators. It also firms up NARAL's liberal credentials by taking a gratuitous swipe or two at Richard Nixon who had offended abortion advocates by expressing his personal abhorrence of abortion in a letter to Terence Cardinal Cooke on May 6, 1972.

But the statement and the charges contained within it were entirely compatible with the NARAL "Catholic strategy". That strategy depended on the exploitation of two major historical events in the 1960s: the campaign and election of John Kennedy to the presidency in conjunction with the Vatican II Council called by Pope John XXIII ("the two Johns revolution"), and the Vietnam War resistance. John Kennedy had gained the presidency as the first practicing Roman Catholic in the nation's history by portraying himself as a "cool" Catholic unencumbered by the fetters of traditional Catholicism, by emphasizing the distance between his religious duties as a Catholic and his civil duties as president, and by thoroughly publicizing his pledge to respect that distance. Kennedy became the model of the modern, enlightened twentieth-century Catholic, thinking for himself without obeisance to church dogma. The old-style anti-Catholicism had drawn on immigrant fear, class snobbery, and an inchoate Protestant distrust of the ethnic, that is Catholic, invasion of this country in the nineteenth century. But Kennedy-style Catholicism made that sort of mindless, all-encompassing bias unfashionable. With increasing numbers of young Catholics entering colleges, joining the professions, enlisting in the ranks of liberal causes such as feminism, civil rights, and the Vietnam War resistance we perceived in the NARAL councils that there were two classes of Catholics now in the United States: the educated, fashionable Kennedy-style, and those who were still bluecollar, only one generation removed from immigration, and uncritically subject to the dictates of the church. Our strategy was to use the "modern" Catholics to persuade the others to our cause.

The "modern" Kennedy Catholics needed little persuasion from us. They were already using contraception and it was not a long step for them to the public position of "pro-choice." To maintain their appearance as enlightened and progressive while still retaining their bona fides as Catholics we provided them with the now classic straddle for Catholics in public positions: abortion is personally abhorrent, but everyone must be free to make their own choice. Now we were ready to use them to call over the more traditional, less trendy Catholics to our cause.

Pope John XXIII had called Vatican II to modernize the church, to bring it into the twentieth century. In a sense his efforts synergized quite nicely with what Kennedy had done for us. Although he was adamantly against abortion, his generally liberal thinking polarized Catholics in the United States along the same lines that Kennedy had, creating a liberal and a conservative Catholic constituency. The stage was set for the portrayal of the Catholic Church as a political force, for the use of anti-Catholicism as a political instrument, and for the manipulation of Catholics themselves by splitting them and setting them against each other. From those same minutes of that high-level meeting in Chicago:

> In the past year or two not only support for repeal but brilliant leadership has come from Catholics. In New York, Catholic Women for Abortion Law Repeal played an influential role in the campaign. Catholic legislators have given moving speeches. In Hawaii a Catholic state senator was the leader of repeal forces. A Catholic nun gave a touching testimony for repeal at the legislative [in Hawaii]. A Catholic governor allowed the bill to become law. All devout Catholics, *they do not believe in abortion themselves but do believe abortion is a private decision that every woman must make for herself.* . . . [italics added]

Anti-Catholicism and its political uses have had a long and inglorious history in the United States, with its roots in reformation Europe and Tudor England. As far back as 1700 the province of New York passed a law which contained the following preamble:

> Whereas divers Jesuit priests and Popish missionaries have of late and for some time had their residence in the remote parts of this province and others of His Majesties adjacent colonies who by their wicked and subtle insinuations industriously labor to debauch, seduce and withdraw the Indians from their due obediance to His Most Sacred Majesty and to excite and stir them to sedition, rebellion and open hostility to His Majesty's government, therefore for protection thereof. . . .

The law which followed required that all Catholic clergy ordained by the Pope leave the province of New York by November 1, 1700. And those clergy who elected to remain there in violation of the law:

> . . . shall be deemed and accounted an incendiary and disturber of the public peace and safety, and an enemy to the true Christian religion, and shall be adjudged to suffer perpetual imprisonment.

That law further stipulated that any person convicted of knowingly sheltering or harboring Catholic clergy would be fined two hundred pounds. The law was passed in response to the successes that Jesuit priests had had in proselytizing the Indians of the state and encouraging them to leave the orbit of English influence.

The Native American Party, an avowedly anti-Catholic, anti-immigrant movement, sprang up in the 1830s and was led by United States Congressman L. C. Levin. Its bible was the virulent anti-Catholic tract *Foreign Conspiracies against the Liberties of the United States*, penned by Samuel F. B. Morse, the inventor of the electric telegraph. The book was particularly vicious in its treatment of the Jesuit order, accusing it of plotting to seize control of the United States government by manipulating the Irish Catholic population at the ballot box. The Nativist movement culminated in a series of bloody riots in Philadelphia in May of 1844 in which a number of people were killed and much property destroyed.

A decade later the Know-Nothings, a secret society dedicated to anti-Catholicism and led by a lapsed priest named Alessandro Gavazzi, came to prominence largely on the strength of a false rumor that President Franklin Pierce was about to convert to "Romanism." Gavazzi lectured widely through the eastern half of the United States and Canada and his society was responsible for another series of religious riots in 1854 ranging from New York to St. Louis. The riots in New York were so violent and uncontrollable that the National Guard had to be mobilized and deployed. The mid-nineteenth century marked the crest of the flood of immigration from Europe into the eastern seaports of this country and the vast majority of the immigrants were Catholic. Incidentally, the Know-Nothings got their name by virtue of their strict secrecy: when asked about their society, its aims, and its membership all members were instructed to say "I know nothing."

The shameful excesses of the Ku Klux Klan in alliance with the Anti-Saloon League and the Southern Baptist and Methodist Churches in opposing the 1928 candidacy for president of the Catholic Governor Al Smith, using anti-Catholicism and anti-Popery as the theme of the attack, are still tender lesions on the American political corpus. Smith, like Kennedy, repeatedly denied a blind and unreasoning fealty to the Roman Catholic Church, affirmed on innumerable occasions his unqualified recognition of the absolute separation of church and state, and ringingly rejected any political role for the Catholic Church in the law-making mechanisms of the nation. The Republican party not only tacitly encouraged the anti-Catholic forces, but also threw in accusations that Smith was pledged to the "wets" in the Prohibition controversy, and that he was a tool of the corrupt Tammany Hall machine of New York City. Smith of course lost the election rather decisively. He was a man of the streets, a poor man who had fought and clawed his way through the political jungle. He was not Harvard educated, did not have a vast fortune at his command, and his electorate was not nearly as sophisticated as Kennedy's would be thirty years later—that electorate which we in NARAL manipulated so artfully.

In a position paper entitled "An Outline For Action" Lader and the Executive Committee of NARAL undertook to analyze their loss in the results of the Michigan referendum on abortion, and accounted for it this way:

> The Catholic strategy concentrated a huge radio-TV campaign in the last two or three weeks, built around the "killing of five month old infants" and the emotional impact of horror pictures of twenty week and older fetuses. . . .

and further on, in paragraph eight on that paper:

> In exploring picture sources [to counter the pictures of dead fetuses which he found effective but apparently not at all offensive to *his* sensibilities] I have not been able to find pictures of a dead woman with a catheter or knitting needle still protruding. Pathologists say they would be removed before any photograph. A picture of a dead woman on a bathroom floor does not tell the real story. It could be a case dead of other causes. The best possibility seems to be pictures of horribly ravaged uteri from needles, chemicals, etc. These would be compared with pictures of the normal uterus. The case history attested by doctor

and hospital would be appended for credibility (which the Catholics lack). Admittedly the uterus lacks the human impact of the fetus . . . this might be countered with a picture of the dead woman on the morgue slab, a fifteen or sixteen year old, medically attested case. Or by a diagram of comparative size: the twelve week fetus would have to be enlarged to a huge apartment building if on the same scale as the dead woman. . . .

There is a remarkably chilling quality to this mulling of campaign tactics, a clinically distancing tone which brings to mind the calculations of those who play nuclear war games at the higher levels of government. And in addition one should note that the mask has slipped here: instead of referring to anti-abortion cadres as the "opposition" Lader comes right out and calls them the "Catholics."

Further on in that paper there is an amusing and uncharacteristic concession:

Among our shock pictures might be those of battered children with attested case histories, or of infanticide cases. *Although the link between the battered child and the unwanted child may not be too firm statistically* [italics added] and infanticides are not common, we may have to stretch the point if need warrants it. . . .

Here is NARAL conceding that abortion may not be the panacea for the battered child problem. The next time abortion advocates claim that "every child a wanted child" will eliminate the battered child, in addition to reminding them that figures on battered children have doubled in the ten years since the dubious blessings of permissive abortion have fallen upon us, you might read that passage from the Founding Father's pen.

Turn if you will to a strategy directive emanating from the Executive Committee of NARAL entitled "Profile of the Opposition." Paragraph thirteen of that document, in discussing how pro-life groups pursue their ends, stated it thus:

Exerting tremendous pressure on legislators: This election year legislators claim they were invited to speak at more Catholic churches than at any time in the past, and asked to either justify a vote on the abortion issue or commit themselves to a position on pending legislation. Catholic legislators particularly are targets for severe pressure. In New York, those who voted for repeal were condemned from the pulpit as murderers and punished by church efforts to defeat their bids for re-election.

The opposition is a threat because it operates within a powerful, influential and established organizational framework with a communications network that can command quick and obedient action; it has substantial funds; its arguments are built around emotionally loaded words that confuse the uninformed; its approach encourages a religious polarization damaging to a democratic society.

Another paragraph in the same paper continues in this manner:

Meeting the polarization threat: As we all know opposition to repeal comes from the church hierarchy, not from most Catholics. Polls confirm time and again that most Catholics do want reform and one out of three favors total repeal. In a religious breakdown of women using the Clergy Consultation Referral Service Catholic women have abortions equal to the Catholic ratio in the total U.S. population.

These passages are notable for the subtle appeal to enlightened modern Catholics to foreswear their allegiance to that shadowy foreign conspiracy and its agents in the United States and to come over to our side. To sweeten the appeal and support those wavering Catholics who wanted to look around and see others of their ilk joining us, NARAL supplied them with fictitious polls and surveys designed to make it appear as if American Catholics were deserting the teachings of the church and the dictates of their consciences in droves. NARAL policy regarding the structuring and use of polls was expressed in these discreet and circumspect terms in the minutes of the Chicago meeting of January 9, 1971, on page five:

It was pointed out that constituent support for the issue [any abortion issue before the public] is best shown before the vote than after. To that end the various [NARAL] groups were encouraged to run local opinion surveys (*careful wording of questions is essential to achieve favorable results*) and to make the results available to the legislators involved.

It may be instructive to look at Lader's writings on the relationship of the Catholic Church to the abortion issue in order to understand more fully the genesis of the Catholic strategy as it was employed by NARAL. In his book *Abortion*, written and published in 1966, he alludes to the "Catholic hierarchy" as a force inimical to what he terms "Legalized abortion—the final freedom." But in his later book, *Abortion II: Making the Revolution*, he really takes the gloves off and roots out the demon in the form of the "Catholic hierarchy." Interestingly, he persists in identifying every anti-abortion figure according to his or her religious affiliation (usually Catholic), though he studiously refrains from characterizing neutral or pro-abortion figures in those terms. Lader's own religious beliefs are never discussed or mentioned but he identified Malcolm Wilson, the lieutenant governor of New York State in 1970, as ". . . a Catholic strongly opposed to abortion"; Hulan Jack, a New York state legislator, as ". . . a black and a Catholic"; Justice William Brennan as ". . . the only Catholic on the [Supreme] Court"; Governor Thomas J. Meskill of Connecticut as ". . . a Republican and a Catholic"; one Dr. James V. McNulty as a ". . . fashionable Los Angeles obstetrician, member of the State Board of Medical Examiners and a Catholic,"and on and on. Neither I nor Assemblyman Albert Blumenthal was ever identified as a Jew, nor was Governor Nelson Rockefeller ever recognized as a Protestant.

The theme persists throughout the book. At one point Lader quotes the *Denver Post* of April 4, 1967, as it described the turmoil in the Colorado senate during the debate on liberalizing the abortion statute:

> A pugnacious, quarrelsome and sometimes shouting crowd dominated by members of the Roman Catholic Church jammed a state senate hearing room Tuesday morning. . . .

Again he quotes Lorenzo Milam, at that time a columnist for the *Seattle Post-Intelligencer*, who commented on the quashing of a proposed liberal abortion bill in the Washington legislature:

> . . . the seven Catholics who help run our state from the comfort and power of the Senate Rules Committee in Olympia . . . two more who are married to Catholics and a handful of others who quiver every time they get a call from the local representative of El [sic] Papa. . . .

and later on in the same column:

> Maybe some day the disciples of El Papa—at least those who sit on the Senate Rules Committee—maybe some day they'll realize that their God may not be the god of the rest of us. . . .

Lader characterizes Milam's outburst as a "blunt attack" and states that Milam refused to retract the column and "left or was fired from the paper." In the report of the executive director of NARAL of September 18, 1969, Milam was explicitly invited to join NARAL, having persumably won his spurs in the anti-Catholic Derby.

The suggestion that Catholic public officials are fatally hindered in their duties by their religious affiliation has its parallels in American history. In 1910 the Georgian congressman and publisher Thomas E. Watson, himself a Baptist, dashed off an editorial in his own weekly newspaper the *Jeffersonian* entitled "The Roman Catholic Hierarchy: The Deadliest Menace To Our Liberties and Our Civilization." In the editorial piece he firmly rejected any suggestion that he bore any prejudice to individual Catholics but regarded the Catholic organization as ". . . an object of profound detestation." Watson had run for vice-president of the United States on the Populist Party ticket in 1896, and in 1904 had been the candidate of that party for president. He and his party were soundly thrashed on both occasions.

The Reverend James B. Dunn, secretary of the Committee of One Hundred in Boston in 1894, asked in a tract published by that august society:

> . . . can a good Romanist be at the same time a loyal American citizen? . . . the Vatican claims absolute and supreme authority in all things civil as well as spiritual, and every member of that church is bound to render to the Pontiff absolute and unquestioning obedience. This being true, is it not quite certain that whatever his personal opinions and feelings might be, he must support the church against the state? Can a Romanist be a good citizen of America?

Paul Blanshard, a respected lawyer and journalist and a soi-disant student of church/state relations, brought anti-Catholicism into the mid-twentieth century fitted out with a tasteful literary style and the furnishings of a first-rate mind. It was anti-Catholicism for the intelligentsia. Books such as *American Freedom and Catholic Power* and *Communism, Democracy and Catholic Power* are putatively serious explorations of the role of the Vatican in American politics, but the preoccupation with the "Catholic hierarchy"—indeed it would not be overstating it to call it an obsession—is unsettling.

However, in all justice, it is unarguable that from the very beginning of the abortion revolution the Catholic Church and its spokesmen took a considerable role in the opposition. This stemmed in part from the doctrine of the church, placing it uncompromisedly and implacably against the destruction of any manifestation of human life. It also stemmed from a failure of leadership from other quarters. Fundamentalist Protestants had not yet discovered their political muscle, and other such disparate groups as Mormons and Orthodox Jews simply didn't have the numbers. Conservative Republicans had been swept away by the Vietnam War Resistance, student riots on college campuses, and the civil rights turbulence.

As NARAL saw it, the Catholic opposition to abortion surfaced publically with a pastoral letter from the Archbishop of Seattle, Thomas A. Connolly, dated April 14, 1970, three days following the signing of the historic new liberal abortion law in New York State. A referendum on abortion in the state of Washington was scheduled for November, 1970, and Connolly exhorted his communicants to ". . . tool up for the Catholic effort." In another communication to the faithful five months later he pleaded for funds to finance the resistance:

> The state committee for the Voice of the Unborn is desperately in need of funds at the moment to continue its excellent campaign on into October, and they would appreciate any financial assistance you may be able to give or procure for them.

In April, 1971, fourteen Catholic bishops in Texas published an open letter in which they stated:

> In June 1970 a Federal court in Dallas declared the abortion laws of Texas unconstitutional. If the judgement of this court stands there will be no law in this state that either prohibits or permits abortion. Whether such a legal situation would be allowed to stand, if it develops or whether new legislation will be passed is not for us to determine, but if abortion is not to be dealt with as the crime we hold it to be, then we are of the opinion that silence in the laws of the state is preferable to positive legal authorization of abortion. . . .

In addition to splitting Catholics into liberal and conservative sects, and using the former to disarm the latter in the abortion conflict, NARAL's Catholic strategy hinged on luring the Catholic

Church out into the open to declare publicly its opposition to abortion reform. Once we had isolated the church in that public posture we would draw attention to its position in support of the war in Vietnam. Since they were the last major institution in the country still uncritically supportive of the war, we would use that unpopular position to prove to those still resistant on the issue of abortion that American public opposition to abortion reform was tantamount to support for the Vietnam War. Disillusionment with the war had peaked by 1970 and with the country intoxicated with the excesses of the "Authority Crisis" it was easy to portray the church as an insensitive, authoritarian war-monger, and association with it or any of its causes as unendurably reactionary, fascistic, and ignorant.

Let it be said: the church helped us in NARAL. The Papal encyclical of 1968 denying both abortion *and* contraception to Catholics was a bonanza for us at NARAL at precisely the correct moment in history. By linking abortion and contraception in the encyclical the Vatican made it impossible for those Catholics who were using birth control to split off the abortion issue, therefore leaving them to pick their own way through the confusing ethical and theological landscape. Many of them ended up in our camp, and we used them with great effect.

Even now United States Catholics retain a significant role in the abortion opposition. Dr. John Willke is the past president of the National Right to Life Committee and a Roman Catholic. But the pro-life group is now a far more ecumenical force than it was ten years ago. The most conspicuous figure in the anti-abortion phalanx is Ronald Reagan, a Protestant president. Fundamentalist Protestant groups such as the Moral Majority and the Religious Roundtable are now the shock troops. It's a reasonable probability that had the Fundamentalist Protestants been active in organized abortion opposition in the late 1960s and early 1970s, we at NARAL would have had a considerably more difficult time selling abortion to the American public. In the public mind Protestant America *is* America, and had Protestant opposition been organized and vociferous early on, permissive abortion might have been perceived as somehow anti-American, the spawn of a cadre of wild-eyed Jewish radicals in New York City.

What continually surprised us in the planning sessions and strategy meetings at NARAL was not only the comparatively mild quality of the organized Catholic opposition but also the virtual absence of response to what was blatantly an anti-Catholic campaign. Even though our artillery was trained on the "Catholic hierarchy," i.e. the prelates and the Vatican, the religious bias was unmistakable. There was no Catholic equivalent of the Anti-defamation League of the B'nai Brith or the NAACP. Even the organized church itself did not directly respond to our flagrant xenophobia and virulent anti-Catholicism, but confined itself decently, (though as it turned out disastrously) to the issue of abortion. It was not until 1973, in the wake of the Roe v. Wade decision, that such organizations as the Catholic League for Religious and Civil Rights were organized. The CLRCR was founded by the Reverend Virgil C. Blum in that year and since then has for the most part devoted itself to three areas of activity: abortion, educational rights, and immigration. The CLRCR is independent of the organized Catholic Church and privately funded.

Had such organizations as the Catholic League for Religious and Civil Rights begun functioning in 1968, I doubt that NARAL and allied abortion advocates could have prevailed as easily as we did. Among other things, it's reasonable to assume that in answer to our portraying the Catholic Church and, by implication, most Catholics as medieval, reactionary, and archaic, they would have pointed to such as Dorothy Day's and Peter Maurin's Catholic Worker movement of the 1930s and 40s as more advanced and more truly progressive than many of the ultra-liberal causes of the 1960s. The *Catholic Worker* was a newspaper as well as a social movement, and it was directed mainly at the huge army of unemployed during the Great Depression. Latterly, the *Catholic Worker* established hospitality houses in large urban areas where the hungry and the needy could sleep, eat, and rest with no social or governmental pressure upon them. The *Worker* supported union activity, pacifism (even during World War II), civil rights for black Americans, and was an early and outspoken foe of nuclear weapons and the war in Vietnam. But by the mid-1960s it was a small and inconspicuous movement with none of the flash or panache to attract media attention.

Currently the CLRCR might cite such enterprises as the *National Catholic Reporter*, a Catholic newspaper published in Kansas City, Missouri, and distinguished by its independent, liberal posture on many issues affecting Catholics, including national issues such as third world problems and Latin American politics. The paper supports the concept of married priests, the nuclear freeze movement, and the diversion of funds from armaments to poverty relief. It is vocal in its criticism of many of the policies of the Reagan administration and follows closely in the enlightened, strong-willed tradition of the *Catholic Worker*.

Had the CLRCR been founded earlier they might have recruited Michael Harrington, author of an extraordinary book entitled *The Other America*, published in 1962, as the spokesman for an involved Catholicism. This was a graphic and dramatic disclosure of an America most of us preferred to ignore: the down-trodden, the disenfranchised, the hungry, and the hopeless. The book was sufficiently influential among policy-makers and social architects in the mid-1960s that it is generally credited as having been a major stimulus to the war on poverty of the Johnson administration.

Instead, NARAL was busily thrashing the Board of Directors of the Catholic Church with an odd farrago of devices ranging from rhetoric, resembling at times the notorious Protocols of Zion, to outright intimidation of key legislators purely on the basis of their religion, and there was no public outcry against these and other equally fulsome tactics. The media discreetly ignored the carefully crafted bigotry we were peddling. Many media people were young college-educated liberal Catholics, just the kind we had succeeded in splitting off from the faithful flock, and they were not about to disgrace their newly-won spurs as intelligentsia by embarrassing the liberals with anything as crass as an accusation of prejudice. Prejudice was something evil directed at Jews and blacks, not Catholics. But had our fulminations been anti-Semitic or anti-black there would have been the most powerful keening in the media—strong enough to have destroyed NARAL.

Not only did we execrate the Catholic Church as the demonic opposition to our crusade, but on the infrequent occasions when the church did summon up the courage to respond to our mostly intemperate attacks, we would accuse them of polarizing the country along religious lines. Here was NARAL churning out pamphlets, circulars, white papers, and media handouts excoriating the church and accusing it of turning the abortion issue into a religious war, and meanwhile we were guilty of precisely that, except on the side of the liberal angels. For sheer chutzpah it had no modern parallel. It reminds one of the old story about Charles "Racehorse" Haynes, the phenomenally successful trial attorney in Houston. It is said that he would instruct his students in courtroom tactics that if all logical argument failed, sheer gall must be the ultimate weapon. He would illustrate his lesson with the following example:

> Say my dog bites you, and you take me to court. I will defend myself with the following arguments: 1. My dog never bites anyone, and 2. my dog was tied up that day, and 3. I don't believe he did bite you—show me your bite, and 4. I DON'T EVEN OWN A DOG.

NARAL had at least one Protestant minister on its executive committee (Jesse Lyons), and a number of other ministers and rabbis on its board of directors. It welcomed, even actively solicited, the support of such organizations as the National Council of Churches. It was wheeling up all manner of heavy religious guns to fire at the Catholic Church while simultaneously screaming out accusations of religious polarization.

NARAL opposed on principle the involvement of religious groups in politics, conveniently ignoring the leadership role clerics had played in that other pivotal revolutionary movement of the 1960s—the civil rights action. No one needs reminding that the Reverend Martin Luther King was a Protestant clergyman, as were many of his cohorts. When the Catholic bishops speak out strongly against abortion they are polarizing the country along religious lines and attempting to subvert the Constitution and the Bill of Rights, but let those same bishops formulate a strong public position against the manufacture, deployment, and use of nuclear weapons and they are considered concerned citizens exercising their democratic right of free speech and participation in the democratic process. What is one to say in the face of such unimaginable gall except maybe: "I don't even own a dog."

Addendum: from the minutes of the meeting of the Executive Committee of NARAL of June 15, 1970:

> Chaired by executive committee member Dr. Jesse Lyons, pastoral minister of the Riverside Church, this meeting of nineteen participants was held . . . on June 15. Included were representatives of the National Council of Churches; YMCA; Women's Division of the United Presbyterian Church; Union of American Hebrew Congregations; Lutheran Church in America; Women's Division of the United Method-

ist Church; United Church of Christ; United Methodist Church; United Presbyterian Church in the U.S.A.; Clergy Consultation Service; American Jewish Congress; American Friends Service Committee; American Ethical Union, and American Baptist Convention. Interested but unable to attend: Church Women United; Episcopal Churchmen of the U.S.A.; Unitarian Universalist Association; Women's Federation Episcopal Church; B'nai Brith, and the American Humanist Association.

Purpose of this meeting: to explore ways of implementing organization positions on abortion and increasing pressure for repeal . . . nationwide. NARAL at the same time . . . would work through them to flush out support and action from churches, synagogues, and other religious-affiliated social and welfare organizations.

A fine secular band of clerical latitudinarians, lacking only Scientologists and Moonies on the list.

Long before the Reverend Donald Wildmon and his group threatened to boycott the products of advertisers sponsoring especially violent and/or sexually explicit television shows, to the howls of the liberal media who accused Wildmon of censorship and a myriad of other un-American sins, consider this appendage to the executive director's report of the minutes of the meeting of the Executive Committee of NARAL. We were discussing the local furor erupting over the contents of a CBS TV show called "Maude" in which abortion had been disparagingly presented as an acceptable alternative for an unplanned pregnancy. These minutes read as follows:

The *National Catholic Reporter* of January 26, 1973, reports that two sponsors of the Maude show [Thomas Lipton Inc. and Norelco] have withdrawn their commercials in response to protests by opponents of abortion. Get out letters to the presidents of these two companies expressing shock at this action as reported by NCR, saying that it amounts to censorship of relevant programs on social issues, and asking them to re-evaluate their ill-advised decision, particularly in view of the [1973] Supreme Court decision. You might also mention *boycotting their products.* [Italics added]

In this tumultuous second half of the twentieth century American society has yielded itself to an impressive number of radical social changes. A partial list includes such movements as civil rights for blacks, feminism, loosening of divorce laws, abolition of laws regulating contraception, gay liberation, and consumerism. Robert Nisbet, in his monumental study *Social Change and History* instructs us that the social behavior of a given society or civilization tends to persist, to resist change; forces which necessitate change precipitate crisis of some degree and that crisis cannot be peaceably resolved until the society makes a new adaptation based on a synthesis of the old pre-change condition with the new. Quite obviously the more sweeping the change, the slower the process of adaptation. Racial matters and civil rights have surely precipitated a broader and deeper crisis than, say, consumerism, and this society has still failed to arrive at a pacific adaptation to them. But adapt it will, as it has to feminism, principally because the arguments on their behalf were based on indisputably decent, logical tenets and ineluctably sound biological data. Unlike the abortion revolution they were not sold to the American public through a combination of religious bias and scientific sleight-of-hand.

Has there been any similar major social change or political movement dependent to some extent upon an anti-religious warp for its success? Abortion was, of course, not merely a sweeping social change but was also an integral part of feminist politics and later a hotly debated plank in the Democratic party platform; in recent years some candidates for elective office have lived or died by it. Or is abortion a sui generis, a one-of-a-kind in modern history?

Oscar Wilde once said that he could resist anything but temptation. The temptation to dredge up once again the National Socialist movement in modern Germany in attempting to answer these questions is undeniably enormous, but the historical roots of the modern German state, the parlous condition of Germany in the immediate post-World War I years as it labored under the revisionist conditions, the stated aims of the National Socialist party, and the incomparable Holocaust, all forbid us to succumb to that temptation. I have long felt that the Holocaust was an event so unspeakably evil, so unique that it must be held apart, quarantined in perpetuo in history. To use it as a basis for comparison with any other malevolence in history is to trivialize it. Further, the crime of permissive abortion is such an unmitigated evil in its own right that it stands on its own, requiring comparison with nothing else.

American history yields up nothing quite like the abortion issue in terms of the uses of an anti-religious warp as a successful political instrument. The sizable immigration of the Irish into the United States in the 1840s and 50s stirred up a cauldron of xenophobia and anti-Catholicism which resulted in the consolidation of school systems throughout the Northeast, the area in which most of the Irish immigrants settled, into a state-run enterprise with heavy emphasis on Protestant teachings. Catholic parochial schools were denied taxpayer funds, and Protestant prayer and the King James Bible were staples of the public school system. America had always been a Protestant country but the reorganization of the public school system into a formally Protestant mode signalled a recrudescence of anti-Catholicism in the mid-1800s. The Protestant character and coloration of the public school system persisted until 1963 when the United States Supreme Court outlawed prayer in schools, and it is significant that the main thrust for the re-institution of school prayer has come not from Catholics but from the Protestant groups. In 1925 in Oregon there was an attempt to force all children into the public school system, in effect illegalizing the Catholic parochial schools, but the attempt was defeated in the Supreme Court. This, too, was a thinly veiled foray by the anti-Catholic elements.

Immigration legislation has long been a target for anti-Catholic feeling. The majority of immigrants entering the Atlantic seaports have been from largely Catholic countries and there have been periodic attempts to have their numbers sharply limited or even excluded. The Reed-Johnson act of 1924, proceeding from irrational fears of the "swamping" of America with immigrants from Southern and Eastern Europe, imposed heavy restrictions on immigration from those predominantly Catholic areas.

Because immigrants into the Atlantic ports settled for the most part in urban areas and were generally unskilled laborers, they were recruited into the burgeoning labor union movement. The resistance to that movement was, at least in part, a response to the threat of Catholic power. Much of the anti-labor activity, and even legislation, was streaked with anti-Catholic bias. Even the bizarre anti-Communist raids known as the "Red Scare," instigated by Attorney General A. Mitchell Palmer in 1919–1920, were tainted with the xenophobic anti-Catholic warp.

But the anti-Catholicism which contaminated educational politics, immigration legislation, and labor legislation in the nineteenth century was invoked in *resistance* to social change. Heavy ethnic immigration into the United States threatened to upset the comfortable Protestant status quo, and was to be fought by the xenophobics here at all costs.

In 1834 Samuel F. B. Morse published his *Foreign Conspiracy Against the Liberties of the United States*, warning that ". . . all America west of the Alleghenies will eventually be a Catholic country" and urging Americans to close the doors of immigration forthwith to keep America "pure."

The only use of anti-Catholicism to further a social change previous to the abortion issue may be found in the unfortunate Prohibition experiment. Prohibition was the creature of the Baptist and Methodist Churches and was forcefully resisted by the Catholic Church. James Cardinal Gibbons of Baltimore spoke publically against it, and for his pains was roundly savaged by the New York Anti-Saloon League. Prohibition was upheld as the great Protestant reform. Opposition to Prohibition in the 1920s was a politically dangerous enterprise especially if one happened to be Catholic, as Governor Al Smith of New York learned in the presidential campaign of 1928.

But even Prohibition, though it incorporated generous drafts of anti-Catholicism in its successful move to amend the United States Constitution, did not design its strategy around its anti-religious appeal. At its core was an undeniable nostalgia for the Puritan simplicity of colonial, uncontaminated, pristine America, combined with the jejune strictures of down-home Protestantism, and Catholics did not present an institutionalized opposition. In fact it was not even important to the Prohibitionists whether or not Catholics opposed them. Anti-Catholicism became casually, almost accidentally, a tactic that would be later used as an amendment in the campaign.

But as we have seen from the position papers, anti-Catholic warp was a central strategy, a keystone of the abortion movement. It was, in a sense, the self-fulfilling prophecy: knowing that the Catholic Church would vigorously oppose abortion we laced the campaign with generous dollops of anti-Catholicism, and once the monster was lured out of the cave in response to the abortion challenge and the nakedly biased line we could make the Catholic Church the point man of the opposition. The more vigorously the church opposed, the stronger the appeal of the anti-Catholic line became to the liberal media, to the northeastern political establishment, to the leftist elements of the Protestant Church, and to Catholic intellectuals themselves.

The anti-Catholic tactic was not only fruitful in rallying the most influential and the most articulate elements of American political life to our side in the late 1960s, it was also central to the maintenance of unity within the High Command of the movement. In providing a palpable, visible opposition it allowed those of us setting policy and devising strategy to occupy ourselves with an enemy. We were kept too busy to contemplate in any critical way the quintessential brutality of permissive abortion. There was always another bishop to denounce, another pastoral letter to be rebutted, another cardinal to excoriate. Even for those of us like myself, who were convinced first-hand of the medical merits of permissive abortion and didn't really require any shoring up on the issue, there was still a comfort in the notion of such an unenlightened authoritarian opposition as the Catholic Church. It felt good to be on the side of the intellectual angels. It was the dark elitism of the Knights of the Great Forest, of the cohorts of Professor Nilus.

There has been, then, no social change in American history as sweeping, as potent in American family life, or as heavily dependent upon an anti-religious bias for its success as the abortion movement. Could it have succeeded without the use of the Catholic card? And has the use of the anti-Catholic strategy fatally flawed the movement? Has its moral stature been dangerously weakened by the use of such a morally detestable tactic, leaving aside for the moment the morality of abortion itself?

There are of course no simple answers to such complex socio-political and ethical questions. By the mid-1960s, laws regulating the availability of contraceptives had been largely set aside, and there had been none of the blatant and virulent anti-Catholicism which marked the abortion movement. This is not to say, of course, that the Catholic Church was silent on the issue of contraception: papal encyclicals, pastoral letters, and public policy statements sprang forth in opposition. But liberal social reformers had not yet dared cross the line which divided courage from audacity, sexual adventurousness from destruction of life. Further, substantial numbers of educated second and third-generation American Catholics had been using contraceptives covertly and the church could not afford to commit its tactical reserves to that campaign; perhaps the Church suspected even then that another, more critical battle was to be fought on the ground of abortion. Feminism was on the march, and the woolly-headed Malthusiasts of the population panic (remember Zero Population Growth, and Ehrlich's Population Bomb?) were all preaching The End Of The

World a week from next Monday and persuading credulous, susceptible youngsters in their late teens and early twenties to have themselves sterilized in the interests of controlling population growth in India. (I and many other gynecologists who do micro-surgical tubal reconstruction are still busy undoing the reproductive damage these poor children were cajoled into inflicting upon themselves.) Unrestricted access to contraception for adults was an unstoppable reform, principally because there were no compelling life-and-death issues inherent in it, and because effective opposition to it could be based on nothing more than nostalgic appeals to the joys of large families, and the stern disapproval of sex qua pleasure.

But the foray into the abolition of abortion laws was a far more daunting, far more audacious enterprise. Public support for unrestricted abortion, according to our sources in NARAL, was certainly less than one tenth of one per cent of the United States electorate. Compared to the tens of millions a year who covertly bought and used some form of contraception, perhaps a hundred thousand or so procured abortions. Contraception was cheap, carried with it no surgical risks, and the flouting of the laws did not make page four of the *New York Daily News*. Who can ever recall an article beginning:

> A vicious ring of condom purveyors was broken in the Bronx yesterday, as a result of a coordinated effort on the part of the police and the district attorney's office. According to a police spokesman the ring had been selling condoms from a dingy kitchen in a small flat in west 176th street and the Grand Concourse. The ring, headed up by a man previously jailed for having smuggled ten thousand diaphragms through the Port of New York, was said to be clearing thirty-five dollars a day in its illegal operation.

True, the first tentative steps had been taken to loosen the abortion laws with the passage of the model A.L.I. statutes in states such as California, Colorado, North Carolina, and Hawaii; still, these laws were light years away from unrestricted permissive abortion. They clothed this liberty in the respectable raiments of medical judgement, and passed on the burden of decision to the historically conservative medical profession. To propose that the decision be ceded to the individual woman was a political audacity of an unparalleled degree in America, even in the tumultuous 1960s. Even those of us devising strategy at NARAL recognized that such a proposal was unsaleable and softened it with the slogan: "a decision between a woman and her doctor." Giving it just the barest patina of a medical judgement made it infinitely more acceptable and politically more palatable. In actual fact, the abortion decision is no more the doctor's than a nose job is. It is the woman alone who decides if she wants her nose fixed, or her breasts done, or her child destroyed, and she merely involves the doctor as the instrument of her decision. In fact there are jurisdictions in the United States which allow nurses and/or midwives to perform the abortion, where there is no requirement of a physician. So much for that slogan.

We have an instrument in the practice of clinical medicine called the retrospectoscope. The view through the retrospectoscope is almost always clear, precise, and correct. It is a favorite instrument for use in staff conferences, teaching seminars, and medical publications. But for once it fails me. Even through the retrospectoscope I am not sure whether or not it was necessary to "play the Catholic card" in the selling of permissive abortion in America. There is no question that it was an incalculably powerful tactic, especially because there was no effective, coordinated political or legal opposition to it. Prelates of the Catholic Church might occasionally complain that we at NARAL were unrestrained and immoral, but at that time there was no Catholic League for Religious and Civil Rights which might have challenged us publically, taken us to court on anti-defamation and civil rights issues, and put the lie to the factitious and often nonsensical medical and scientific claims we were making (five to ten thousand women dying annually from abortion, a million abortions a year). But was this tactic vital to the selling of abortion?

I doubt it. By the late 1960s historical momentum in the form of the authority crisis was irresistible in areas of social and political reform. I believe that had we confined ourselves to the medical issues, as deceitfully as we presented them; to the feminist appeal; to the population issue; to the persuasive, seductive argument that laws which are flouted a million times a year ought to be wiped off the books (how many people cheat on their taxes or break the speed limit?); to the argument that there were rights to privacy (indeed to abortion itself) to be quarried from the United States Constitution; and to the impetus of the sexual revolution, we would probably have succeeded anyway.

And it would have been a cleaner, less tainted victory. From the vantage point of fifteen years I carry with me a heavy baggage of emotion. The loss of life as a result of my efforts is of such massive scale that I have no words which adequately express my feelings. They transcend guilt (a pop-psych word so over-used as to be meaningless), remorse, regret, contrition, even sorrow and grief. As a Joycean, I am drawn to the phrase "agenbite of inwit." It most accurately depicts the splanchnic pain of the unforgivable crime.

On a lesser level, I am heartily ashamed of the use of the anti-Catholic ploy. It was grubby, dangerously divisive, and probably superfluous. It was a reincarnation of McCarthyism at its worst. We were seeing Catholic demons everywhere, where Joe McCarthy had seen communists twenty years earlier. And we were those liberals who most vehemently had execrated McCarthy. Instead of waving spurious lists of communists from the State Department we were busily fabricating casualty lists of women killed in the abortion wars. Our slogans like "a woman's right to control her own body" were as misleading and as incendiary as his slogans like "soft on communism." And I bear a special onus in that I had been caught up in the McCarthy madness myself, even though only peripherally, fifteen years before. My aged, revered father would call it a "Shandeh fah yidden" (scandal for the Jews).

Concededly, the parallel to the McCarthy phenomenon of the 1950s cannot be pushed too far. McCarthy's war on the communists in government was a fever that had no purpose except the constant roiling of the body politic, the thirst for headlines, and the satisfaction of perpetual chaos. Our anti-Catholic chase was a keenly focussed weapon, full of purpose and design. But like McCarthyism it claimed its victims. Not just the millions of tiny bodies sent through the remorseless choppers of the Berkely suction machines (why aren't the nuclear freezniks and the napalm protestors of other years out demonstrating in front of the Berkely plant?), but those innocent, well-meaning persons who had the courage to resist the madness and to put their bodies against the machine and be brutalized by it.

Consider the case of Robert Byrn. Perhaps the most nakedly bigoted, fecklessly anti-Catholic campaign NARAL ever mounted was the Robert Byrn affair. Byrn, characterized in the *New York Times* as ". . . a forty year old Roman Catholic bachelor" had gone before Justice Lester Holtzman in the county of Queens on December 2, 1971, to have himself declared guardian of unborn infant Roe, that is special guardian for all unborn infants vulnerable to abortion. In this regard it is interesting that the *New York Times* did not characterize Justice Holtzman as a married Jew. Having legally established his relationship as advocate for the unborn, Byrn then brought suit in the New York Supreme Court for an injunction on abortions in New York's municipal hospitals. On January 5, 1972, Justice Francis X. Smith issued a temporary injunction to ban such abortions. In the *Times* coverage of the hearing, it's stated that Attorney General Louis Lefkowitz vowed to do everything in his power to keep the abortion mills grinding. Lefkowitz's marital and religious status were ignored. In that same article one Nancy Stearns, a lawyer for the grandly-named Center for Constitutional Rights, was quoted to the effect that Mr. Byrn should put up a forty-thousand dollar bond for each woman "forced" to have a child as a result of the granting of the injunction. Apart from the question of what Pickwickian mathematics Stearns employed to arrive at this truly astonishing figure, one also notes that Jane Brody to whom the article was attributed failed to describe Stearns as a single Jewess.

But that article is most noteworthy for its utter lack of balance and for its shameful, supine surrender to the NARAL line. Consider the rest of the article:

> In a statement issued yesterday the National Association for Repeal of Abortion Laws [NARAL] said: "A Roman Catholic judge [Smith] has initiated a disgraceful incident in judicial history. He has followed religious dogma in deciding a case in a court of law."

Though Brody failed to comment specifically on Justice Smith's religious affiliation, the identification is pellucidly clear. So, while Roman Catholics Francis X. Smith and Robert Byrn were clearly identified by their religious affiliation, Justice Holtzman, Attorney General Lefkowitz, and Counselor Stearns were not so designated. Ms. Brody herself chose to remain shrouded in journalistic anonymity though in justice shouldn't she have declared her own religious and marital status? This was an egregious inequity in a newspaper which some years before had banned identification of criminal suspects with respect to race.

But to give her her due, Brody, or at least her rewrite people, appear to have exercised a modicum of restraint in failing to quote the entire text of the NARAL statement on the affair. It was, in fact, the embodiment of the most vicious and undisguised bigotry on the American political stage in recent memory, calculated to make George Lincoln Rockwell sick with envy:

> A Roman Catholic judge has initiated a disgraceful incident in judicial history. He has followed religious dogma—and at that the belief of only a minority of Catholics—in deciding a case in a court of law. He has permitted a few religious fanatics to frustrate the will of the people, and their legislators. No judge in American history has ever held that a fetus is a person in the meaning of the Fourteenth Amendment to the United States Constitution.

NARAL was, as usual, guilty of mis-representing the facts. A Massachusetts court in 1969 had held that: ". . . the evidence clearly establishes that the product of human conception, whether it be in the state of embryo, zygote, or fetus, may properly be classified as human life. It is a human being in and of itself in the sense that it is an individual, entirely human in origin, human in its characteristics and human in its destiny." The NARAL text continues:

> Religious belief alone should not disqualify a judge if he is able to put it aside in reaching his judicial decision. But where he cannot free himself from prejudice in his conduct on the bench, his oath of office requires him to disqualify himself from sitting on such a case. NARAL therefore urges that the appropriate authorities should investigate Judge Smith's failure to disqualify himself from this case.

This is of course vintage Lader. In his book *Abortion II: Making The Revolution* Lader described the Byrn affair as ". . . another Catholic offensive."

The Appellate Division of the New York Court system subsequently overturned Justice Smith's temporary injunction on abortion by a 4–1 decision, ruling that the unborn child was not a legal person. The majority opinion declared the following:

> In our opinion the extent to which fetal life should be protected is a value judgement not committed to the discretion of judges, but reposing instead in the representative branches of the government. . . .

At least there is no reference to Romanism here. And although we at NARAL chortled over this decision at the time, had this exemplary line of legal thinking been followed by the United States Supreme Court it would have nullified the pro-abortion argument in the Roe v.

Wade decision, indeed there may never have been a Roe v. Wade case, and would likely have changed the course of social history.

Byrn appealed the case in the New York State Court of Appeals, the highest court in the state, and was defeated by a 5–2 margin. An effort was made in January, 1973, to bring the case before the United States Supreme Court but Justice Marshall, acting for the Second Circuit, denied the application. Roe v. Wade was about to mushroom up and over the country.

Today, eleven years removed from those turbulent days, Robert Byrn reflects calmly and without rancor on his historic, doomed bid to halt the abortion juggernaut. The Bronx born and bred professor of Criminal Law at Fordham University (still a bachelor and a Roman Catholic) sits quietly in his cramped office on the second floor of the Law Building. His back is to the single window which overlooks the cluster of neo-Mussolini behemoths that comprise the Lincoln Center. His hands rest contentedly over his spreading paunch as he replies to his questioner with answers as direct and responsive as the ideal witness in the box. No, he was neither surprised nor embittered by the patently unfair and ad hominem treatment he was accorded by the press. "You can't go into something like this prepared to resent it," he says. "It's like the army; you're either amused by it, or you hang yourself. I don't think the bachelor part was malicious— that was even amusing. But the constant harping on my Catholicism was malicious."

Generously he declines any credit for having devised the tactic of applying to become the guardian of all the unborn between four and twenty-four weeks facing extinction in the New York abortion lazarettos of 1972. That was the brainchild of Thomas Ford, his counsel during those proceedings, and of A. Lawrence Washburn, another attorney working with him at the time. His diffident laugh emerges as a soft bark and he says: "They're both Roman Catholics, you know, but married and with children."

Though ridiculed and savaged by the media of the era, Byrn looks back almost contentedly on the affair, as a great general might look back on a classic campaign modelled on the best of Clausewitz, though it resulted unfortunately in the decimation of his forces. Of course he would have liked to have won, think of all the lives that could have been saved, but at least legal form was preserved impeccably throughout; the system functioned perfectly though it failed to work. He gazes over the legal caricatures framed and hung on the long side wall of his office, particularly pleased with a Hogarth he picked up for five dollars and a Daumier he paid only fifteen for many years ago, and reflects: "I think it was something that had to be done, and I'm glad I did it." He is regretful that the issue is no longer within the exclusive and tidy purview of the professionals, the doctors and lawyers, but has been spirited away by feminists, entrepreneurs, political candidates, and TV producers. In the old days, he muses, he didn't even mind the ". . . occasional Larry Lader."

Byrn is still involved in the anti-abortion cause, working on the constitutional questions. Twisting the large Fordham ring (class of '53) on the third finger of his left hand he offers this: "The Human Life Bill is the best bet, but there *are* constitutional questions and doubts. . . ."

As the visitor leaves his office, he notices bookshelves to the left of the door which contain a great many volumes on the abortion issue. There is one shelf of bric-a-brac. A brown larger-than-life coffee cup squats there, and across its belly:

> Old lawyers never die
> They just lose their appeal.

It's almost reassuring to know that, like diamonds, some political distempers are forever. Lawrence Lader, whose fertile brain devised the Catholic card in the abortion revolution of the 1960s, is still at it fifteen years later. Like a heat-seeking missile, mindlessly locking on those steamy scarlet robes, Lader is still chasing the foreign Vatican devils, this time with his own little band of Narodnicki called the Abortion Rights Mobilization. This dissident splinter faction has little or nothing to do with abortion rights but is fervently dedicated to the proposition that the tax exemption of the Roman Catholic Church be revoked on the grounds that it involves itself in secular political affairs such as abortion, though curiously they took no umbrage from the American Catholic bishops' recent policy statement favoring a nuclear halt. His single-minded vendetta, almost an indée-fixe, is not only massively irrelevant given the current players in the abortion struggle, but is pathetically telescopic in that it scants the leadership role of the Protestant fundamentalists in the pro-life cause. Like Castlereagh he persists doggedly in his obsession, locked eternally in a late 1960s esto perpetuo.

Abortion Rights Mobilization is a one-celled creature, a political paramecium. It occupies a tiny office at 175 Fifth Avenue in New York City, and is staffed by a single secretary and a part-time worker. When one peruses the list of the names of the board of directors, there are no surprises. The executive vice president is one Lana Clark Phelan, a former vice president of NARAL, and an old confidant and political doppelgänger of Lader. Phelan co-authored the infamous *Abortion Handbook* with Pat Maginnis, a primer on do-it-yourself abortion methods. That book, published in 1969 by an obscure publishing house in North Hollywood, was required reading for new recruits in NARAL and has a rather grisly chapter on the use of such instruments as knitting needles, coathangers, raw spaghetti (yes, pasta), and douches of kerosene, turpentine, and leaded gasoline.

Other old reliables, refugees from the bitter and divisive internecine warfare in the NARAL ranks in the mid-1970s, include such familiar names as Dr. Edgar Keemer, an obstetrician-gynecologist practicing in Detroit and another ex-vice president of NARAL, Councilwoman Carol Greitzer, a one-time president of NARAL, and Susan Brownmiller, a writer known chiefly for her spleeny diatribe on rape entitled *Against Our Will.* Brownmiller is a prominent feminist, and her book was about as daring a literary and social treatise as an all-out attack on herpes. Two other grizzled veterans on the board are Manfred Ohrenstein, minority leader in the New York State legislature, and Percy Sutton, former borough president of Manhattan and another NARAL apostate. There are also two token Catholics on the board, one Joseph T. Skeha and the other Reverend Joseph O'Rourke who styles himself as president of Catholics for Free Choice.

Predictably, ARM literature putters endlessly with the usual Lader line: anti-Romanism. From time to time it pauses to take an absent-minded swipe at the fundamentalist Protestant right (Moral Majority, Religious Roundtable, and so forth), but it's clear that its heart is still in the Roman highlands. Here is a published policy statement from ARM:

Destruction of Church-State Separation
Pushed By Catholic Bishops

First Attack on United States Law Banning Religions From Political
Campaigns Looms As Major Threat To First Amendment

In a startling attempt to overthrow a traditional safeguard of church-state separation long considered a bastion of the First Amendment, the National Conference of Catholic Bishops' U.S. Catholic Conference has asked the Federal Court in New York (Southern District) to declare a crucial tax law unconstitutional. This attack by a leading religious group would seriously endanger the First Amendment prohibition against religious intervention into political campaigns that has been an American tradition for two hundred years, states Lawrence Lader, ARM President. "It is clear that some churches want to take over the governing of this country. It would mean that the vast money and organizing power of the Catholic hierarchy—and of fundamentalists, the so-called Moral Majority as well—could be thrown against office-holders and candidates running for President, Congress, or the local City Council."

This rather dyspeptic eructation is the overture to an announcement that ARM has instituted a suit against the Roman Catholic Church in America for abuses of tax laws which prohibit participation or intervention in any political campaign on behalf of any candidate for public office by tax-exempt organizations (Sections 501-C3 and 501-h of the IRS Code). In this almost endearingly quixotic enterprise Lader intends nothing less than the revocation of the tax-exempt status of the Catholic Church. Why he slights the fundamentalist Protestants is unexplained. Conveniently Lader forgets that in the early days of the NARAL wars we Jedi knights unapologetically recruited and exploited such tax-exempt church groups as the National Council of Churches, the Unitarian Church, and the like.

And the pro-abortion tactic is dismayingly unchanged. In another ARM pamphlet there is a headline: "Victorious Italian Abortion Rights Leaders in U.S. To Reveal Strategy of 70% Landslide." Here ARM declares that it intends to bring three prominent women members of the Italian Parliament in addition to an Italian Catholic priest and a professor of Public Health in Rome to the United States to explain how the Italian electorate in a national referendum in May, 1981, defeated an attempt to repeal the Italian abortion law by an alleged seventy per cent. The prevailing law in Italy permits abortion up to ninety days of pregnancy for all women of eighteen and older and the abortions are at government expense. I was in Italy at the time of this referendum. I arrived there the day Pope John Paul II was shot and spoke publically at many large gatherings on behalf of the Italian pro-life movement. The truth is that the portion of the referendum which proposed rolling back the permissive early abortion law was defeated two to one, but a more important proposal on this same referendum advocating legalizing abortion throughout the entire pregnancy, a condition we have in the United States, was overwhelmingly defeated by a margin of eight to one.

Where was ARM when the Rabbinical Council of America, a major American Orthodox Jewish organization, held a five-day meeting in Miami Beach in which it urged that this nation re-examine permissive abortion laws, endorse federal aid for private schools, and concern itself with the general deterioration of moral values in American society? The rabbis specifically proposed that legislators in the separate states ". . . should submit their abortion statutes to a serious evaluation in view of the experiences of several states in the past year." It is almost unnecessary to point out that the anti-abortion position has never been identified in the liberal media as a Jewish plot and that when Justice Holtzman granted Mr. Byrn his request to become guardian of all the unborn in risk of abortion in the New York City hospitals he was not attacked as an unwitting Jewish tool of a ferocious Hebraic cabal working its will on the American body politic and conspiring to destroy the Constitution.

The Holocaust in Europe has, I suppose, worked to establish anti-Semitism unfair and un-American, much as slavery and its sequel in the civil rights movement of the 1960s have designated racism infra dig. Not that anti-Semitism has disappeared any more than racism has, but that it is intellectually unfashionable at this time and no "educated" person would permit him or herself to succumb to it. But Catholics, despite all the brutality and killing attributable to anti-Catholicism in history, have known nothing comparable to the Holocaust. Thus anti-Catholicism is tolerated and even encouraged in America at the close of the twentieth century. Revisionist historians may find permissive abortion to be the Catholic Holocaust (even though most of the bodies are not Catholic) until something worse comes along.

Did the anti-Catholic tactic fatally stigmatize the abortion revolution? What does the use of such a despicable tactic tell us of the moral stature of the movement? After all, the tactic clearly violates the spirit of the Constitution, and would in effect set up a two-class system in America separating observing Catholics from the rest of us. Is this social change an end so fatally flawed by its means that it is fundamentally unstable and reversible?

Not even the most zealous defenders of the pro-abortion cause claim a lofty moral stature for their side. The most they can claim is a questionable and undependable political right vulnerable to nullification by a less ultra liberal, more biologically enlightened Supreme Court, and an irrational brand of medical utilitarianism in which 1.5 million unborn infants are destroyed annually to bring the maternal mortality rate down from twenty per hundred thousand live births to ten per hundred thousand live births and to reduce sharply the number of injuries to women suffered as a result of septic abortion. The reasoning here is roughly as sound as proposing that the breasts of all women be amputated at the age of thirty in order to reduce the toll from cancer of the breast. The maternal mortality rate was falling sharply even before the era of permissive abortion, as Hilgers has demonstrated repeatedly in his rather elegant bio-statistical studies on the question, and there is every reason to believe that it would have continued to fall as our therapeutic weaponry became increasingly more efficient and sophisticated.

As for the political liberty won by the Abortion People, the woman's right to control her own body, we have already analyzed in another section how biologically specious and misleading this slogan is. Even if, in a moment of grand generosity, one were to grant its validity, the control of the means of reproduction was won with the abolition of contraceptive laws, aided by the loosening of divorce laws and the passage of equal rights laws in the various states. To seize the factory at night with no one inside it, and to turn it over to the people may be a moral cause in the eyes of those so politically inclined, but to seize the factory in the middle of the day when only a group of defenseless children is manning it, and to line those children up against the wall and shoot them (and to repeat the assault and the shooting daily for ten years) can hardly be considered in the same category of morality. In any civilized person's lexicon, it has the ring of Stalinist morality, which is no morality at all.

Lader, in his book *The Bold Brahmins*, recounts the history of the Abolitionist movement in the years 1831–1863 and speaks almost reverently of the leaders of the movement: Wendell Phillips, William Lloyd Garrison, Theodore Parker, and Thomas Wentworth Higginson. Indeed, he points out that although they were dismissed in the beginning as annoying fanatics, they were great men who: ". . . moved the nation toward its greatest moral decision." In his comprehensive account of this movement and in the biographical sketches of these leaders there is no trace of bigotry in these great men, no appeal to religious polarization in their cause. To their eternal credit the Brahmins of the Abolitionist movement spurned the support of the anti-Catholic Know-Nothings who voiced Abolitionist sentiments. One finds no fabrication of data, no deceitful manipulation of the public, no suppression of relevant material here. For Lader to have equated himself with these great men, even by implication, and drawn parallels between the abortion monster and the ineffable purity of the Brahmin cause, is a despicable claim in itself.

In the most febrile era of the civil rights movement in the United States from 1955 to 1965, the Church of the Latter Day Saints (Mormons) would not permit blacks to become priests. The church line was that blacks were the direct descendants of Ham, and thus unworthy of participation in the most solemn rites of the church. This line has been repudiated, and blacks are now welcomed into the priesthood, yet none of the leaders of the civil rights movement— Martin Luther King Jr., A. Phillip Randolph, Whitney Young, Ralph Abernathy—none of these luminaries had to stoop to anti-Mormonism and accuse the Mormons of fomenting infinitely complex conspiracies designed to thwart their purpose. There was never even reference to Mormon policies until quite late in the civil rights crusade, and even then it was a tempered and measured criticism with none of the sulphurous vitriol of the NARAL style anti-Catholicism. The leaders of the civil rights movement were largely as exalted as their cause, and it is quite literally impossible to conceive of Martin Luther King Jr. battening on a poisonous diet of religious bigotry.

I believe the abortion ethic is fatally and forever flawed by the immorality of the means of its victory. A political victory achieved by such odious tactics is at best an unstable tyranny spawned by an unscrupulous and unprincipled minority. At the very least this disclosure of those odious tactics should compel those who are uneasy with permissive abortion to re-examine the issue. I believe that an America which permits a junta of moral thugs to foist an evil of incalculable dimensions upon it, and continues to permit that evil to flower, creates for itself a deadly legacy: a millenium of shame.

EPILOGUE

On June 15, 1983, the United States Supreme Court struck down as unconstitutional laws requiring hospitalization for late abortion, a mandatory twenty-four hour waiting period before the performance of any type of abortion, and an informed consent provision requiring a detailed explanation both of the nature of the unborn child (victim of the proposed operation) and of the precise manner of the surgical destruction of the child. The Court upheld laws stipulating that a minor must have parental consent or the consent of a juvenile court before submitting to abortion.

On June 28, 1983, the United States Senate defeated by a vote of 50–49 the stripped-down, relatively feeble Hatch-Eagleton Amendment which stated simply: "A right to abortion is not secured by this Constitution." Hatch-Eagleton was a legislative chimera, a classic demonstration of the old saw that a camel is a horse designed by a committee. It was the 1982 Hatch Amendment trimmed, deboned, and filleted by conflicting elements in the pro-life movement. Not only did it fail to obtain the two-thirds vote necessary to pass it as a proposed constitutional amendment, but it even failed to pass by a simple majority. Although the Human Life Bill and the "Paramount" Human Life Amendment are still on the Senate calendar for debate, in practical legislative terms their prospects are exceedingly dim. It is no wonder the Abortion People are rejoicing in this dismal summer of our defeat and disarray.

In national reportage the media have taken the predictable line that the United States Supreme Court has conferred a mantle of respectability and saintly altruism on the abortion industry and has removed abortion from the national agenda. Linda Greenhouse, writing in the *New York Times*, articulated the mega-press line thus:

As it turned out, the majority of the Court might have hit on the best weapon against the specter of endless litigation . . . a reaffirmation forceful enough to persuade people that further efforts to change the rules will be futile. *Indeed, the legacy of last week's ruling may be to defuse abortion as a political issue.* (italics added)

Please note that Greenhouse used the word "defuse," and not "end." The word "defuse" means to make less dangerous, tense, or hostile. Even the Abortion People understand that until the United States Supreme Court categorically denies the humanity of the unborn child, an issue the Court has not faced squarely in ten years, the issue is insistently alive. In the Akron decision the majority sideswiped that question, referring here and there to "potential human life" in the familiar 1973-style straddle and dithering about "one theory of when life begins," but nowhere addressing the core of the conflict: The nature of the unborn child in sternly neutral, politically impartial, and antiseptically scientific terms.

Greenhouse, her Abortion People, and the majority opinion of the Supreme Court sense that this is no flat earth controversy. They understand that they can *never* adduce some dramatic or arresting piece of scientific evidence so compelling that it will forever inter the issue. To the contrary, as the enlightened minority opinion takes pains to explain, the scientific evidence is mounting relentlessly to establish more and more clearly that the human unborn is a person in its own right and that the issue, far from being settled, demands a broader and deeper ruling.

The Court's decision has not, by some amazing legal sleight-of-hand, changed the nature of the abortion procedure and magically nullified the stark reality that human life is being destroyed on an unimaginably vast scale. Greenhouse and her ilk delude themselves to think that the millions who resist the abortion ethic and find the casual destruction of human life abhorrent will miraculously discard their traditional values and submit meekly to this unprecedented tyranny of the national media and the Federal Court. Dreading the increasing mass of politically neutral scientific data which supports the concept of prenatality as one of the many passages in our lives, the Greenhouse gang struggles desperately to keep the abortion conflict focussed on the question of political rights rather than biological reality.

By contrast, the Canadian Campaign for Life has determined that the biological nature of the human unborn is the sole critical issue in the entire abortion conflict and has moved the matter into their Supreme Court on that issue alone. Joseph Borowski, a former minister in the cabinet of the government of Manitoba, has challenged the constitutionality of the abortion statute contained within the Criminal Code of Canada. Briefly, that statute permits the performance of "therapeutic abortion" by a licensed physician in an accredited hospital based upon an application by the petitioning woman and her physician that the pregnancy constitutes a threat to her life or health. The application must be approved by a therapeutic abortion committee of the hospital, a committee of course composed of staff colleagues of the petitioning doctor, with whom that doctor socializes, and to whom he refers patients requiring care in other areas of medical practice. In short, the committee enjoys a cozy arrangement of "you scratch my back and I'll scratch yours," an arrangement which we in the high councils of NARAL exposed as ludicrous and infinitely exploitable in New York State in 1969-70.

Among other glaring deficiencies in the current Canadian statute is the interpretation of the word "health." In most hospitals in Canada the word is taken in its cosmic or United Nations definition: A woman who fails to resemble Miss America, who lacks the financial resources of Jacqueline Onassis and the talent of Liza Minnelli is disadvantaged and does not enjoy perfect "health." Predictably the statute has been ruthlessly abused and exploited. In many provinces, therapeutic abortion committees have rubber-stamped virtually every application for abortion presented to them, making abortion on demand a prevalent practice throughout much of Canada. Disrespect for the statute has become so pervasive that a particularly offensive entrepreneur named Henry Morgenthaler has set up abortion clinics in three provinces which do not even pretend an obeisance to the form. These clinics have no formal affiliation with any accredited hospital and they bypass completely the therapeutic abortion committee requirement. Morgenthaler, a gnomish creature who has developed sputtering, snarling, and screaming into a high form of argument, and who is adored by the Canadian mega-press, has spent ten months in jail on illegal abortion charges and is quite as devoted to malignant anti-Catholicism as our American exorcist, Lawrence Lader.

Borowski, who resigned from his post as cabinet minister in Manitoba over the abortion issue and at one point even carried on a fast in protest of the widespread abuse of the statute, has instituted a suit against the Ministers of Justice and Finance of Canada charging that the Canadian abortion statute violates the new Canadian Bill of Rights which holds:

> Everyone has the right to life, liberty and security of the person, and the right not to be deprived thereof except in accordance with the principles of fundamental justice . . .

> Every individual is equal before and under the law, and has the right to the equal protection and equal benefit of the law without discrimination on race, national or ethnic origin, color, religion, age, sex, mental or physical disability.

At the center of Borowski's suit is the claim that the unborn child is indisputably "everyone" and "every individual," and may not be denied the right to life in a free and democratic society. The success of his suit, and with it the fate of the pro-life cause in Canada, hinges on the proof that the human unborn is a person and an individual within the definition of the Canadian Constitution.

Borowski's attorney, the brilliant and charismatic Morris Shumiatcher, invited me to testify on his behalf, assuring me that it was to be one of the most important constitutional trials ever held in Canada and that the decision would have important bearings on similar statutes in other countries, such as Australia and New Zealand. He proposed to confine the evidence strictly to the issue of the humanity of the unborn child and reassured me that this court would give a full and fair hearing to every bit of scientific evidence I could marshall to that effect.

In company with the late Sir William Liley, Dr. Jerome Lejeune, and Dr. Patrick Berne, I testified in that trial on May 16, 1983. Judge Matheson listened intently to the evidence, allowed me to present the data unhurriedly and in full, and posed shrewd and penetrating questions at the appropriate junctures. It impressed me that for the first time in an English-speaking national courtroom advocates for the unborn were being given a fair hearing. The cross-examination by the attorney for the crown was carping, brief, and even perfunctory as if the evidence which had been presented was all but unanswerable on a purely biological basis.

At this writing the verdict of that court is not in. I am not so naive as to think that this case will be decided as it should be, purely on its bio-ethical merits, or that as a result of that verdict abortion will once again be proscribed in Canada. No matter how compelling and how persuasive our evidence for the pro-life cause, this judge, and the full complement of nine judges in Ottawa who will review the evidence and render the final decision, will be heavily influenced by the shrill keening of the radical feminists, the pro-abortion mindset of the Canadian national media, the clever machinations of the Planned Parenthood strategists, the redoubtable economic clout of the physicians and entrepreneurs of the abortion industry, and by the pernicious example of the United States experience. Great legal decisions are not made in a political vacuum and liberal judges are irresistibly attracted to liberal public policy-making. Still, I believe that at the very least the national Canadian judiciary will recognize that at the heart of this matter is the unconscionable stripping of the civil rights of a voiceless and invisible segment of the population without the due process of law which every civilized society demands, and will insist on a more rigorous, less imprecise definition of the conditions under which the unborn may be destroyed. It is impossible to predict whether this will take the form of judicial review of every proposed abortion; therapeutic abortion committees composed of laypersons, lawyers, doctors and nurses from other hospitals and even other cities; or elimination of the economic motive in the procedure by making it truly free without reimbursement to the abortionist. However, it may be all we can reasonably expect at this time.

On the surface the notion of judicial review of each proposed abortion is patently impractical and impossibly cumbersome to the already ailing court system, but it may in fact be the only logically acceptable resolution of the issue if the court should accept the irrefutable scientific data which demonstrates that the unborn is a person in the law, but refuses to proscribe permissive abortion. It is fundamental to this society that due process be observed before a person is deprived of his or her life. To do less is to sanction the ultimate violation of a person's civil rights. In the question of capital punishment the proposed termination of the prisoner's life is subjected to endless judicial review and interminable legal wrangling, invariably ending with the highest courts' determination that for all practical purposes society does not endorse the taking of human life, no matter the provocation. The courts forbid the taking of a life which has been pledged to a lethal war with society, but the life taken in the issue of abortion requires no judicial review whatever though it is as innocent as any can be. I admit that judicial review of every proposed abortion would be enormously burdensome for the courts, but we are speaking of life and death. Courts generally have consented to arbitrate similar critical bioethical issues such as the question of when life support systems should be turned off. Further, most serious critics of the judicial system agree that the courts are bogged down in a great deal of litigation of lesser import which could and should be moved into a referee-arbitration setting, leaving the courts free to handle more pressing matters.

I believe that the Supreme Court of Canada, and inevitably of the United States, will be *forced* to accept the notion of legal personhood of the unborn, though they will probably couple this belated recognition of the unborn's civil rights with some unfortunate waffling to the effect that a woman's right to the abortion procedure overrides the civil rights of the unborn, even the right to life. But once the legal door is open and the unborn is a person in the law, then judicial review of every proposed abortion flows naturally from the demands of due process. One and a half million advocates for the unborn should crowd the courts annually, demanding due process for their clients over whom the sentence of death hangs, and doubtless the judicial system of the United States and Canada will grind to a halt. Flooding the courts and bursting the jails was a most fruitful tactic of the black civil rights movement, the Vietnam War resisters, Gandhi's disenfranchised millions—why not the pro-life movement?

Abortion is the most bitterly contested civil rights issue of our time. The nature of the oppressed, a defenseless, mute, and invisible minority (though increasingly less so with the advent of realtime ultrasound and other technologies) sets it apart from all other civil rights conflicts. The most eloquent angry spokesmen for the black civil rights movement are black themselves. Women speak and write passionately for the feminist cause. Gays parade through the streets of our cities decrying sexual prejudice and demanding the nation's approval. The human unborn is the ultimate civil rights victim. It cannot be heard; it cannot be read; it cannot demonstrate or parade through the streets. It cannot even be arrested and thrown into jail for civil disorder. The victim's silent anguished pleas are heard only by the pro-life cause. Paradoxically, Americans who have historically been deeply sympathetic to the plight of the oppressed and the downtrodden turn a deaf ear to these pleas. Congressman Henry Hyde, that lion of pro-life, has characterized the movement as one of the most admirable in history since those who labor in this cause reap absolutely no material gain from its success. It is a movement distinguished from all others in this nation's history, excepting perhaps the Abolitionists, by its pure and perfect altruism. Compare the crystalline selflessness of the pro-life cause to the shabby materialism of the abortion industry and the ruthless self-gratification of the Abortion People.

The pro-life movement has been tragically hobbled by factionalism and disunity. This more than any other factor may be responsible for the recent legislative and judicial defeats. No social revolution, or even counter-revolution, can succeed without the public appearance of unity and harmony within the ranks. In NARAL in the 1960s we preserved a fictional unity for the media and the legislation despite a critical split between the forces of the left (the Lader-Nathanson group) and those of the right (the Smith-McClintock group). The black civil rights movement had fissured into the Southern Christian Leadership Conference, the Student Non-Violent Co-ordinating Committee, the Congress for Racial Equality, and the NAACP, but it remained functionally united, if for no other reason than that its blackness set it apart and forced it together.

I am only a relative newcomer to the pro-life scene and perhaps it will appear presumptuous of me to offer prescriptions to organizers and workers who have dedicated ten years or more to this cause. Still, I cannot help but feel that it may be time to pull back a little on the legislative and judicial fronts and invest energy and funds in a massive educational campaign to educate the public regarding recent developments in the controversy such as the concept of prenatality, molecular genetics, fetal medicine, and fetal surgery. Martin Palmer, the pro-life attorney in Hagerstown Maryland, who argued the landmark Fritz case so brilliantly, has proposed the construction of a Freedom Train to traverse the nation with a cargo of educational materials and exhibits relating to fetology and futuristic technologies in bio-ethics. Foundation Genesis, organized and administered by Patricia Judge in Australia, has devoted itself to educating the people of Australia on complex bio-ethical questions from a strong pro-life posture. It has been a remarkably successful venture and has earned considerable respect not only from the Australian people but also from the Australian media. Mrs. Judge is confident in her belief, a belief I share, that when faced with complex public questions in a free and democratic society an educated electorate will always make the morally correct decision.

I have no doubt that the pro-life cause will ultimately prevail, if for no other reason than that the population of the nation is aging and the graying of America will move us back to more traditional and conservative values. Combined with the increasing weight of the scientific data indisputably confirming the humanity of the unborn, this will suffice to see the reimposition of a ban on abortion. It may even be that technology such as surgical embryo transfer from one human uterus to another or to a marvelously sophisticated life support system may finally remove abortion from the national agenda, only to replace it with a host of equally perplexing though less incendiary concerns. But we cannot afford to wait passively for this relief. The decimation of four thousand innocent lives daily imposes a crushing urgency upon us to find a solution now.

And it may be time to sort out the factional differences in the pro-life ranks and resolve the dissidence in this glorious movement. I fear that without unity we will condemn ourselves repeatedly to the bitter dregs of disappointment and defeat.

* * * *

Mahatma Gandhi, an enormously clever politician and the personification of the Indian resistance, was once asked how so humble a man could rally a third of a billion of the most downtrodden people on earth to bring the mighty British empire to its knees in the subcontinent. "By love and truth," he smiled. "In the long run no force can prevail against them."

APPENDIX A

INTRODUCTION

This paper was written by the author and a young pro-life obstetrical resident at the St. Luke's Hospital Center in New York City, Dr. Frank Chervenak. It was written in protest against the practice of destruction of hydrocephalic infants in utero. The paper was written in early 1980, immediately prior to the era of intra-uterine surgery which today preserves the lives of these infants. Predictably, the paper was rejected by both the *New England Journal of Medicine* and the *American Journal of Obstetrics and Gynecology*.

MORBUS ABORTIENSIS
AND THE QUAQUAVERSAL ETHIC

Practicing at the southern borders of life, the obstetrician has traditionally been pledged to the dictum: Primum Non Nocere. Whether in treating the dying fetus in utero (as in severe iso-immunization disorder) or in resuscitating the profoundly depressed newborn in the delivery room, the deontology of obstetrical practice has cleaved unswervingly to the undiscriminating and unshakable resolve to first do no harm, to preserve and protect life in all of its manifestations, actual, probable, and even "potential."

Regrettably, the modern obstetrician is now engaged in carrying out medical procedures for para-medical or social purposes: elective abortioneering. The obstetrician is in danger of becoming de facto and de jure another social engineer. A new ethic for society at large, deriving in part from the soothing and accommodating embrace of the situational ethicists, has infiltrated the healing arts. This collapsible, multidirectional, or Quaquaversal Ethic, anatomized rather resignedly in an editorial in *California Medicine* in 1970, would have us all to come to terms with the necessity to "place relative rather than absolute value on such things as human lives, the use of scarce resources, and the various elements which are to make up the quality of life or of living which is to be sought."[1] This poisonous doctrine subjects each of us to cost-accounting and social worthiness analyses and leans precariously on the slippery and ultimately unreliable concept of "quality of life." To imply that any of us, individually or collectively, possessed the Huxleyan technology to measure the unimaginably complex quiddity of life is scientific arrogance, even hubris.

One of the more controversial spawn of the Quaquaversal Ethic is permissive abortion. The author's views on abortion are a matter of the public record[2] and need not be elaborated upon here, but to illustrate in at least one significant area the philosophical ullage of the Quaquaversal Ethic it might be useful to examine the abortion issue from a different perspective than the customary incendiary one of "rights" and examine it instead through the lens of intent.

The term "abortion" is defined as the separation of the fetus (unborn child, products of conception, alpha) prematurely from the mother. The definition does not include within it a purposeful destruction of the fetus. Yet, because of our present technological limitation we now have no means of carrying out early abortion without the simultaneous destruction of the fetus. The commonly expressed intent of early abortion is to remove the fetus from the mother's inhospitable body so that she may be spared the toll of bearing and raising the child. Whether it is the intent of the woman submitting herself to early abortion also to destroy knowingly and purposefully the fetus is at present probably unascertainable. If the technology existed to carry out early abortion without the destruction of the fetus, allowing an atraumatic removal of the fetus from the uterus into some marvelously efficient life support system where it could grow and mature, how many women seeking early abortion would elect to have this type of abortion rather than the current method in which the fetus is destroyed? How many physicians would encourage the former method as an ethical alternative to destructive abortion?

The intent of the late or "genetic" abortion, that done for fetal disorders such as Down's Syndrome or neural tube defects, deserves careful scrutiny. The intent of this abortion is a different one. Its purpose is not merely to rid the mother of an unwanted pregnancy, but to eradicate an imperfect product, a product which fails to meet the nebulous standards of cost-accounting and social worthiness tests. Indeed, many physicians feel that in these circumstances termination of fetal life is an act of kindness. That the intent of this type of abortion is primarily destructive is made clear by the fact that the majority of the "genetic" abortions are still carried out by the method of intra-uterine saline instillation. This method is most often fatal to the fetus and is used despite the evidence that the prostaglandin method is considerably safer for the mother and frequently results in the delivery of a live, though usually immature, fetus. It is curious that though the participation of women in the management of all aspects of their reproductive functioning is increasing, the choice of method for late abortion is tacitly ceded to the physician. Whether this represents a failure on the part of the physician to give that choice to the pregnant woman ("freedom of choice" turned inside out) or whether it represents a disinclination on the part of women to participate in this perplexing question is not clear. One can only state with reasonable assurance that the continued adherence to the saline method is strongly suggestive of the deep inroads the Quaquaversal Ethic has made into medical practice.

The authors feel that it is important to emphasize that they do not espouse an anti-intellectual or fundamentalist approach to modern medical genetics and today's obstetrics. Unfortunately, the therapeutic and humanistic contributions of medical genetics are often overshadowed by the destructive consequences of prenatal diagnosis. Genetic amniocentesis need not be used for destructive purposes but can allay the fears of an anxious family or can help the family prepare for the birth of the deformed child.[3] Further, the successful prenatal treatment of a patient with methylmalonic acidemia has been documented[4] and successful neonatal screening and treatment of phenylketonuria without resort to antenatal triage has become an integral part of modern medicine.[5,6] Gene therapy with the potential of inserting new genetic information into diseased genomes is the new frontier.[7,8]

* * * *

In his presidential address Dr. William H. Kirkley called upon members of the South Atlantic Association of Obstetricians and Gynecologists to strive for a "quality product."[9] He has in effect demanded that physicians involved in the area of perinatology (obstetricians, pediatricians, neonatologists) make judgements regarding which infants shall live and which shall die according to their biological integrity and future value in the labor market. These judgements are often made on the spot in the delivery room or intensive care nursery and are therefore individual and nonappealable. In developing this thesis he relies in part on the work of Dr. John Lorber of the Department of Child Health of the University of Sheffield, England.[10] Lorber has written extensively on the medical and ethical aspects of the treatment of infants with neural tube defects. In the corpus of his earlier work he strongly advocated a highly selective approach to the surgical correction of these defects based upon the "quality of life" standard. For those infants who after correction will not be able to walk, will probably not be able to work, and will be consigned to a life of pain and suffering as a result of their handicap, Lorber has held that it is ethically sound, medically desirable, and economically imperative that they be denied surgical correction, be allowed to die. Kirkley would extend this dubious charity to hydrocephalics and to sick premature infants as well, reasoning: "At times the present concept that everything that is alive (even in utero) has a right to live at all costs, even with greater risks to the mother, bothers most of us who practice obstetrics."[9] Quite apart from his immodesty in designating himself as a spokesman for some phantom majority, he has embroiled himself in an ethical controversy in which his principle ally, Lorber, has lately and inconspicuously defected, as we will discuss later. Let us for the moment turn to the question of hydrocephalus and the Quaquaversal Ethic.

Until the middle of the twentieth century, Caesarean section was considered a formidable procedure that carried with it an unacceptable risk to the mother's life. When confronted with the delivery of a hydrocephalic infant it was considered far safer to reduce the size of the head and deliver the infant vaginally than to resort to the hazardous Caesarean section. In order to effect a vaginal delivery the hydrocephalic head was decompressed by a transvaginal destructive operation carried out in the later stages of labor and for this purpose there was a remarkable array of the most fulsome instruments in every delivery room. They had in common the task of perforating the fetal skull, draining off the excessive amounts of fluid, and crushing the skull for delivery. They were, au fond, alarmingly efficient instruments.

Now, in the ninth decade of the twentieth century, the maternal mortality rate for Caesarean section has been dramatically reduced to approximately one in a thousand, roughly comparable to that for a varicose vein ligation, and perhaps one-twentieth of that for a chole-cystectomy. Mutatis mutandis, the obstetrical management of the hydrocephalic infant is still a destructive operation. I concede that the operation does not involve the use of those loathsome instruments of the past. Now the obstetrician simply thrusts a large-bore needle through the maternal abdominal wall into the fetal skull and the accessible pool of cerebro spinal fluid is entirely drawn off. This results in a significant reduction in the size of the skull to allow for vaginal delivery and also, invariably, in the death of the fetus. Not only is there a considerable amount of literature advocating this Procedure,[11,12,13] but if one is to judge by the Sixteenth Edition of *William's Obstetrics*,[14] it has become the standard of practice for the obstetrical community in this country.

However, the rationale for the destructive operation has subtly changed. Formerly it was done to spare the mother the risk of Caesarean section, but now that that risk is almost nonexistent, indeed Caesarean section has been performed for far more insubstantial reasons, the destruction of the hydrocephalic fetus in utero is justified on a "quality of life" basis. If the ultrasound examination done on the pregnant woman measures a mantle of brain tissue in the fetus judged by reference to some recondite nomogram to be inadequate for a socially functional, marketable "unit", or if that "unit" will require unacceptable sums of money for salvage, then instead of a Caesarean section with the delivery of a live hydrocephalic infant, the destructive operation is performed.

This practice of the prenatal destruction of defective infants who fail to meet the Pickwickian standards of some social engineering stress test exemplifies the Quaquaversal Ethic in action. That it is ethically impermissable and legally unsound is undeniable. Even the current United States Supreme Court has decreed that the third trimester fetus is at least a "potential" life and that the state has a compelling interest in protecting that life except where the mother's life is in jeopardy. Moreover, this practice is deeply flawed medically.

There is now a substantial body of literature on the prenatal diagnosis of hydrocephalus by ultrasound.[15,16] The technique has been refined to the extent that the mantle of brain tissue can be measured with impressive accuracy. However, Sutton, Bruce, and Schut point out that hydranencephaly, a condition of infancy in which there is total absence of the cerebral hemispheres with an intact skull and in which there is no reasonable expectation of improvement with any known surgical procedure, can be readily confused with maximal hydrocephalus by ultrasound.[17] Maximal hydrocephalus, however, offers a surprisingly good prognosis for recovery of brain functioning with shunting. The authors caution that it can be extremely difficult to distinguish between the two conditions in the neonate. How much more difficult, if not impossible, must it be in the fetus.

Lorber himself seems to be edging uneasily away from his former position. In a recent issue of *Science* he recounts the discovery of a young hydrocephalic student at his university who had an I.Q. of 126 and had achieved first-class honors in mathematics, though he had virtually no forebrain as determined by ultrasound. Instead of the usual 4.5 centimeters thickness of brain tissue he had only the most fragile shell of cerebral cortex, a millimeter or so in thickness. This case does not appear to be unique. Lorber rather ruefully concedes that even an apparently hopeless hydrocephalic has a good chance for recovery and that the brain in fact may: "not be necessary at all."[18]

The destruction of a living being, whether embryo, defective fetus, or neonate, is an act of irretrievable finality. One life is not fungible with another, and the value of each human life transcends ordinary mensuration. To justify the destruction of a life by invoking the puny reach of our current scientific knowledge, as the Quaquaversal Ethic would have us do, is to traverse a pool of quicksand on ballet slippers. Physicians should declare a moratorium on the destruction of life until we have explored every feasible alternative and until we more fully comprehend the inexpressible divinity of existence.

1. "A New Ethic for Medicine and Society." *Cal Med.* 1970; 113:67-68.

2. NATHANSON B N. *Aborting America.* New York: Doubleday and Co, Inc. 1979.

3. ELIAS S, AND MAHONEY M. "Prenatal Diagnosis of Trisomy 13 with Decision Not to Terminate." *Obstet Gynecol.* 1976; 47:75s–76s.

4. AMPOLA M G, MAHONEY M, NAKAMURA E, TANAKA K. II Prenatal Therapy of a Patient with Vitamin-B$_{12}$-Responsive Methylmalonic Acidemia." *N Engl J Med.* 1975; 293:313–317.

5. SCRIVER C R, CLOW L C. "Phenylketonuria: Epitome of Human Biochemical Genetics." *N Engl J Med.* 1980; 303:1394–1400.

6. MERYASH D L, LEVY H L, GUTHRIE R, WARNER R, BLOOM S, CARR J R. *N Engl J Med.* 1981; 304:294–296.

7. ANDERSON W F, FLETCHER J C. "Gene Therapy in Human Beings: When Is It Ethical to Begin?" *N Engl J Med.* 1980; 303:1293–1297.

8. MERCOLA K E, CLINE M J. "The Potentials of Inserting New Genetic Information." *N Engl J Med.* 1980; 303:1297–1300.

9. KIRKLEY W H. "Fetal Survival—What Price." *Am J Obstet Gynecol.* 1980; 137:873–875.

10. LORBER J. "Ethical Problems in the Management of Myelomeningocele and Hydrocephalus." *J R Coll Physicians Lond.* 1975; 10:47–60.

11. BORNO R P, BON TEMPO N C, KIRKENDALL H L, ET AL. "Vaginal Frank Breech Delivery of a Hydrocephalic Fetus after Transabdominal Encephalocentesis." *Am J Obstet and Gynecol.* 1978; 132:336–338.

12. JACOBS J P. "Transabdominal Drainage of Hydrocephalus Associated with Breech Presentation." *Obstet Gynecol.* 1965; 26:557–559.

13. LAUDERDALE J M. "Transabdominal Decompression of the Breech Hydrocephalus." *Obstet Gynecol.* 1964; 23:938–939.

14. PRITCHARD J A, MACDONALD P C. *Williams Obstetrics.* New York; Appleton-Century-Crofts, 1980; 690–693.

15. HYNDMAN J, JOHRI A M, MACLEAN N E. "Diagnosis of Fetal Hydrocephalus by Ultrasound." *New Zealand Med J.* 1980; 91:385–386.

16. UEMATSU S, WALKER A E. "Ultrasonic Determination of the Size of Cerebral Ventricular System." *Neurol.* 1967; 17:81–84.

17. SUTTON L N, BRUCE D A, SCHUT L. "Hydraencephaly versus Maximal Hydrocephalus: An Important Clinical Distinction." *Neurosurgery.* 11 1980; 6:35–38.

18. LEWIN R. "Is Your Brain Really Necessary?" *Science.* 1980; 210:1232–1234.

APPENDIX B

ABORTION LEGISLATION

From the *Journal of the American Medical Association*,
August 20, 1982.

IMPLICATIONS FOR MEDICINE

At present there is congressional activity in Washington, DC, that poses grave danger for the future of medical practice in the United States. It involves the desire of certain politicians to limit the rights of both physicians and patients to decide whether an abortion is required or desirable. Through the use of a proposed constitutional amendment or federal statutes, the federal government could be put in the position of telling physicians what medical procedures they can or cannot perform. This is dissimilar to the ruling that the federal government will not pay for abortions for indigent women (a physician could still provide an abortion although payment is an issue).[1] It is more restrictive than the Food and Drug Administration's regulation of drugs that involves the interstate shipment and sale but not their prescription for specific patients.[2] This new government action could outlaw, or permit the outlawing by states, of a widely used procedure.

Although *Roe v. Wade*[3] was in many ways a clear victory for women's rights, it also involved the rights of physicians. Thus, In *Roe v. Wade*, the court specifically held that "the abortion decision and its effectation must be left to the *medical judgement* of the pregnant woman's attending physician"[4] (emphasis added). Elsewhere the court states that before fetal viability "the abortion decision in all its aspects is *inherently, and primarily, a medical decision,* and basic responsibility for it must rest with the physician"[5] (emphasis added).

227

It is this decision, and these principles, that would be abrogated by the new legislation.

Individual physicians and their patients may decide that abortion is the treatment of choice for a variety of reasons. Pregnancies are not uncommon among rape victims, the seriously retarded, the very young, and those impregnated through incest, as well as among those couples at risk of bearing children with severe genetic defects. Invariably painful and tortured dilemmas are spawned. Great sensitivity and compassion are prerequisite qualities (among many) for helping these persons or families. Individual decisions must be made by and for each patient on the basis of their needs, not federal law. Notwithstanding likely and general agreement on the latter premise, we have now witnessed the introduction in Congress of bills (such as S 158 or HR 900), constitutional amendments, and joint resolutions, all fundamentally aimed at stopping abortion. The effects of these constitutional and statutory proposals, in our opinion, would involve deprivation of fundamental freedoms.

At present, one active piece of legislation before Congress is the Hatch Amendment (SJ Res 110). It would amend the Constitution to say that

> A right of abortion is not secured by this Constitution. The Congress and the several states shall have the concurrent power to restrict and prohibit abortion, provided that a law of a state which is more restrictive than a law of Congress shall govern.

As can be seen, there is no exception to protect a woman whose life could be threatened by the continuation of her pregnancy. Under this amendment abortion could be forbidden even in the following circumstances: (1) the woman could die or suffer irrevocable physical damage because of the pregnancy, (2) the pregnancy resulted from rape or incest, (3) the fetus had a serious genetic defect, (4) a young child were pregnant, or (5) the woman would suffer serious psychological damage from the continuation of the pregnancy. In none of these circumstances could a physician exercise his medical judgement that an abortion is appropriate for the patient.

It would be difficult to outlaw abortion where maternal life is endangered by the pregnancy. In such situations, especially when maternal life is threatened early in the pregnancy, both the mother and fetus would die. Second, when a fetus endangers the life of the mother, one can make a self-defense argument that the fetus must be destroyed to save the mother. One is entitled to use deadly force against a person who threatens one's life. As strained as this argument sounds, it is the kind of argument that will have to be made to permit abortion if certain anti-abortion legislation is enacted.

One anti-abortion argument holds that human life begins at fertilization and that the fertilized ovum is a person entitled to complete constitutional protection. One bill (S 158) declares that "human life shall be deemed to exist from conception" and specifically gives the conceptus the rights of a "person" under the Fourteenth Amendment. While the proposed laws and constitutional amendments that confer personhood on fertilized ova have been tabled for the moment, it is useful to examine the consequences of such premises, since they are inherent in the proposed anti-abortion amendment and will unquestionably arise again.

Should a fertilized ovum be deemed a "person," contraceptive techniques that take effect after fertilization, such as intra-uterine devices and certain oral contraceptives, will most likely be outlawed. This is because homicide is "the killing of a human being by another human being"[6(p28)] and the terms "human being" and "person" are likely to be used synonymously in this context. It would be difficult to argue that a fetus is a person but not a human being. Thus, one who intentionally kills the fertilized ovum (person) has committed a homicide. Under this reasoning it is arguable, if unlikely, that a woman who suffers a spontaneous abortion could be subject to criminal investigation, since we may have the death of a person under suspicious circumstances. Of course, physicians who performed abortions would clearly be guilty of a homicide, as they would directly and intentionally cause the death of a person. This makes abortion a much more serious crime than it was before *Roe v. Wade*, when abortion was a separate and much less serious crime than homicide.

There are a variety of other legal ramifications that result from deeming the fetus a person. The possibility of wrongful death suits would be expanded after the death of a fetus or fertilized egg. Issues would arise about the possibility of fetuses being heir to their deceased father's estates and about the estate of the fetus itself if its father should also die before its birth. Questions of tax law (is a fetus a dependent?) and payment of welfare and other benefits must arise. The Fourteenth Amendment states that representatives shall be appointed among the several states by counting "the whole number of persons" in each state—how does one count fertilized ova? This is a partial list, and it is impossible to determine what further legal complexities would arise. At the very least, it seems inappropriate to give the rights of persons to entities we cannot even tell exist—just when is an egg fertilized? Just when does conception occur? How can we know when this person exists?

The conferring of personhood on fetuses and fertilized eggs and the outlawing of abortions would have a negative impact on fetal research. In 1974, Massachusetts passed a law[7] that states in part:

> No person shall use any live human fetus, whether before or after expulsion from its mother's womb, for scientific, laboratory, research, or other kind of experimentation. This section shall not prohibit procedures incident to the study of a human fetus while it is in its mother's womb, provided that in the best medical judgement of the physician, made at the time of the study, said procedures do not substantially jeopardize the life or health of the fetus, and provided said fetus is not the subject of a planned abortion.
>
> For purposes of this section, the word "fetus" shall include also an embryo or *neonate* (emphasis added).

Therefore, any research on a fetus *or* neonate associated with "substantial" risk was specifically barred. The very pregnancies that were to be aborted by elective parental decision were also specifically precluded from study (for example, by amniocentesis or fetoscopy) because of the caveat that the "fetus is not the subject of a planned abortion." Since the development of safe techniques (eg, fetoscopy) depended on physicians being able to study pregnancies just before elective abortion, all such progress was stopped in Massachusetts.

Research and development of fetoscopy, whose goal would be to treat, save, and diagnose the fetus, are interdicted today in Massachusetts. Citizens of this state must travel elsewhere for such diagnostic or therapeutic studies. The newly developed treatment of the fetus with hemophilia or Rh disease by direct blood transfusion using fetoscopy[8,9] is now denied to citizens of this commonwealth because the necessary testing required to perfect techniques cannot be done. In Massachusetts a similar fate faces any effort to develop safe techniques for fetal surgery or "genetic engineering" approaches to fetal therapy. The proposed congressional bills and amendments are designed to achieve even more extreme goals—this time on a national scale.

Indeed, one of the lessons we can learn from the existence of the Massachusetts legislation is that unclear laws have an extremely chilling effect on those who might be subject to them. The first sentence of the law prohibits "research" on the fetus—the second sentence permits "study" in some circumstances. What is the difference between the two? The law uses the phrase "substantially jeopardize" the life or health of the fetus. What does that mean? As a result of this lack of clarity, much research designed to benefit fetuses, which would be technically legal, has not been performed. Who wants to take a chance of being wrong and being subject to five years in jail and a $10,000 fine—the maximum penalty prescribed by the law? Indeed the law is so uncertain that, two years after its enactment, it was amended to include a lengthy and burdensome procedure by which investigators could petition the local district attorney and superior court for a before-the-fact determination of the legality of proposed research. As far as we know, this costly and time-consuming procedure has not been utilized.

At the very least, we believe that people should retain the freedom of reproductive autonomy and, in particular, the rights to save the life and secure the health of the mother rather than the fetus, to enable victims of incest or rape to abort a pregnancy, and to allow parents the option of aborting a pregnancy when the fetus is seriously defective or deformed. We believe that physicians and patients must not allow the life and health of a mother to become subordinate to her fertilized ovum.

AUBREY MILUNSKY, MB, BCH, DSc, FRCP, DCH
LEONARD H. GLANTZ, JD

1. *Maher v. Roe*, 432 US 464 (1977).

2. ANNAS G, GLANTZ L, DATZ B. *The Rights of Doctors, Nurses, and Allied Health Professionals.* New York, Avon Books, 1981, pp 123-124.

3. *Roe v. Wade*, 410 US 113 (1973).

4. *Roe v. Wade*, 410 US 164 (1973).

5. *Roe v. Wade*, 410 US 166 (1973).

6. *Perkins on Criminal Law*, ed. 2. New York, Foundation Press, 1969, pp 28, 997-1018.

7. Mass General Laws chap 112, §12J.

8. RODECK C, KEMP J, HOLMAN C. Direct intravascular fetal blood transfusion by fetoscopy in severe rhesus isoimmunisation. *Lancet* 1981; 1:625-627.

9. MAHONEY M J, HOBBINS J C. Fetoscopy and fetal blood sampling, in Milunsky A (ed): *Genetic Disorders and the Fetus: Diagnosis, Prevention and Treatment.* New York, Plenum Press, 1979, pp 501-526.

APPENDIX C

ABORTION LEGISLATION: ANOTHER VIEW

> "The first precept was never to accept a thing as true until I knew it as such without a single doubt."
>
> RENE DESCARTES: *Discourse on Method*

The question of legislation in the area of abortion is an exquisitely sensitive one, embracing as it does perplexing matters of social, legal and political importance. Hence it is imperative that in pondering this question one adhere to the most punctilious standards of academic exposition, without recourse to simple sloganeering or heuristic cant. I have no wish to debate here the thorny issue of the ethical acceptability of abortion on demand, my views on this issue are a matter of public record[1,2], but I am moved to examine more fully the arguments adduced in Milunsky's and Glantz's "Commentary on Abortion Legislation"[3] and put to rest some of the more chiliastic prophecies therein.

I was co-founder of the National Association for Repeal of Abortion Laws (now the National Abortion Rights Action League) in 1969, and served as medical consultant to that organization until my resignation in 1975. As one of the key architects of abortion political strategy in the United States I was responsible for the coining of the many passwords and shibboleths, such as "freedom of choice" and "a private matter between a woman and her doctor," which have too long passed for serious argument in this infinitely complex and incendiary issue. The burgeoning of the field of fetology and fetal surgery, and the increasingly insistent questions raised by in vitro fertilization, embryo banks, and genetic engineering require more of us than the dreary litany of 1960-ish pro-abortion fustian.

If there is one thing that is certain in this maddeningly uncertain conspiracy we call civilization, it is that abortion is quite simply not a medical matter. If we are to believe that abortion is done for medical reasons, then we must assume that because the number of abortions has doubled in the past ten years since the Roe v. Wade decision of the United States Supreme Court (750,000 to 1.55 million annually), either the pregnant population of the United States has become twice as ill as it was ten years ago or medical science has become half as efficient. And if unplanned pregnancy is itself a disease and abortion a ". . . treatment of choice," then where are the papers in the medical literature reporting the cure rates for this "disease," the five year survivals, or the indications and contra-indications for this "treatment"? Just because physicians are the technicians involved does not make abortion a medical matter any more than the use of sodium pentothal for execution in some states makes capital punishment a medical matter.

No. Unplanned pregnancy is a social problem and demands social solutions. It is as inappropriate to cope with this particular social problem with destructive surgical means as it would be to "treat" violent criminals with lobotomies or rapists with surgical castration. Vexing social problems call for imaginative and humane social responses, not surgical holocausts.

With respect to the abortion legislation introduced into the ninety-seventh Congress, the "Commentary" unwittingly misleads its readership by implying that the proposed Hatch Amendment sets out restrictions on abortion practices. The Hatch Amendment reads as follows:

Section 1.
The right to abortion is not secured by this Constitution. The Congress and the several states shall have concurrent power to restrict and prohibit abortion.

Section 2.
That a law of a state more restrictive than a law of Congress shall govern.

This proposed amendment to the Constitution would restore the power to legislate on abortion to the elected national representatives in the United States Congress and to the separate states where it has historically resided, removing the power from the hands of an un-elected judicial elite. It stipulates that each state legislature may formulate its own laws regarding abortion in conformance with the will of its people and further asserts that the federal law would establish the national standard which could be strengthened by the separate states but not weakened. This Jeffersonian model contains NOT ONE WORD regarding specific exemptions, medical practices, or punitive measures.

The other major piece of abortion legislation proposed to the ninety-seventh Congress was the Human Life Bill, an attempt to define the beginnings of life. Regrettably, both the pro- and anti-abortion camps quickly politicized the bill, and its intrinsic worth was lost in the hailfire of partisan battle. But such a definition has become vital for those who work at the southern borders of life: fetologists, pediatric neonatologists involved with life support systems for pre-mature infants, and in vitro fertilization groups. Curiously, many scientists with the confidence of an Euclidean certitude in other bio-ethical matters suddenly dissolve into coy disclaimers and anguished humility when confronted with defining the beginning of life, fearing the political fall-out. Yet when the definition of death became a pressing necessity for those working in the fields or organ transplant, life support systems, law enforcement, and the criminal justice system, a Presidential Commission for the Study of Ethical Problems in Medicine and Biomedical and Behavioral Research was promptly appointed, and its comprehensive report[4] on the definition of death was fearlessly issued to national approbation in July, 1981. I submit that should the Congress fail to define the beginnings of life with the appropriate legislation a Presidential Commission be appointed to carry out this task in a similarly unheated, non-political manner.

To deplore the role of the federal government in the regulation of abortion on the grounds that the federal government should have no presence in medical politics and practice is to advocate a finely selective ox-goring indeed. The senior author of the "Commentary" has published fifty-two papers in the medical literature in the past ten years, several on amniocentesis and prenatal diagnosis, and virtually all have enjoyed substantial funding from various governmental agencies such as the United States Public Health Service, the National

Institute of Child Health and Human Development, and the Maternal and Child Health Project. The requirements and standards which attend the granting of each of these subsidies surely places the federal government squarely in the center of American medical research, and lest anyone remain unconvinced regarding the federal nose in the medical tent, let him try to read his way through the murky bureaucratese of Medicaid standards regulating the delivery of obstetrical services or sterilization procedures, to cite examples within my own professional purview.

The issue of fetal research, on which the "Commentary" dwells at some length, is a viscerally disturbing one, especially in the wake of the squalid public disclosures of the Tuskegee "experiments" on poor blacks with untreated syphilis and the Willowbrook "researches" involving injection of live hepatitis vaccine into mental retards. The Department of Health and Human Services in conjunction with the Food and Drug Administration published in January, 1981, a new set of guidelines[7] regulating research on human subjects. These guidelines require researchers to distinguish between "minimal risk; greater than minimal risk; and greater than minimal risk, but only by a minor increase" in planning and carrying out projects on humans. Therefore, it seems somewhat disingenuous for investigators who carry on federally subsidized clinical research to protest that the phrase "substantial jeopardy" is excessively vague when applied in the Massachusetts statute on fetal research. And to plead that fetal research planned within the allegedly vague, though to this viewer eminently reasonable and humane limits of "substantial jeopardy" carries with it an unacceptable risk of heavy fines and imprisonment, though no one has ever been penalized or even charged under this statute, is to cry "fire" in an empty theatre.

Commendably, the federal government was concerned enough about the welfare of experimental animals to pass legislation known as the Laboratory Animal Welfare Act of 1966. The Act is a seventy-nine page document setting forth rather stringent standards mandating decent care and treatment for experimental animals, even to the extent that it demands the use of anesthetics, analgesics, or tranquillizers when the animal might suffer unduly as a result of the experiment. The National Research Council published a guide for the care and use of experimental animals, stipulating that ". . . animals intended for use in research facilities receive humane care and treatment."[8] Can we now afford to persevere in this profoundly disturbing antinomy: administering drugs to one ailing fetus and performing life-saving surgery on another while simultaneously conducting experiments on a similar fetus that are regulated to a lesser standard of compassion and humanity than that which we apply to laboratory animals?

Let us by all means continue to examine this agonizing dilemma of abortion. But let us do so rejecting ideology, eschewing politics, and confining ourselves to the Cartesian ideal: the pitiless light of reason.

1. NATHANSON B N. "Deeper into Abortion." *N Eng J Med.* 1974; 291:1189.

2. NATHANSON B N. *Aborting America.* New York: Doubleday and Co, Inc. 1979.

3. MILUNSKY A, GLANTZ L. "Abortion Legislation, Implications for Medicine." *JAMA.* 1982; 248:833–834.

4. President's Commission For the Study of Ethical Problems in Biomedical and Behavioral Research. "Defining Death: Medical, Legal and Ethical Issues in the Determination of Death." Washington D.C. 1981: 84 pp. plus six appendices.

5. MILUNSKY A, ATKINS L, LITTLEFIELD J W. "Amniocentesis, for Prenatal Genetic Studies." *Obstet. Gynecol.* 1972; 40: 107.

6. MILUNSKY A, LITTLEFIELD J W, KANFER J N, KOLODNY E H, SHIH V E, ATKINS L. "Current Concepts in Genetics. Prenatal Diagnosis of Genetic Disorders." *N Eng J Med.* 12 Aug 1976; 295(7):377–80.

7. Department of Health and Human Services. Final Regulations Amending Basic HHS Policy for the Protection of Human Research Subjects. *Fed Register 1981:* 46(16 part 2):8366–8391.

8. Committee on Care and Use of Laboratory Animals of the Institute of Laboratory Animal Resources. National Research Council. Bethesda Md. 1978; 70 pp.

APPENDIX D

22 Feb. 1983

George B. Lundberg, MD
Editor
Journal of the A.M.A.
535 N. Dearborn St.
Chicago, Ill.

Dear Dr. Lundberg:

The 20 August 1982 issue of the *Journal* contained an opinion piece authored by Milunsky and Glantz entitled "Abortion Legislation." Measured by even the most charitable standards it was an aggressively political, unarguably pro-abortion tract. Occupying as it did two full pages of the *Journal* I felt it required a full-scale, point-by-point rebuttal, and submitted same to the *Journal* several weeks ago.

The piece was returned to me with unseemly haste, accompanied by a profoundly disappointing, astonishingly inadequate explanation of the rejection. Indeed, the Meyer rebuff was a flagrant insolence, not only to me personally (I am a Board-certified obstetrician-gynecologist, was a founding member of the National Abortion Rights Action League, and have testified in the United States Senate on this issue twice in the past year) but also to the tens of thousands of physicians on the membership rolls of the A.M.A. who share my views on this matter.

I categorically deny that the two short letters published in the letters section of the 28 January 1983 issue of the *Journal* deal in any detailed manner with the substance and assertions of the Milunsky-Glantz piece.

239

Further, I fail to understand what Meyer means when she airily refers to: "opinions frequently aired in the general news media." She offers no examples or citations for this rather fatuous observation. Does she think that Milunsky's views on abortion have never found their way into the "general news media"?

The abortion question is a uniquely perplexing, exquisitely sensitive issue before the nation—and the medical community. To bar the responsible expression of a carefully developed dissident view from the pages of the *Journal*—equal time, if you will—using as an excuse the Pickwickian triticisms of an obvious ideologue such as Meyer is an intolerant and undemocratic act, one not in the great tradition of the JAMA and, I daresay, not acceptable to that great portion of the membership which welcomes full and frank examination of *all* aspects of difficult bio-ethical dilemmas.

I respectfully request that this piece be re-considered for publication in the *Journal*.

Sincerely,
BERNARD N. NATHANSON, MD, FACOG.